Diary of a South Coast Walk.......*with a freedom pass*

By

Neil Edington

By the same author

Sisters,Saints and Queens [2015] [amazon/create space]

Published by Neil Edington [2016]
Printed by Amazon/Create Space
neiled11@btinternet.com

To Roger Cline and Richard Curtis for kind help in putting this book together: and to the good company of people on the journey.

The walk.........

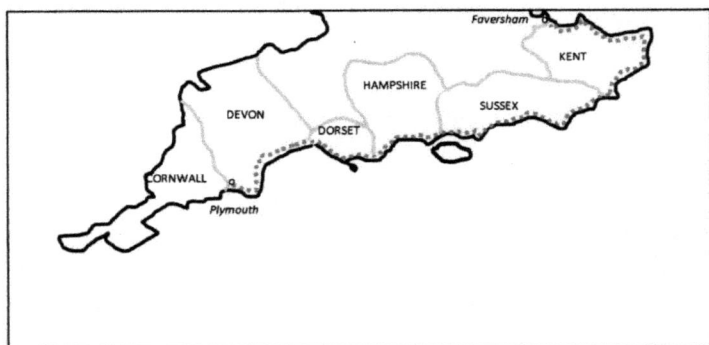

INDEX...page

Prologue: 26 August 2008.

Winding myself up to start this journey along the coast, I realise that there are two obvious questions. Firstly, why walk round the south coast and, secondly, why start at Faversham?

The first question is simply answered by the fact that we are an island and the coast is there to be walked, to be enjoyed in its infinite range of variation. The dialogue between land, water and sky seems endless; blue- green to grey- brown seas; serene calm waters to crashing waves; sweeping bays of sand; craggy cliffs; seaweeded, rocky shores; salt marshes; and all of them changed by the stage of the moon- tide, the blowing of the wind, the pattern of clouds, and the shining of the sun or the falling of the rain. There is a special sort of exhilaration here, which is something more than an extra dose of ozone. That the coastline is both popular and useful is also confirmed by long stretches of urbanisation and shorter stretches of industrialisation. The latter is immediately less attractive to the walker; but it does become an intriguing and acquired taste after some exploration, as well as a sometimes barrier. I am not so sure that I can be equally enthusiastic about golf courses: but, even as they are more frequent than industry, they are often more generous in allowing hazardous rights of way!

However all this lies ahead of me; to say nothing of the numerous estuaries which, apart from adding walking miles when you cannot cross them, are generally the source of habitation, and thereby of sustenance and a comfortable bed: for it is not my intention to put up in a tent, or even carry a tent, more than is absolutely necessary, at my ripe old age. Three score and ten we are given: and I am but a footstep away. It is also the age of the 'freedom pass' that now gives the 'grey pounders' free access to all the coastal bus routes. This transport is a great asset in designing a day's walk, or even a sequence of walks: and certain long distance bus routes acquire the familiarity of good friends as I get further from a London base.

I say that estuaries have most of the towns, but the exception is the south east coast, where the walk seems to be one long sprawl of habitation with beach huts, punctuated by golf courses, interspersed with rare interludes of white cliffs or salt marshes. Uninhabited beaches seem as rare as the small white egret.

As to the second question [why Faversham as a starting point?] the south coast was chosen because, as I am based in London, there is ready, radial access to most of the south east coast [rail access rather than buses!] and pretty good connections to the south west. Modesty and time decided me not to aim for the whole of the island's coasts [I think that I started a little too late for that!]. So practicalities say that the south easterly coast is where I chose to start, mainly because I can get home quickly if things do not work out [I should say that I have had walking holidays for 60 or so of my nearly 70 years – so I hope not to get caught out too often!].

Faversham seemed an appropriate place because it is sufficiently out on the Thames estuary to think of it as coast [even if it is more north easterly than southern in aspect!]. It is certainly tidal. It has a good Saxon name, and while Gravesend is the beginning of the designated 'Saxon Shore Way'. I feel that Gravesend seems a more appropriate place to finish a walk than to start it! So tomorrow I catch a train to Faversham.

A word to the reader might be that this diary might best be tackled in the manner of the episodic walking that it describes: for there is no love story or crime to be resolved in this journey! Yet much incidental pleasure was had in small doses!

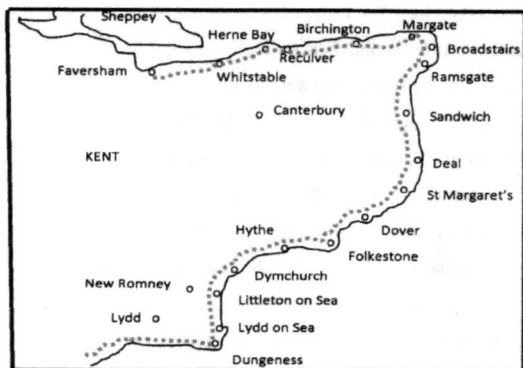

27, August,2008: Faversham to Whitstable.

So I set off.

An inauspicious start, as my watch must have caught on something in the night, so that the clocks at Victoria are an hour later than the reading on my wrist, with the consequence that I arrive at Faversham closer to lunch time than I had intended.

I remind myself that this is no longer a competition driven life. Nevertheless, full of good intentions, I pass by the temptation of too many delightful Shepherd-Neame pubs [I have visited them on previous occasions: the brewery being a major source of employment in the town and I, once, a very minor shareholder], head on past the handsome clock tower of the town hall, with its scattering of market stalls clustered under comfortably reassuring arches, and I make for the attractive row of period houses that form Abbey Road. At the end of this road the choice is to go down towards the river, my future destination; or to turn back to the tranquility of the old abbey grounds.

Faversham clock tower & market. Sept. 08.

The charm of the old town generally increases in a direct relationship to the distance from railway station, but is contrasted with a rather clinical development of new townhouses on the far side of the river; which, in turn, is in direct contrast to the scrimmage of boats, in various shapes and states of seepage, on the nearside river bank. To call this a boatyard would be something of a euphemism. My rather dated ordnance survey map emphasises this sentiment by having the purple diamonds marking the 'Saxon Shore Way' covering this area, but fails to make a dotted line to join the diamonds over this particular stretch. It admirably expresses the task that the intrepid explorer faces: the way through is not clear. But as locals occasionally appear walking in the opposite direction it is assumed that there is a way through! Sometimes, amongst nettles, there is, on a fairly rotten piece of fencing, a rather tattered yellow pointer [often pointing to the skies, suggesting that flying over this area might be more appropriate!]. However the area is full of interesting clusters of people, apparently either working or living there, while many of the boats seem to be, like many actors, 'resting'.

After I had negotiated some fairly impressive cranes in a more organised area, a clear path emerges; just where the dots start again on the map. Moreover this path is planked and, in turn, covered with antislip wire netting, so that one feels 'back on course'. The tide is low and there are oyster catchers and peewits among the ever-present herring gulls. Sea dill and mustard are in their autumn yellow with black seeds, while still-green sedges and rushes fill the undrained gullies.

11

I know that to the left, across the estuary, I might see the spire of St Thomas at Harty, an isle within the Isle of Sheppey. Harty, with its tranquil St Thomas, is a scattered little hamlet that has a breeding colony of terns, and a Ferry inn that used to know, and use, all the tides to Faversham.

Nagreb Hamlet + Estuary. Sept 08.

But today I must follow the Saxon Shore way and head for the even smaller hamlet of Nagden. The path is unambiguous until you approach the market gardens of Nagden and Broom Street. Here there are diversionary tracks and pathways [mainly for cyclists], which will take you to Whitstable via Graveney rather than the Saxon Shore Way; and other unlabelled yellow arrows point in many directions. It would be a shame to miss this part of the estuary, as it is one of the wilder parts, with views across to Harty Island. But you do need to persevere, and head towards Nagden. This is one of those hamlets that has been privately done up, and the walker excluded from the shore line. Keeping the house, the cottages, and the redeveloped barn on your left, you will eventually reach the river estuary again, and it is a fine raised pathway that curves right round the Swale and Thames estuary to head for Sea Salter. There are fewer walkers here and good cornland [below sea level?] along with a wild habitat mix of rushes and weeds, while there is a serious concrete sea wall bounding the estuary side. The Swale sanctuary has protected nesting sites for terns, and, at appropriate times, flocks of Kentish plovers with brent geese frequenting the mud and shingle. This stretch is a fine unurbanised beginning to the walk. The sea breeze can be quite vigorous!

Further out an off shore wind farm makes its spasmodic semaphores that hopefully divert most of the flying wild life, and hopefully also light up the lives of people in Southend. It is an individual, if marshy, beginning to the flat estuary walk.

The beach huts start where the Graveney marsh road reaches the coast: and the Sportsman Inn half hides one of the sites of caravans and chalets that pepper the south east coast. Having walked from Faversham I was ready for refreshment, but it was not a walkers' place [I gathered it was Michelin-rated]. So, with feet rather sore from not having found my walking socks, I soldier on. Here begins a fairly continuous sequence of habitations as far as Dungeness, apart from the cliffs at Ramsgate, Dover and Folkestone. A concrete sea barrier which doubles as an esplanade for walkers and cyclists separates the sea from what originally was marshland, close to sea level, if not lower. It would surely be very susceptible to seasonal flooding without this defence. Global warming and a rise in the sea level could easily transform this area!

The shore here consists of a mixture of mud and shingle, with the former luring odd solitaries [humans!], or clusters of twos and threes, to splash out and ferret around in a fairly knowledgeable manner for what must be worms for bait: trophies to be bucketed. The Seasalter architecture is initially uninspiring but then becomes much smarter and more expensive, sealed off into Stepford-wives estates with contented wives, happy children and plastic bags for their dogs' droppings. I began to develop blisters walking on the shingle here. If you obey the 'Private Beach' signs you end up on the rather narrow coastal road, but after passing the pub with the unusual name of 'The Rose in Bloom' you can return to the seafront by an alleyway to the left which dives down over the railway [via a footbridge].

The Lower Island of Whitstable appears and the path runs seamlessly into the town, an attractive tumble of old streets to the east of the rather bleak harbour, with local oysters, fresh fish, crab, whatever you will, tempting the visitor.

I end up in the Cumberland Hotel, more attractive inside than its rather grim exterior suggests, and an interesting cross-section of society. An elderly mother and daughter on a late holiday, with the daughter fussing round the mother and looking to be but two twinsets away from old age herself [but twinsets may last a considerable time!]. A dapper bearded George V look-a-like with an older companion; and three local youths for whom this is obviously but one of their stopping places this evening, all add to the mix. Good seabass and almost crumbly new potatoes; Pinot Grigio perhaps a little sweet, but at the end of what has been a longish half days walk, most welcome.

Feet definitely blistered.

28 August, 2008: Whitstable to Birchington -on -Sea.

Well now I am on my way; and some old dear twitched her lace curtains at the sight of me sitting down in the nine o'clock rush hour to take off my shoes and socks in order to tape up blistered heels with elastoplasts just bought at the chemists in the hope that doing so might help them to last the day.

Sea catches are being loaded into refrigerated lorries in the confines of the harbour: the modern world. Stalls begin to assemble in the square that houses the Thursday market; and I start out on the concrete barrier that goes from Whitstable to Birchington-on-Sea via Herne Bay. The only relief from this easily negotiated sea barrier is around the suggestion of sandstone cliffs leading into Reculver, considerably further on. But on the exit from Whitstable there are almost continuous beach huts lining the path, with the occasional remnant of an old grand café, or an out-door paddling pool, or a modern sailing club, making temporary interruptions: and, on the seaward side, always a goodish belt of shingle before the mud or sand. However, the sea and the sky are undiminished in their uncluttered splendour.

Septon. Beach huts, Herne Bay.

At the end of this promenade of beach huts, Herne Bay is something of a pleasant surprise. A terrace of gracious Georgian houses and generous hotels has been masked by less attractive shops, but, so far, the beautifully laid out and maintained, esplanade gardens remain a strikingly handsome feature of what looks as if it were a resort for the gracious pleasure of the sometime brass bands and cream teas, rather than the remains of a working fishing and trading community as at Whitstable. This general demeanour of gentility is however not maintained by the monstrosity, on what might have been a pier, by what might be a civic theatre. This large, out of proportion, box could well have been an inspiration for the Power Station at Dungeness: but this might be to insult the industrial architecture of Dungeness.

However, refreshed by an hot chocolate at a rather popular Italian cafeteria on the sea front, I continue along the esplanade until the shingle beach peters out and sand dunes struggle to form crumbly cliffs which, despite warning notices, seem to be a favourite scrambling site for local adolescents; and possibly not only for scrambling. But even the local youth only go so far, and then there is a stone strewn stretch where there is sufficient unattended cliff to provide home for sand martins, and sufficient solitude, until I crunch along, for cormorants to perch on the rocks in the shallows of the lapping sea, spreading their wings to capture the sun's heat. Ring collared doves peck at insect life in the swathes of seaweed that plait on the shore at low tide, the plaits doubtless uplifted into elegant and swirling dances when the tide comes in, but now just a little smelly!

Then, round the corner, you catch sight of the dramatic ruins of St Mary's at Reculver.

St Mary's at Reculver,
Sept 08.

St Mary
at Reculver. Sept 08

From afar on a grey day, they look as if they are the remains of a Norman fortress or a great abbey. In fact it is an 18th century local parish church, now in ruins. As the outcrop was originally also home to a Roman garrison of some size, it is obviously a strategically imposing site. This is emphasized by the fact that the 'Saxon Shore Way' takes this promontory to turn inland and slip behind the Chislet and Monkton Marshes, which historically cut off the Isle of Thanet from mainland England. These marshes run right through to Sandwich on the south coast, embracing the tributaries of the river Stour that runs from no lesser a place than Canterbury. But, as a coastal walker, I am left with the big corner of the Isle of Thanet [now part of the mainland] to walk round.

At Reculver an appropriately named hostelry 'King Ethelred' serves to emphasise the Saxon connections here, and cares well for visitors and locals from the hidden caravan site.

Replenished at the inn, henceforth to the marsh sea wall; now named 'Wantsum Walk', [which actually does go past Plum Pudding Island! -as corny as true: it sounds very 'Alice in Wonderland!'].

The land side of this stretch of coast does have the appearance of fen or marshland: some of it preserved as wild marshland: some of it well farmed, even fish

16

farmed: and some of it, sadly, a bit of a tip. But there are quite well marked circular walks of varying lengths for those who have over indulged in the King Ethelred. The beach side is a mixture of shingle, sand, and mud; and without beach huts. There are yellow horned sea poppies flowering in their grey green foliage, and an escaped rugosa rose is tough enough to throw in a splash of magenta red. Teasels have colonized the landward side of the esplanade.

It is not far to Birchington-on-Sea, where a better class of beach hut appears, along with the first stretch, in my walk, of good, sandy beach. But such a shame that so much of this is spoilt, in the name of conservation, by rather large mounds of near-to-rotting seaweed; unsavoury, both by sight and smell. Being green is one thing: but not smelly, rotting green, where children play, surely? A shame, as otherwise it is a quite charming bay of sand with open well- kept grassland: and a bus to the railway station. Birchington feels like a comfortable suburb by the sea, without any centre, and therefore a heart, of any description. But, this may just be approaching it from the sea; and, like a lot of suburbs, I presume that the inhabitants are happy to keep it that way.

Yesterday's blisters have burst, and I think that my feet need a rest. Birchington station is being redecorated, doubtless as a result of one of the changes in franchise in the local network systems. But it means that the ticket office is closed, so I have to work out how to use plastic in the all-singing-and-dancing ticket machine. I wonder if I am quite as quick as the 6-year-old girl in front of me who helps her father with tickets for two adults and two children [I can see it is what they call problem solving learning!]. I justify my delay by the fact that, although only needing a single ticket, I do have to key in 'Senior Rail Card' at the right stage of my options!

A train back to London soon follows, with the hyperactive children reminding me of my age!

15th September, 2008: Birchington-on-Sea to Broadstairs.

Back to Birchington-on-sea on a fine September day. The lack of blisters, the presence of walking socks and of a pale blue sky with a fresh breeze definitely improve one's outlook.

It seems that the most easterly of the white chalk cliffs start here and rise in a parallel course with the number of golf courses and cashmere sweaters. I am on the Isle of Thanet: the marsh hinterland has been crossed via the pleasant concrete esplanade! Here the nascent cliffs do really look as if they are built from cubes of soft chalk bricks, like a huge barricading dry stone wall: impressive, exposed geology.

What was the Wantsum Walk has now been named, imaginatively, either ' the Viking Way', or the ' Viking Coastal Trail'. I say imaginatively because it seems to me to be very similar to the concrete esplanade that started at Graveney. However I can well imagine that the Vikings would have applauded the gentle slopes from beach to esplanade for buggy and disabled access, and the frequent runs of steps which would have been so appreciated by tired limbs that had just tacked and rowed from Scandinavia against prevailing south westerly winds.

But in the white cliffs there are now some interesting concrete in-builds, which I imagine to be the remnants from a combined outlook and defence system from a much more recent war.

This walk round to Margate certainly gives the first feel of the geological thrust of the chalk cliffs pushing the Isle of Thanet out of the sea. The white of the cliffs contrasted by a beautiful blue sky and scudding blue green sea, in which the odd wave rises to break spray over the barrier; the spray matching the white of the cliffs; and the surge occasionally splashing across the esplanade, eliciting gurgles of delight from a pink-clad toddler being pushed at a brisk place by a plumpish mum. A fine approach to the daily shopping at Tesco's in Margate? I wonder if she gets the bus on the way back when she is more heavily laden?

Margate has improved since I last saw it twenty years ago. It has something of the air of a north facing Blackpool, without the funfair, or quite such a good spread of sand: but nevertheless the best spread of sand that I have seen so far.

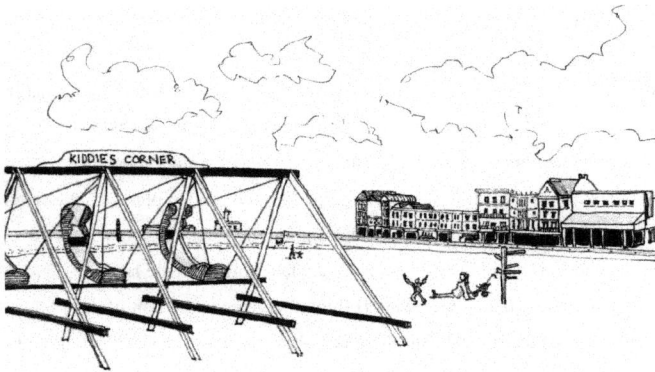

Swings up at the end of the season.
Margate 03.

Margate obviously did have a Victorian hey-day, as there are some good pieces of architecture, not least the ' Sea Hospital', and a cluster of ex- ' Grand Hotels' at the west end of town. But a central sixties tower block does nothing for the town, even if it gives its inhabitants fine views. Doubtless it is a product of the redbrick universities churning out a new breed of planners who saw the vertical as the American answer; but forgot about context? Hey-ho!

While it is fair to say that Margate does have the best stretch of sand that I have seen on the north Kent coast so far, the shops seem to reflect the struggle for survival here, in spite of the bravely cheerful municipal flower beds. An empty shop, still with a notice, 'Senior Service Satisfies' [a brand of cigarettes – for those too young to remember; nothing to do with local pensioners eking out a living!], seems as dated as it is dilapidated. A neighbouring shop, rather garishly labeled, 'live out your fantasies', leaves me even surer that things have changed since the Victorian era. However there are positive signs of a struggle to re-establish Margate; and a faster train service to London [and. now, a new Turner Art Gallery], may well transform it: deservedly.

There is also a reasonable pier for fishermen; and an imposing clock tower on the sea front. As you exit eastwards, well past the pier, there is a ghostly dilapidated lido that somehow looks like a disused Ealing Studios film set, peeling cream coloured plaster, with small clusters of over-bright ceramics; water trying to be deep enough to paddle in;

but a hovering whimsical echo of past fun. I wonder if Margate will ever struggle thus far again.

Eastward and onwards takes me to no wild place, but the cliffs become marginally higher, and the concrete finally peters out even as the tide is coming in, so that the cliff path is, for the first time, the only alternative. There are some encouraging belts of untouched cliff vegetation, which shows an odd mix of escaped garden plants challenging 'natural vegetation', such that valerian gives colour among the seedheads of wild parsley, wild carrot, and lilac scabious flowers amongst late purple thistle heads.

Houses are never more than a tee away. [I think that a tee is the unit of measurement on this part of the coast!]. But there is a glimpse of a wader, a wagtail, and a cormorant: even if Corsas and Citroens are easier to spot. There occurs again a single small white egret, which caused me to rub my eyes when I first saw one near Whitstable, and another at Herne Bay. I understand how people believed in omens in the unexpected. But it is a most elegant omen: the more singular for being an apparent solitary.

There is a distinct breathing space as Foreness Point and North Foreland are approached; although again one has to wonder whether the 'Fore', represents a true Saxon word origin, or relates to the cries from the golfers on a course embracing some of the most sumptuous sea views and small coves yet encountered. Botany, Kingsgate, and Joss bays are all distinctive small treats; and at this time of the year, and mid-week, they are virtually empty; apart from the odd spaniel or labrador walking its owner.

I think that I have finally rounded the northern corner; and the coast is facing east, and I am walking south at last. In this quiet corner, before it runs into Broadstairs and Ramsgate, there are the first set of rolling hills and woods, with isolated striking buildings which have the resemblance of fortifications, even if the main building looks as if Lutyens could have done a better version. But at last there is an imposing, uncluttered interlude. The first, really, since the estuary at Faversham.

It is something of a shame that what once was a moderately grand hotel is now split into apartments, giving it a feeling of somehow 'deshabillé'; but still probably very comfortable to live in. Where carriages, coaches and charabancs once may have stopped, cars now whizz by: trade has always needed trade.

That this part of the coast is select rather than wild is made clear by the fact that parts of the cliffs are privately owned by biggish houses, hidden in substantial grounds, with high trees and rhododendrons.

I suspect that, if I could afford to own [and to run] such a property, I would fight for the pleasure of that privacy. But meanwhile I part wish them well, welcoming diversity, but also rather resent having to traipse along stretches of the B2052 until I can get back onto the East Cliff walk. This eventually becomes a minor road of suburbia facing the sea. It runs for a mile or so until it goes straight past the back of Dickens' splendidly situated 'Bleak House' on the north side of Broadstairs Bay. When you know that Dickens has plaques on something like 106 houses, one wonders how he ever managed to write so much. But apart from the dramatic situation, and idiosyncratic architecture of Bleak House, it is also slightly spicier than the other 105 dwellings inasmuch as Dickens lived here with his mistress.

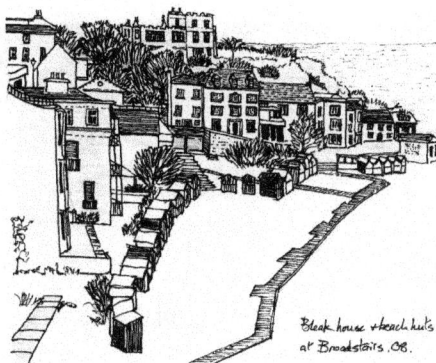

Bleak house + beach huts
at Broadstairs .08.

Having observed previously that I had just rounded the corner of Kent I was interested to note the curious nomenclature of cliffs in this area. The 'East Cliff' of Broadstairs is north of what is appropriately called the 'South Cliff' of Broadstairs: and

21

this in turn is north of the 'East Cliff' of Ramsgate, which is north of what is called the 'West Cliff' of Ramsgate, which actually faces south. Very Alice in Wonderland! But they are all fine chalk cliffs. I wonder if the naming of these cliffs is where Humphrey Lyttleton got his idea for the rules of his radio game 'Mornington Crescent'!

By the time that I reach the enclosed bay of Broadstairs I have had a longish walk without an indulgence; so I am somewhat weary of foot, and ready for a hot bath, and some liquid refreshment. Broadstairs seems quiet at this time of the year, retiring into its comfortable shell. One or two obvious B & Bs have notices saying 'No Vacancies', which can be interpreted as having closed for the season, or gone off on holiday themselves. So I try for the rather imposing and well-situated Royal Albion Hotel, which has a notice I read as 'Shirts and Ties must be worn at all times'. This slightly surprises me in this day and age; and makes me wonder if a rather bedraggled elderly walker will be allowed in. But there is no problem from the antipodean manager; and when I later get my glasses out I realize that the notice says 'Shirts and Shoes must be worn at all times': and that it obviously refers to a different time of year, and a different sort of trade!

The present clientele savours of long haired daschunds, whose female owners sip large glasses of white wine, while some of the gentlemen wear tweedy green checked jackets, and obviously long to be able to smoke a pipe or a cigar with their half of bitter or whisky and ginger: but smoking is no longer allowed! There is also a smattering of anoraks drinking lager; and retired couples, the latter mainly in the restaurant; while round the corner a coffee and cake area attract a younger group. The situation of the hotel encompasses the sea and the whole bay, so it has obviously adjusted well from the grand Victorian to modern trends. The skate was not fresh; but they were appropriately confessional and reparatory.

16th September, 2008: Broadstairs to Deal.

Refreshed by a good night's sleep and a fairly substantial breakfast, I leave the comfortably ordered feel of middle-class Broadstairs at about 9am to walk round the esplanade [which has reappeared] towards Ramsgate. This makes me realize that I have hit the dog- walking rush hour. Nobody but me is just walking on their own: but there are various and numerous combinations of humans and hounds. It seems like a variation of

22

the man walking to St Ives, except there are seven leads rather than seven sacks; with each lead a separate breed; so how many breeds are there going to Ramsgate: sort of thing?

There is a stretch in the middle third of the walk between Broadstairs and Ramsgate where there is some solitude: then the reverse happens, and you meet the packs of hounds coming out of Ramsgate. Both sets of ambulations have subsets of walkers who quietly ignore the frequent and prominent notices that dogs are not allowed on the beaches between April 1 and Sept 30. All part of the English character, no doubt; but I suspect it is also the subject of some local feuding too. I take no photographs.

The walk on the sea front esplanade is easy. However the chalk cliffs really do rise to Ramsgate and anticipate what I shall find, and have to climb, at Dover and Folkestone.

Ramsgate is the peak of the Isle of Thanet. The chalk now forms in larger slabs, and they in turn show signs of stress, with long fissures and fractures. A further variation is that there are thin horizontal strata of flint. Given that the chalk represent years of compressed marine crustaceans, I wonder what epochs or ice ages these interludes of flint strata represent. It is amazing how some plants are tenacious enough to root in the fissures: and ubiquitous pigeons find safe nesting in the cracks.

But Ramsgate looms. The original lido, at the end of the East Cliff, is now a tarmacked car park, with an informative ' natural sea plant garden' as a token gesture at the end. It has to be said that Ramsgate does have character and variety in abundance. There is a large harbour, full of boats, but nowhere near the percentage of fishing boats there used to be and one remaining ferry connection to the continent. But it is a vibrant presence, and the harbour does not overpower the town, as the terminals at Dover do.

After the base of the east cliffs and the bustle of the harbour the road rises towards the top off the West Cliff past a splendid series of Victorian red brick arches, giving space for a treasure trove of chandlers, paint shops, mariners' cafés, and, at its steepest point, a church for sailors, whose high nave must underpin the road above. Adjacent to this is a ' Home for Smack Boys'; raising questions that can be second only to the one prompted by the fine building on the rising road that still bears the inscription ' Royal Sailors Rest'. Whatever happened to non- royal sailors? Perhaps I don't want to know the

23

answer to either question. But I reflect that while we might admire the influence of the victorian architecture and selective philanthropy, other aspects of that age are well left behind.

The West Cliff looks as if it were once the smart place to live. There is a fine row of Regency terrace houses, some of which are now peeling, and have washing variously draped over erstwhile elegant balconies, and curtains that suggest that all the interior furniture does not match the original architecture. Nor do the gardens do the houses justice. But the situation is grand; and there are better properties and municipal spaces further on. This is not to forget the imposing Pugin monastery, church, and house in their splendid isolation; which I have visited on a separate occasion, but are now under restoration.

This imposing west end of Ramsgate terminates rather abruptly, and one finds a way to the right, slightly inland, that takes the pedestrian through walkways onto the road to Pegwell and Pegwell Bay. Comfortable houses here, but a narrow road, and a feeling that this once was a smaller separate village. A couple of pubs have imposing south views over Pegwell Bay.

A quick look at the map had told me that there might be problems henceforth as Pegwell Bay is the outlet of the river Stour, running all the way down from Canterbury through what once was marsh land. From the cliffs at Pegwell the large towers of Richborough Power station prefigure the omniprescent bulk of Dungeness Power station, which is just round the corner at the end of the Romney marshes.

But the sun is shining across the Sandwich flats, and the whole area, designated a nature reserve for tidal mudflat life, was, allegedly, the landing place for St Augustine, many centuries ago. So I decide to tackle it; ignoring my instinct that this is one of the areas where to make progress you get on a bus!

Once off the Pegwell road, there is a shortish walk along a lower cliff that is almost meadowland, with a charming cluster of what might have been fishermen's cottages.

All too soon this runs on to the A257, which I fear might be the only way of crossing the Stour [and this turns out to be correct]. My common sense said use the freedom pass to take a bus from Ramsgate [or pay for a train], to Sandwich as the A257 will be a dreary road: and it is. Sprawling industrialised dual carriageway, with even the Richborough Power Station a ghost of a place, all rusted and surrounded with barbed wire. [By the time I finish my walk I learn that this iconic structure has been demolished – and a motorway ploughed through the area].

I fail to find any indication of where St Augustine landed; but there is an impressive but strangely placed replica of a Viking ship on a green before the dual carriage way of the A257. Perhaps marking the end of the 'Viking Way'?

However, not to tackle the A257 on foot would be to miss out the splendour of the nature reserve at Pegwell Bay, which is a combination of well-laid-out paths and a labyrinth of pathways in a tidal and wild life zone, in which it is easy to lose all sense of direction [except that the tall poplars and wire netting of the Pfizer sports ground are a quite distinctive landmark! …[and now Pfizer have moved on!]]. But it is not possible to cross over to the Sandwich flats. The sensible thing would be to spend half a day at least in the nature reserve with binoculars, and with flora and fauna guides, then hop on a passing bus from Ramsgate to Sandwich. A warning is needed here. Do not try and get down onto the nature reserve until you are well past the replica Viking boat. There is a strange no-man's-land at the foot of the Pegwell cliff. This looks as if it was once a ferry terminal, but now the concrete is being reclaimed by nature. Here brambles and buddleia disguise the original concreted lay out. It looks like a magic playground for children; or a good sixth form project on mapping the 'natural' recovery of an ex-industrial site. But it ends as a dead end of unpassable marsh land. Not a place to be on a windy, moonless night.

The trundle of the A257, busy with lorries, cars, enthusiastic cyclists going to the recreation grounds, and more lorries, is one of those passages when one wishes one could recite long verses of poetry to pass the time of day and to lift the spirits. But finally it approaches the industrial side of Sandwich, which seems mainly to be more of Pfizer's land. Thanks to the exploits of animal rights activity, this estate now has the appearance of an internment camp, with high security mesh fencing, topped with three strands of barbed wire and CCTV monitoring. Solitary interned figures plough round the boundary in their lunch break, emphasizing the prison like feel. But some cabbage white butterflies flutter along the road side, in and out of the meshing, and oblivious to this wholly depressing interlude: and I do sing a little to bring some cheer; even if it is generally drowned out by the heavy traffic.

Sandwich, at last, is due recompense: quaint and charming; and but a golf course away from the sea. Here the River Stour is quite narrow, and well boated. The two round gate houses are pillars to the arched toll gate entrance to the town, leading to gabled overhanging houses where rooves curve with ancient red tiles; and beamed or mellow-red-bricked hostelries are to be found. Ancient narrow streets dictate one way systems for traffic and narrow pavements for pedestrians.

The Toligate, Sandwich 08

It seems a somewhat sad comment on the good people of the town that the main church of St Peter is ghosted, but preserved by the Church Conservation Trust, with a 13thcentury Carmelite friary undercroft. There are also delightful details of the history of the Earls of Sandwich on the walls of the church - museum, of which the 4th Earl seems a most colourful character. Of his partners it is written:

'Judith Fane bore him many children, and they lived contentedly for many years. She eventually…. was confined to a mental asylum……….

………For 17 years the Earl lived openly with his beautiful mistress, Martha Ray, who bore him five children…. She was subsequently murdered on the steps of Covent Garden by a rejected suitor.'

I could only think that it was a strange notion of contented living. Not only that, but the Earl also managed to be three times first Lord of the Admiralty. Questionably admirable: but certainly lived life to the hilt!

Sandwich is also the first of the real Cinque Ports, all of which I shall subsequently visit. So it is perhaps worth dealing with a fragment of their history here; particularly as there seems to be a slightly different version, let us call it local bias, at each place.

That there were five of them originally seems to be agreed; and, going from east to west, they were Sandwich, Dover, Hythe, Romney, and Hastings. They seem to have been commissioned by Edward the Confessor, whose Saxon ancestors had either driven out, murdered or married the Celts and now wished to have some sort of naval defence for themselves when they, in turn, where invaded by the Franks or French. So Edward created a Lord Warden [also Constable of Dover Castle], who had overall jurisdiction of each of the five ports, with freedom to levy taxes with which they would each, theoretically, provide boats and men for the defence of their country. There is also a most curious link with the herring fair of Yarmouth; and the Court of Sheppway [remember the Isle of Sheppey as I started out from Faversham?]. But, as if these were not curious enough aspects, a great storm in 1287 took up the shingle and closed off Romney [and Lydd]. The result was that both Rye and Winchelsea escaped the jurisdiction of Hastings and became ports 6 and 7: but Sept Ports does not have the same ring! So they have stayed as the Cinque Ports, and in addition Deal and Ramsgate have been included, along with 'Corporate members', Faversham, Margate, Folkestone and Lydd. It all reminds me of the growth of the EU in present times!

So Edward had a fine strategy. But since history's hindsight tells us that Normandy William came in via Pevensey, west of Hastings, it was more prophetic than protective. Methinks the French did something similar in their defence strategy against Germany in the second world war. Do we ever learn?

This stretch of the south east coast remained an Achilles heel in the time of the Armada, the Napoleonic wars, and even the great wars of the last century.

But I am still only at Sandwich, and rushing ahead of myself. It seems that the Sandwich family are still here, and owners of a considerable estate. While Broadstairs and Ramsgate seem to be conjoined by dog walkers, Sandwich and Deal seem to abut via two golf courses, the Royal George and the Royal Cinque Ports: enough said. But walkers are allowed a way through to the coast, even if you have to be fairly wary of being in the line of golf ball fire: 'fore' play has an aggressive aspect here! Of the foursome that I give way to, two seem to have proceeded pretty well down the fairway, whereas the other two seem to be foraging in some long grass on a hillock to the left. I wonder if my 'I am waiting, and watching' body language discouraged their normal fluency: or perhaps they just had a 'natural' handicap! I made the shingle shore feeling a little relieved, and a little smug.

Sandwich golf runs into Deal golf with a few dog walkers pounding out the distance along the shore on a blowy day. Where the Deal golf course ends there is the usual transition from outer twentieth century suburban architecture to the old town houses in the centre. There is a pier in the coastal middle of the town. But Deal also suffered from the might of the tidal waters changing the nature of the sea bed, with the result that there is a three mile sand and shingle bank in the bay that effectively prevents safe sailing. However the bank of shingle in the bay used to be a favourite picnic site in the summers of the late Victorian era: with appropriate photographs to illustrate the family teas in full dress, out on the shingle.

I plump for the Clarendon Hotel on the sea front and am comfortable. Breakfast is dominated by eight male golfers, all Daily Mail readers, and all retired. They all have instant coffee, full English breakfast, and golden shred marmalade. I have no idea about their other handicaps, but I do return by train, having investigated the very curious circular castle associated with Henry VIII.

Henry's Castle at Deal.

22 September 2008: Deal to Dover in reverse.

This is the beginning of an accommodation strategy that I shall increasingly adopt as I am further from London: no more easy day returns, or a single overnight stay. I now plan to travel to a place which is at least a day's walk further west than my last destination. By doing this not only can I stay in one place for several nights, but I can also leave most of my luggage at one abode. I thereby also become an expert on the coastal bus routes, whereby I can bus back to base at the end of a day's walk; or even bus out at the beginning of a day's walk, and walk back to the hotel. The 'freedom pass' comes into its own!

So, having last been at Deal, I take a return ticket from London to Dover; [and find it a little strange not to be dashing for the Channel Ferry]. I settle for a B&B somewhere near the foot of the castle, away from the ferry rush. Access to the multiple boat terminals does carve up the town, and the docking berths dominate the estuary. Having arrived late afternoon on the Sunday, taking care to be in the last 4 coaches from Victoria – lest I go back to Ramsgate, I have time to look at least at the hostelries of Dover, and to find the White Horse, next to the ruins of St James, and also close to where Wellington had his offices as Warden of the Cinque Ports [which until quite recently was also held by Elizabeth, the Queen Mother]. Apart from a selection of fine ales, the White Horse is distinguished by being the place where those who have swum the Channel come [assuming that they arrived at Dover rather than Folkestone!], and sign the walls or the ceiling with their name, date and time. The swim seems to take anything from 12 to 20 hours. In some ways I have more admiration for those taking 20 hours. How do they manage to stay in the water for so long? Some swimmers have even done it more than once; which almost seems foolhardy. It makes my pottering along the coast feels very mediocre. I am duly chastened.

The next day is very windy and threatening rain. My intention is to walk back to Deal over the Dover cliffs. Picking up the trail is not so straightforward going out of the town [perhaps it would have been easier to bus or train to Deal and walk back!]. My route involves skirmishing with the dual carriageway to the eastern Dover docks, periodically full of juggernauts as they are disgorged from the ferries. But there is a strange and rather attractive remnant in the form of a street of old buildings, even a pub and a restaurant, hidden from the heavy traffic. When this finishes you have to walk under the large flyover and immediately begin to climb up the chalk cliffs.

It begins to rain. The wind is blustery and up to force six. From being in the midst of a very urban environment it is suddenly quite wild and exposed. The path is very close to the edge of the cliff, and a film of rain makes the chalk path quite slippery in the gusting wind. Thank goodness that the gusts are blowing from sea to land. For the first time on the coastal walk I have a touch of vertigo and insecurity. Once the height of the cliffs is achieved the path moves away from the edge and there is an uncultivated area that is marked as a nature reserve, seeming to cultivate male loiterers at this time of day: but I don't, and in the rest of this magnificent cliff walk through agricultural land I see only one other walker, suitably waterproofed.

St Margaret's at Cliff is about at a third of my journey, and the cliff walk does descend through some very well-laid-out large gardens. Quiet affluence oozes from every pine needle. It is possible to walk round the bay without coming down, but I descend to the cove that feels as if it might have been a smugglers' hideout in times of old. It does boast the English pub that is closest to France!

The persistent rain does not induce me to hang around. So I heave up through another layer of comfortable affluence to find that I am back on the Saxon Shore Way, [which cut through from Reculver to Sandwich - remember?]. But here there are majestic views of the sea and land all the way to Kingsdown, where the walker descends on the edge of the inevitable golf course to a long run of shingle beach that will run into Deal, and Henry's strange castle of circles.

Kingsdown seems to be several different places. The coastal community seems to be quite separate from the more suburban component which is perched up on the higher ground. The coastal community seems to consist of the original sailing/fishing houses at the west end attached to a grid like system of later houses, separated by unmade roads in some cases. The Rising Sun, standing in the older part of the collection of smallish houses, is as welcoming as it is welcome: and Deal and the end of the day's walk does not seem too far away on a day of bracing weather.

Suitably refreshed, I found Kingsdown to Deal a shingle beach walk; some of it passing an unremitting new development of apartments, but with an easy footpath away

31

from the minor road. It eventually leads past some farm land of an estate, which, I subsequently learn from my South African landlord in Dover, was the erstwhile residence of the Duke of Wellington in his heyday: a most comfortable looking abode, without needing to impress, as seems to be the aspiration of so many stately homes.

The path runs into the more aspiring end of Deal. Here are older, gracious houses, with private gardens across the quiet road, as in some of the more established London Squares. There are even weeping silver pear trees; a contemporary sign of good taste. A plaque indicates that Lister, the surgeon, lived in one of the houses. A little further on a well-maintained hedge and sign indicate that this is Archery Square 'for members only': such is the neighbourhood. Then Henry's castle looms [the perennial 'french problem'] and I am back to where I finished my last walk.

Thence a train ride back to Dover Priory [no freedom pass here!].

23 September, 2008: in Dover.

The next day but one I did make Folkestone; another serious, chalk, cliff top, walk. But with rain dominating my second day I ended up with a day in Dover and, apart from the obvious morning in the splendid castle, found the local museum in the town centre to be well worth a visit. Not only does it show how Dover was an important roman settlement, with lighthouses on either headland, but, on the top floor of the museum, there is a superb exhibition of a bronze age boat, and a well-documented account of both its discovery when they were enlarging the A20 road, and an attempt to reconstruct a model with similar instruments and tools for that period from local timber. Thus no saws for felling and planking; and all tight-fitting pegged, all-wood, joints: no nails. This was a display well worth a rainy day!

As I was staying in Dover in accommodation at the foot of the castle my western exit [a preliminary exploration for tomorrow] ran along the sea front where there is actually an area of green

Richborough miner
in Dover

between the sea and the major roads full of traffic hammering   towards the ferry
terminals. The open space here has a striking life-size figure of a crouching man, which
from a distance I assumed to be a war memorial: the stoic trooper soldier defending the
harbour. But no, it is dedicated to the miners of Richborough power station, whose
ghostly skeleton so eerily dominated the skyline between Pegwell Bay and Sandwich.
This memorial is a fine casting; even if a somewhat strange placing.

24 September, 2008: Dover to Folkestone.

The cliff walk to Folkestone does not compare favourably to the eastern cliffs of
Dover, even if it is the ending of the North Downs Way. The first difficulty is finding
where it starts as you exit Dover. There is an obligatory, penitential stretch of very busy
dual carriageway with flyovers that force the pedestrian to cross at awkward points. Then
the footpath to the cliffs is very poorly indicated. It goes off to the left, very steeply, at a
roundabout, and again, is very close to the cliff edge, with the railway seeming hundreds
of metres below [shades of Moira Shearer and the 'Red Shoes' ballet film?]. In its favour,
bits of the very narrow path are concreted and intermittently stepped; it is also securely
fenced with wire netting and hand rails. Somewhat oddly the narrow strip of land

between this and the A20 has well-padlocked, terraced allotments; and higher up, when you have scrambled through gorse and blackthorn that make the pathway almost into a tunnel, a notice saying that this is known as 'Lear's leap'! The story goes that Shakespeare came down for a sojourn, and this high place inspired the suicidal thoughts portrayed by the recently eyeless Gloucester in the great late tragedy of King Lear [although actually Edgar, Gloucester's son, disguised as Tom, manages to deceive him into harmlessly jumping from one piece of flat land to another- as I recall?]. However, I quite understand the propensity for inducing a jumping feeling by the vertiginous drop here. But the path does get better and more rural once the top of the first undulation is achieved: a distinct sigh of relief from this walker.

For several minutes a sense of isolation is achieved; the space of a minor haven. But a little further round a small thicket and meadow and you realize that they were but screening out the A20 with its tail to fin lines of killer whales pounding out from the ferries disguised as juggernauts. These remain as one's companion for the best part of the walk to Folkestone, while the railway below temporarily disappears into a tunnel. However the landward busy road contrasts with the magnificent sea views right across to France from the peak of these cliffs. The scudding clouds allow those magical bright beams of sunshine to spill silver patterns onto the sea; slowly changing; even as a finger painting on the water: quite transfixing. Blot out the traffic, and this spectacle is the reason for walking alone; to just stop and stare. Photographs can capture an image, but are only a memory of the whole, ever shifting dynamic of such a situation.

The cliff edge walk is here signposted as the end of the North Downs walk, and the cliff top, a strip of land between the sea and the A20, has the feel and botany of downland, with bits of it variously grazed by sheep and ponies. The map says that the Saxon Shore Way runs down below, but how that is accessed or where it runs into the sea or the rail tunnel remains a mystery to me. Anyway the haunting sea views quite justify the high cliff route at this time.

Fortunately, as the cliff contours rise, the A 20 goes into an escarpment; and suddenly there is a dramatic coastal site dedicated to the airmen of the Battle of Britain at Capel le Ferne. This is a well-kept, landscaped site with another fine sculpture: this time of a debonair young pilot in his leather jacket, helmet and goggles in his hands; representing the heroic sacrifice of youth and talent.

It is the more moving because it is very sparsely visited [at this moment], and I have come across it unexpectedly; jolting me back into another part of the century. The monolithic blocks, on the land side of the memorial, list too many names: such heroic sadness. But they are lists of all participants as opposed to only those who died: so not all was lost, and all are recognized for their contribution.

The sky is now a radiant blue, scattered with white strung out clouds over a silvery blue sea; and you can almost feel the seated figure listening and watching for a formation of spitfires to fly over. It is the most moving event of the day; perhaps of the walk.

Thence the path begins to descend, and thankfully parts company with the re-emerged A20, while below the railway emerges from its tunnel to run along the lower coastline. The walk is now through what is called the Warrens; which is again a safely fenced walk, with a fall of shrubs seaward, while bare stone rises to houses perched on the top of the cliffs; forwards a distant view of Folkestone Harbour. The path is well signposted and eventually arrives at a hostelry on the road running down into Folkestone. This is a moderately busy road and I spot a signposted footpath and stile leading to a short cut across a field. One foot on the stile I observe that the steep slope below is well populated with long horned West Highland cattle. I reassure myself that they are all placidly chewing their cud, but nevertheless, having accomplished suicidal heights on the cliffs in safety, I opt for conservatism, and continue down the road.

As thirties Folkestone suburbia appears, along with dahlias and fuschias, I am very tempted to get on a bus; but persevere to arrive at another long eastern promenade, running into the harbour and ferry terminal; the latter being nowhere near so domineering, nor as intrusive, as at Dover.

Folkestone around the ferry terminal has the impression of so called 'planning blight', leaving strange islands of next-to-no-man's-land, the vernacular, and, over a very good pint of bitter, the impression that you could buy almost anything around here with the right contacts and ready cash. However, I proceed up the fairly steep incline [it was but a slope when I was descending?], and there are hidden, handsome squares and stately houses, some of which have seen better times. Perhaps I will investigate these a little more on my next visit?

21 October, 2008: Folkestone to New Romney.

On returning, a month or so later, I find that the esplanade at Folkestone runs both at sea level and along the top of the cliff. At sea level there is an extensive shingle beach and some lesser twentieth-century architecture. But on the upper levels the houses are grand, with an almost military bearing, testimony to it being favoured by the Victorians and Edwardians. The conservatory of the majestic 'Grand Hotel' echoes with the ghosts of seven tiered jellies and delicate doilies. Do I hear the muted strings straining through the potted palms, or is it simple the wind humming in the telegraph wires? I think the latter. But the whole area is a gracious space, well maintained, with plenty of width, both in grass and tarmac, to stroll or sit. On this fine late October afternoon two young husbands chat as they push their respective offspring in buggies, sans femmes: an elderly couple potter hand in hand, each with a walking stick poking from the spare hand: a retired cleric zooms around on an electric scooter and homes in on a passively sun bathing pensioner on one of the many tempting seats: seemingly a suitable diversity of upper Folkestone's population.

36

However the utopia of Folkestone does not last, and the esplanade descends towards Sandgate and the busy A259, from which it is even good to get back to struggle on the shingle, only to find that this is still ' the Saxon Shore Way'.

While continuous with Folkestone, Sandgate has more of a village feel, of local sailing clubs and pubs, and even boasts one of the most eastern of the anti-Napoleon Martello towers that will measure out the coast from here westwards [a pleasant change from measuring in golf course tees!]. At Sandgate Rowing Club, on a fine Sunday afternoon, it seemed that on the balcony more alcohol was being consumed than was consistent with Olympic aspirations in rowing. I even felt a twinge of superiority [or was it envy?], as I strode past, crunching the shingle underfoot.

The houses of Sandgate do not so much peter out as become set further back, allowing a heath-like barrier to run parallel to the sea: that is until the inevitable Hythe Golf Club appears as an appendage to the Imperial Hotel.

Hythe is the middle of the cinque ports and makes a tricky part of the coastal walk inasmuch as there is an extensive firing range to the west of the town; and thus a definite no-go area. The town itself seems pleasant enough and rises up on to yet another snake of chalk hills, giving a view of splendid, comfortable, architecture, with the medieval church of St Leonard's sitting conspicuously on the rising hill, beyond the military canal. This latter feature is yet another marker in line with the cinque ports, the Martello towers, concrete hideouts, and Henry's castles, all designed to defend this Achilles heel of England from the invaders, French or German. In this case it was the threat of Napoleon that stimulated the building of this canal, running westwards some miles west of Rye, theoretically to facilitate the rapid movement of troops and supplies, to defend this stretch of coast. Fortunately Wellington, the Prussians, and the battle of Waterloo saw to it that this was never needed. Such a simple sentence, writing off much hard labour in digging out the canal from these marshy lands [to say nothing of the gruesome battles that both preceded and were part of Waterloo!]. However the canal now provides the ideal way of circumnavigating the out of bounds firing range, which takes up the west coast of Hythe. The designers of 'the Saxon Shore Way' had the same idea; although it just might be true that all this land was uninhabitable marshland in Saxon times. But now the canal walk has been well surfaced and provides a leafy and tranquil sojourn through the estates of

37

Hythe and out into the country side. Autumn's leaves fall and for a while float on the still surface, looking almost like water lilies. Coots scuttle; an occasional swan glides sedately; and twos or threes of ducks bob around. The arching trees and shrubs host the suburban portfolio of robins, blackbirds, blackcaps, wrens, and even the occasional yellow hammer or chaffinch. It is a very different feel from the hard marching on coastal shingle. It is pleasant enough to tempt the ambling walker to follow it all the way to Cliff End and Fairlight Cove, thereby cutting off the corner of the Romney marshes and the Dungeness Power station. But I resist, and at the road crossing for West Hythe, I take the road to Botolph bridge and head for the coast again.

I make a note that at some future date I shall complete the canal walk.

The quiet of the canal also shows up the splendour of Stutfall Castle standing on the run of hills that snake into Hythe, and there are the remains of a considerable Roman fort spreading out immediately below the castle: well worth a detour.

But from the canal bridge there is a well- marked footpath, crossing a narrow gauge railway, then the path back to the coast is sort of indicated by blue beacons which seem to peter out into a disused gravel pit! Heading instinctively to the coast, but with no blue markers, all too soon returns the walker to the concrete esplanade, which butts right on to the military firing range. But the esplanade is itself almost like a military fortification, and wide enough to run a windsurfing race on, to say nothing of the tonnage of Norwegian granite that has been transported. The feeling of fortification is enhanced by the fact that the promenade is one or more storeys higher than the caravans and houses that line the A259, running tightly behind the fortifications here. A large rock records that one Michael Howard [local MP & erstwhile Conservative Party leader], was instrumental in achieving this construction; possibly with EU money? Now it begins to make sense!

Dymchurch looms in the distance; and another Martello tower.

Old Dymchurch has a clutch of charming houses with pointed rooves and facades that are either tiled or boarded in wood. There are even sagging tiled roofs and a clutch of mellowed Tudor cottages. It seems to be very much a small coastal town with the A259 running through it; but I do have a very good fresh crab sandwich at the one hostelry I manage to find; and the locals seem sufficiently relaxed not to feel constrained in talking to strangers!

Replenished I head on along this great bend of a bay, with Dungeness power station looming at the end, and the local small gauge [and small carriage size!] railway that runs from Hythe to Dungeness, occasionally peeping its whistle as it takes shoppers and a spattering of tourists hither and thither.

St Mary's Bay is but a continuation of Dymchurch. But then there is a fair stretch of open space as you head to the Romneys which give their name to this whole low-lying peninsula of reclaimed marshland. By now the reader will fully expect this open stretch to harbour a golf course; and they would not be disappointed. Shingle and seakale lie seaward. A ghost of an empty white-faced hotel marks the entrance into what goes as Littlestone-on-Sea, which somehow sets the tone for a strange mixture of what was grand but is decayed, contrasted with some new build flats; some of the latter very like retirement homes. The slightly lost feel might just be that it is very out of season, for there is a reasonable beach here. But it is inevitably compounded by the fact that Romney, as in Old Romney is some three miles inland, while even 'New Romney' feels a good mile and a half inland when walking at the end of the day. This distribution says much about the history of this area, with so much shingle being deposited in 1287 that New Romney became the new coast line, which in turn is some distance from the urbanized present coast line of the twenty-first century. That this is history is emphasised by the attractive medieval houses lining the A259 as it runs through New Romney. These are as attractive as those in the much better known and 'found' town of Rye. Thankfully the tourists do not seem to have found this place. Perhaps not having an official railway connection, [since Beeching's severe pruning!], has preserved it.

I find a medieval inn; of which there is more than one. I also stumble on one of the other inns hosting trannies rather than grannies at five o'clock on a Monday evening. Perhaps this says much about the difference between Rye and New Romney. But there are many attractive old houses with tiled or timbered fronts and an imposing tower of St Nicholas.

House in New Romney

There is a graveyard with a lytch gate some distance from the church, but well maintained and sheltered from the wind by a decent hedge. Sitting there in the shelter and the sun, I had the spooky experience of hearing the most terminal, railing, ghostly sort of gasping.

I hesitated, wondering whose ghost was visiting me; then looked round cautiously, only to realize that there were some Romney Marsh sheep on the other side of the fence that obviously had more than a touch of pneumonia. I felt sorry for them, but the hairs on my neck subsided, and I enjoyed the sun again.

22 October, 2008: New Romney to Lydd.

Back on the coast and striking off to Dungeness after an overnight rest I enjoyed the splendid beach at low tide which hosts flocks of small waders, which I think might be turnstones flitting and skimming away from me, then round behind me in a great arc, feasting on the sand worms while the tide is low.

Walking on the splendid expanse of beach is a world away from the ribbon development of bungalow-itis that runs along the minor coast road, with all the houses having their back gardens defined by the miniature railway behind them; but then looking beyond over the slightly surreal landscape of shingle-scape. The changing nature of this landscape is again reflected by Lydd-on-Sea being some two miles away from the inland old town of Lydd, the two being separated by a mixture of colonized shingle and marshland, making a designated nature reserve which preserves a very particular flora and fauna, and a stopping-off location for migratory birds. This area is rendered even more surreal as the minor road swings right towards Lydd, by the dotted collection of wooden and iron habitations, interspersed with the remains of various ships and their ancillary discarded equipment; all dominated by the massive outline of the Dungeness Power Station, and no less than two lighthouses. In the middle of all this there is also an excellent pub that serves the freshest fish, with chips, that you are likely to get anywhere. The latter very welcome on a blustery and chilly day. The gay film director, Derek Jarman, had a hideout here. Sadly his originally iconic garden and wooden house have now become a shrine of high camp.

Dungeness escarpment.

I visit the well laid out RSPB centre. But it is a little early for the great migrations of water birds; and only a few mallards can be easily seen in the gravel lakes. However there are largish groups of starlings fluttering overhead, dashing towards the coast, then, at the last moment, wheeling back in a large arc. It is as if there is a collective anticipation that they have to cross the water, but, as yet they do not have the common will to make that bold commitment. Starlings are not my favourite bird, but seeing them en masse they do look frail forms for such a formidable flight across the sea. I wonder if it is some sort of mass hypnosis or psychological energy that they work up to. It is easy to see why these mass flights have always fascinated us, seeming to put our own lives into some timid perspective.

Down to earth again, the thought that the lakes are also home to medicinal leeches does not encourage paddling, nor does one wish to disturb the eco system for various local species of frogs and newts. The low level scrub of broom, sedge grasses and the delicate filigree of lichens is not as immediately gripping as the skyscape; so that a wild hare, dashing away from the piercing whistle of the small train, seems like a large mammal. The wind blows keenly. The Power Station, so long a looming shape, is massively domineering, but in its own way, a sort of strange abstraction of grey and green rectangles; if you have a penchant for that sort of industrial architecture.

Since round the corner from the Dungeness monster is yet another shooting range, out of bounds, and thereby cutting off a whole wedge of land south of Lydd, I opt for a return ride on the miniature railway to Hythe, and therefrom back to the metropolis. My next strategy is to visit Rye as a base and to visit Lydd and Hastings from there. But the winter months might intervene!

SUSSEX: 2009

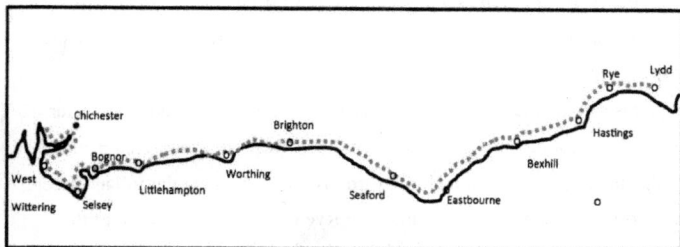

16-17 March 2009: Lydd to Rye

So it is in the lambing season when I emerge from hibernation in the city and take the train to Rye, seeing both Winchelsea and Rye standing out like castles from the surrounding marshes as I arrive at Rye railway station, the latter conveniently doubling as a bus station. But this is in no way as an attractive an approach as arriving on foot from Lydd as I intend to do the following day.

Having booked myself in at the side of the river I have the privilege of making preliminary explorations of this delightfully-preserved, even to the extent of being slightly quaint, town. Because of these features it does suffer from the dual features of tourism and gentrification, which reminded me why I liked New Romney.

Almost any exploration naturally leads up the hill to the finest views, and, fortified by half a pint of fine smoked shrimps and a pint of Harvey's Best bitter, I do get glimpses, between the fine, often timbered, houses, of flat stretches of the marshes. The streets are narrow, often cobbled, and much cornered, so that it is a surprise to find the space of a churchyard and the dignified presence of St Mary's Church at the top of the hill. The interior was filled with scaffolding associated with replacing the organ; but I felt that there is a sense in which the echoes of holiness are more tangible when the building is stripped of its comfortable trappings.

By evening most of the trippers have gone; and the town has almost a surfeit of pubs and eating places for both residents and visitors: there is generally much good fresh sea-food.

The following day I hop on the 100 bus [discovered by yesterday's homework] to head towards Lydd. A useful, even as a pleasant, exercise from upstairs in the bus inasmuch as it gives a foretaste of what to expect walking back from Lydd towards Rye. The privilege of the freedom pass!

Old Lydd is a complete contrast to the tourism of Rye; with Lydd's character strongly modified by the army camp attached to its southwestern aspect. Again, as in Rye, it is the old church and its central churchyard, like a great triangular village green, which seems to form the centre of the old town. In Rye it is the high position of the church that is its making. But in Lydd it is the size of the church in a flat spread of surrounding land that makes it so imposing. It is no surprise that All Saints, Lydd, is known as the cathedral of the marshes.

Various paths criss-cross the churchyard, connecting the various groups of attractive timbered, or white-washed or old-red-bricked houses that edge the green; all of them dwarfed by the size and height of the church. The space inside bears out the cathedral designation. The pillars of the nave bow outwards in a curve that I do not think the architects originally intended. But the heads of their high arches have the jolliest set of carved heads that I have seen in a church; a delightful change from grimacing gargoyles, [or of Suffolk angels, dare I say?!]. The north wall is identified as 'preconquest', and is part of what was possibly a basilica, therefore quite a rarity. The great nave has many brasses and effigies of local notaries, but it was the sheer size, and the fact that I was alone in it, that was the most impressive. I think that I must have been particularly lucky as on another occasion it was locked: albeit there is a notice detailing from where a key might be collected: and well worth a visit!

The George Hotel, adjacent to All Saints, was, and still is, a place of long standing hospitality; and in my case, for suitable refreshment. The immediately local houses retain some of this charm, but the B2075 then runs into a less attractive ribbon development and the estate of the army camp, which in turn excludes access to the coast for the next three miles or so. It is quite tempting to walk a little inland away from the B road in order to investigate the dykes and ditches, even if only to see if the so named 'Jury Gut Sewer' lives up to its name! But I see that the Royal Bank of Scotland, [before the tax payer had to bail it out!], has funded a cycle and pedestrian walkway that runs parallel to the road, yet some 10 metres apart- for safety. So I decide to follow this course.

It turns out to be yet another slightly surreal walk as it is set below sea level, with the coastal view being defined by a military boundary of concrete posts connected by a more than 6 foot high mesh fence topped with barbed wire, while the landward side is a mixture of shingle farm land in which gravel pits seem to have been the main product, with the older ones now showing as mini lakes, even meres? This landward aspect is all surmounted by the ghost-like background of a haunt of wind turbines. The land seems to struggle to produce grass here, and the few cows seem to echo that struggle: it cries out for a few tough Romney Marsh sheep to bring their golden hooves to bear?

However the upbeat side of the obviously remunerative gravel pits is that the water infill has resulted in a natural habitat that increasingly supports a fauna as well as a flora, and the more so the further one gets away from the army camp and its gun noise. A linnet pops out from the brambles, flutters across my path, and alights on a strand of the fence surrounding the still waters. It lifts the spirit, and soon I see a mixture of Canada and Pink Foot geese, along with a solitary swan. I begin to wonder if these are domestic, but then, a little further along this waterway, there are two small islands in the water that are packed out with nesting gulls, with the accompanying cacophony. As I round a corner I also disturb a flock of some thirty wigeon and a smaller group of eider ducks. So there is a reward for persevering with this rather out-of-the-way walk. The RSPB gravel pools at Dungeness do not have a monopoly on local wildlife after all!

The army boundary thankfully ends at Broomhill Sands; and again there is due recompense. Clambering up over a man-made fortified pile of shingle and concrete suddenly there is a vista of the spread of the sea, blazing in the glorious sunshine, and a great sweep of beach through Camber Sands right round to Winchelsea, with the cliffs of Hastings hazy in the distance. At 11.00 am in mid-March there is nobody else on this stretch of beach, and it reminds me of why I am celebrating walking the coast. It reminds me of similar wild stretches on the Northumbrian coast: but it is the first impressive wild expanse that I have encountered on this southern coast. To cap it the tide is well out, so that it is an idyllic walk for half an hour or so.

Gradually figures appear in twos and threes, with and without dogs, and/or prams; or on or off horseback.

Having done the reverse journey on top of a double decker bus I am aware that Camber has both a Holiday Camp and an estate of rather superior immobile 'mobile homes'. But from the beach only twenty or so houses of inoffensive architecture present themselves, so the disguise of an idyll is maintained. Moreover there is a very acceptable café [and a pub!], on the beach. So I have perfectly adequate refreshment without the overkill of a resort. One non-idyllic aspect of this stretch of beach is that the outlet from 'Jury Gut Sewer' has to be crossed fairly early on; and perhaps this could account for the eastern aspect of the beach being less populated!

However, once past Camber, it is quite possible to walk on the now busying beach all the way to the outlet of the tidal river Rother, that swells to and from Rye.

Rye from the Harbour

But the river is certainly far too active and deep for any sort of pedestrian crossing. So it dictates a retreat to Rye.

To approach Rye from this aspect does enhance the image of the town as a fortress of the fens, with the matriarchal church and heroic ruins of the castle perched above rows of houses. Moreover there is a good bridleway along the eastern bank which runs partly through and adjacent to the inevitable golf course, but also alongside a sizeable mere that surprisingly seems to have been largely left to wildlife. The opposite, westerly, bank of the river seems to house a smartish sailing club, but otherwise seems rather bleak and occupied by all the signs of a decayed industry.

Back to a comfortable night in Rye, and some fine sea bass at a timbered pub.

18, March, 2009: Rye to St Leonards.

Having spotted that the west bank of the Rother was mainly industrial estate I was tempted to avoid this route by crossing the military road and the military canal to head across fields on a well-marked path heading for Castle Farm on the outskirts of Winchelsea Beach. This has the reward of passing by the distant ruins of Henry VIII's Camber Castle,which, marooned in a misty field, accentuates its allure of abandonment: such a contrast to the well restored twin castle at Deal.

But the prescribed route down through the industrial site does yield echoes of better times, and splutters into life by the time that you arrive at Rye Harbour, with a decent pub and some quite attractive terrace houses. There is also something of the feel of community here, not quite so invaded by the tourists or the affluent grey pound as in Rye itself. It also leads down to the continuation of the magnificent sweep of Camber Sands; and inland gives you the view of a wild area of marsh and fen, with considerable expanses of water, across which the more distant gaunt ruins of Camber Castle seem even more romantically bleak. On a misty morning one would not be surprised to see the ghosts of Elsinore, [or Henry's deputies?], going for their daily newspaper!

The beach stretches on and on, past the conurbation of straggling Winchelsea Beach, with Winchelsea itself now remote from the coast and raised up above the Military Canal. But, staying on the coast, I see all too soon patches of mud and shale outcrop appear and make pools in the beach; walking becomes a much slower and trickier exercise. Thankfully, the cliffs that form Firehill and the National Trust Land, west of Hastings, soon loom large. So that by the pleasant, but traffic-busy, conurbation of Cliff End I am glad to leave the accompanying coastal road behind. The rising cliffs also mark the termination of the Military Canal, which was first seen in Deal; and also the end of the Saxon Way, first seen at Faversham on day one! That now seems a long while as well as a long way away!

It is quite tricky to find the pedestrian entrance up on to the Fairlight Cliffs. Two locals, kindly having drawn my attention to the finishing of the Military Canal, direct me from the 'Smuggler's Inn' along the narrow road [no pedestrian protection!]. It curves round and upwards, then, where there is a turning to the right marked 'Pett Village'; look to your left. It appears to be a private driveway. But set some 10yards back from the road there is a signpost with a yellow arrow, designating your allowed access to a narrow fenced path bordering the boundaries of a series of private gardens: a route easily missed! For the first time since the cliffs at Folkestone this is an uphill walk; but at least it is through quiet leafy gardens, with no traffic noise. At the top you emerge from the grand suburban feel to open fields and hedgerows, somewhat set back from the cliff edge; and eventually this leads into the comfortable anonymity of Fairlight houses and their extensive gardens. Here you have to find the centre of a centreless place [as far as a coastal walker approaching from the east can ascertain], before you can get back onto the coastal cliff path.

This is a variable feast because much of the cliff path is open to crumbling and therefore, appropriately, fenced off. It is very much a case of heading westwards along the suburban roads until you can find a road leading to safe cliff edge on your left! There is a quite broad walkway when you do find it, and the houses are set back: these finally petering out when the sweep of Firehill rises before you. This sweep of land is something of a relief, and a total contrast to the flat spread of Camber Sands. Here there are suitably placed seats on which to sit and survey the rolling grassland, interspersed with gorse and woodland, dipping into and rising from the several valleys; while the sea glistens and twinkles remotely in the horizon, smudging into the blue of the sky. No sound of breaking waves here. But did I hear the first skylark?

This is a National Trust 'Park' running right up to Hastings. Strictly the cliff coast walk is there for the walking, and is a very scenic walk up and down into the various coves, some of which are only accessible by steep steps, and others not at all. As I have done these before on visits to Hastings, I choose to loop behind all the valleys, staying at the same height and scooting to Fairlight Place and on to the lake above Ecclesbourne Glen. I suspect this is also influenced by the fact that I am beginning to feel a little leg weary, and the prospect of repeated up and downing loses out to strolling a slightly more circuitous route at one level!

The Fairlight Park reminds me of an enlarged Hampstead Heath, with well laid-out paths, so that one can wander at will and find different idylls, hidden groves, still water, running water, sweeping vistas; always something new just round the corner. It also abuts quite suddenly onto the old town of Hastings, with a steep descent via a path and steps; or even a lift if you have to.

From on high the view across Hastings, and on to St Leonards and Bexhill is impressive; but reminds you that the next stretch is a built up esplanade again. The next real interlude of wild coast will be the National Trust Park of Beachy Head, west of Eastbourne!

But I am still at Hastings and enjoy the bustle and charm of the old Town, with its ever diminishing cluster of a fishing industry. It seems but a parody of an industry; more a museum. It is a busy sea front here, mainly hotels and bed and breakfast accommodation, touristy shops, and plenty of hostelries offering a wide range of sustenance. The older grander hotels have thankfully been rescued here, some converted into apartments. But it is a fairly seamless walk into St Leonards, where I decide to stay the night, as I have sung here at St John the Evangelist, further up the hill, and so know the quirky Grand Hotel, with its fine sea views.

St Leonards is marked by the advent of several impressive squares [one side being the sea!], with Warrior Square being the most spacious, even if the ex-large hotel is now a centre for immigrants.

But further along the sea front I have my room with a sea view; and am not going to get into local politics when on a coastal walk!

19 March, 2009: St Leonards to Pevensey Bay.

I am privileged with another bright sunny day to start me on my journey, along with the advice of the hotel manager as to all the tricks of navigating to the hidden cafés on bits of beach that are relatively quiet: valuable local information.

The grandeur of the squares of St Leonards ameliorates westwards into Edwardian architecture, and then a jumble of thirties buildings. The railway also runs progressively closer to the shingle beach until the footpath has the railway on one side and beach huts of various hues on the other: the latter still boarded up at this time of year, with the occasional enthusiast taking advantage of the fine weather to give a touch of bright blue paint to the eaves of his hut. There is an area where there is a virtual squadron

49

of huts, four or six rows of them: certainly very colourful. The path then weaves to the coast to pass a sort of semi-industrial area to emerge onto shingle, still with the railway close by.

An attempt to break out of the built-up area occurs at Glynne Gap, with one of the hidden cafés nestling in a corner, and an attempt by the land to form something of a cliff. Here there is enough of a rudimentary fortification at the base, presumably to minimize erosion, that allows a walk round at sea level and into the beginnings of Bexhill. Now you are definitely back to the residential, mainly purpose-built for comfortable retirement? It follows that there is a well-kept seafront, although not up to the charm of Herne Bay, nor the memory of attempted opulence at Eastbourne [yet to come in the walk, but previously visited].

The centre of Bexhill has a cluster of attractive low houses on the sea front, with longish gardens overlooked by the passerby on the seashore. But by far the most dramatic feature is the revamped De La Warr pavilion, a bravura block of white, 'modern' [as in 1930s] architecture. Here the sweeping staircase leads up to another café where you half expect everybody to be dressed for the Ascot Races as in 'My Fair Lady', in Cecil Beaton black and white mode. Instead they are plumpish retired couples in comfortable coats and shoes, mixed with a sprinkling of kids and mums in trainers and jeans, plus prams and shopping. But the view deserves a coffee stop; even a chocolate cookie.

Westwards from Bexhill the railway and a minor road separate the pedestrian from the statutory golf course, but it does give a feeling of openness, and a view across open fields. This, rather than Hastings, was the landing point for William the Conqueror's Norman troops, and, within the larger sweep of Pevensey Bay, there are a cluster of houses round 'Norman's Bay', with its own Martello tower. All too soon this trickles into the spread of buildings that make up Pevensey Bay, a ribbon development of suburbia, hard onto the shingle; and hard on the feet. As the latter are beginning to feel a little tired I opt for the road running behind the houses. The view of the sea is replaced by one of the backs of gardens and garages, a suffocation of suburbia, sufficiently non-descript to give my boots new walking power. I find a jolly hostelry at the cross roads, where sustenance makes me feel better, but I have the intuition to ask at the newsagent opposite before thinking of walking out to the railway station of Pevensey. This station is some way inland, and I wonder if this is not another example of the coast having moved seawards over time. Was Pevensey and its castle originally coastal too, I also wonder? [On a later visit I find old Pevensey and its castle much more attractive than the coastal strip!].

But the most important outcome of my enquiry at the newsagent was to find that the trains are not stopping at Pevensey at the moment [which would not have been an appealing aspect had I traipsed out there!]. However there is a bus stop across the road from the inn, with 'freedom pass' transport back to the door of my hotel in St Leonards. An half hour wait in the pleasant afternoon sun and I am saved again!

May 6, 2009: Pevensey to Eastbourne in reverse.

Easter and a cluster of birthdays, including my seventieth, have passed by before I am on the coast again, with the strategy of going to Eastbourne, midway between my next two walks, so that I can make a base at a family hotel in a street of hotels near to the pier and the flamboyant flower beds. The seafront hotels of Eastbourne seem to be very grand and spacious, catering for coach-loads of elderly visitors, to which I am in denial. They seem to loom like pastel twin-setted and tweeded ghosts in arm chairs or surrounding tables in all the large Edwardian windows; with rather more twin-sets than tweeds.

51

It is an extremely blustery and cloudy day; so much so that the chilly wind and greyness remind me of February. I wonder about the wisdom of my projected walking. But my hotel is a family-run place with the pleasant authenticity which that often brings; and it is close to the pier.

Eastbourne Pier on a calm day.

I have half a day to walk eastwards out of Eastbourne towards my last destination at Pevensey, passing the handsome sea front of Eastbourne architecture and seeing it peter out into the Groynes, which is an area of open amenity land. This then regroups itself to become the very newly-developed Sovereign Harbour, with overtones of Canary Wharf – on –Sea. Indeed it is something of a magical mystery tour to weave a way through, or more strictly, across this complex on foot, without travelling all the way round the water's edge. But it is possible with perseverance. I do wonder what all these people do for a living: neither fishermen nor bankers: not surely all due to the grey pound?

This stretch of the afternoon walk is also punctuated by a high density of Martello towers, which, from the coast, is the only hint that they thought that Napoleon might sail further west than William at Pevensey! But it is another case of the coast having grown and pushed Pevensey inland, with its ex coastal castle and both Norman and Roman ruins. The present coastal collection of dwellings on Pevensey Bay has little to recommend it, but the beach is fine, and may be its main recommendation.

The number 12 bus sees me back at Eastbourne, and a rather grey and blustery day brightens when, in a pub at the end of the pier, I have watched Manchester United beat

52

Arsenal, with only five other people out on such a chilly night. Returning, Eastbourne is a glitter of lights on the handsome architecture, set against the wildish sea. The journey begins to justify itself.

7 May, 2009: Eastbourne to Seaford.

A good night's sleep and muesli followed by scrambled egg for breakfast see me well disposed to a sunny day and the prospect of the cliffs of Beachy Head. The promenade is boldy colourful with multicoloured wall flowers in full perfume as well as blossom. There is also a quieter lower walkway, away from the traffic, and peopled by dog walkers, the occasional cyclist, and the early morning people out for the first coffee-fix. However the most arresting sight, as I negotiate a curve, is to be swooped round by a rather androgynous, tattooed, young mother roller blading with her baby strapped to her back. The new generation! I can only hope that should the mother fall it is not backwards!

The promenade rises toward the open spaces of Beachy Head and then the road suddenly switches right while the footpath continues forward to big open spaces. Almost immediately there are various options; a fan of paths. Since I am strictly doing a coastal walk [and have taken some of the other options before with friends], I head left to Cow Hole. Not many choose this route so it is a pleasantly solitary walk on this fine morning, and a striking contrast to the bustle of Eastbourne. These humps of white cliff are where the snaking South Downs, that will be a dominant background to much of my next stretch of walk, run here into the English Channel. Being a fairly solid sort of chalk, they seem only to be dusted with a thin layer of soil which does manage to support a particular flora, balanced with a certain amount of controlled grazing. At the time of my walking the grassland is well dotted with the deeper delphinium blue of the creeping ajugas, while the ubiquitous gorse is a mass of vivid yellow.

I find that the reason that this pleasant walk is so relatively under used is that it leads straight to a cliff edge, with the only egress being to the even higher cliff of Beachy Head itself; via quite a stiff climb! This is even more peeving when, as you [or I, in this case!], stagger to the summit, you find bus-loads of pedestrians tottering around in the very blowy wind, having made comfortable access via easier routes!

However, once this height has been scaled it is all relatively downhill to Birling Gap, with a fine spread of bluebells to welcome the walkers.

7 Sisters from inland.

There is time to have a quick cup of coffee here [amongst all the car drivers], before tackling the switchback of the seven sisters.

They are all considerably lower than Beachy Head itself; but they certainly hump up and down. They also seem to be quite a popular sequence for people of all ages, shapes, and sizes: each, wisely, taking it at their own pace. There is also the odd seat where one can catch breath and just absorb the impressive views, if so inclined.

After the final peak the path descends to what seems like the broad estuary of the river Cuckmere, which curves and twists between marsh fields and pasture, most of which look as if they might be subject to winter flooding. The river is certainly not crossable without walking upstream on a well-marked path to the bridge of the A259.

Just across the bridge is the very pleasant 'Golden Galleon' which is, justifiably, a popular pub restaurant: and very welcome after completing the morning's switch back walk.

Refreshed by a fluid-replacing orange and lemonade, followed by a pint of Harvey's Best and a crab sandwich, I start off again on the west side of the river. After a short spell of following the river there is the choice of two paths; the one a raised walk following close to the river bank, while the other goes through a gate, following something of a farm track, lying above the marsh pasture grazing that stretches to the river. The latter is the less-frequented path and, bordered by blackberries and butterflies, with mixtures of sheep and cattle grazing on the lower fields, is the one that I choose. This path rises to go behind a cluster of houses which overlook Cuckmere Haven, which presumably was the original fishing community, and which have quite stunning views of the Seven Sisters cliffs. The headland of these cliffs having been successfully walked by myself earlier in the morning adds to my appreciation of the view!

The coastal path rises steadily to Seaford head, with judiciously placed seats for enjoying the view. It is quite tempting to walk up the hill backwards so that the view of the Seven Sisters is constantly held! However a wind has sprung up, which is quite chilly, and as the path seems to enter a channel seaward of the peak of Seaford Head this funnels the wind, so that today there is no encouragement to stop: but, as ever, the view is instantly captured on a digital camera to make a future screen saver!

No surprise that this path emerges onto the back of golf links and the houses of Seaford. These all seem quite distant from the sea. No grand esplanade here, although there are some late-twentieth-century blocks of flats on the road that eventually runs along the shore towards the railway station, and there is something of a concrete walkway with seats here. But as I am after the 12 bus back to Eastbourne [12A for the scenic route via Beachy Head!], I turn right into the town and find some of the older buildings, and the shop assistant, from whom I buy my mints and a copy of The Times, points me in the right direction for the next bus. This is my last night in Eastbourne; and time to move on to the next ordnance survey map. Real progress: and a most enjoyable day!

14 June 2009: Brighton arrival.

Another piece of staged strategy. I take the train to Brighton as a base; and the coastal bus [still the faithful no. 12 – my freedom pass coming into its own] to Seaford. It was a hot and stuffy day in London, and the Victoria Underground Line was closed for the weekend. All of which amounts to hassle. But an air-conditioned train and the much cooler and fresher air at Brighton restore me, so my step finds a spring to it on arrival.

However it is a Sunday evening, and the weekend beach crowd are just thinking about returning to the metropolis; so, as I leave the station, I feel somewhat like the man going to St Ives.

Once at the sea front I head eastwards, at least facing towards Seaford and tomorrow's walk. I find an attractive smallish square, made up of hotels and private houses. I select one of the hotels from its external appearance. But the red-dyed hair and heavily mascara-ed receptionist, along with the news that there is a conference coming in from Monday to Friday, plus a guy behind me asking if he can change his room because of the noise of banging doors late at night; all these make me wonder if I have been deceived by external appearances!

I venture out to eat locally, and find that I am in a fairly assertively gay part of the town. Definitely a fairly out, pink pound, presence: just a little strong for my taste. But there is very acceptable pasta at the local Italian.

15 June, 2009: Seaford to Brighton

In the morning I find that the number 12 bus departs for Seaford more or less from the bottom of the square where I am, running on the main coast road; while on the other side I notice that the 700 coastal bus runs all the way to Portsmouth. I see my walking problems for some distance all solved, and feel the freedom pass quivering with anticipation in my pocket. Only to be brought down to earth by the fact that I am at the bus stop by 9.15, and I do catch a bus straight away, at which hour the freedom pass is not allowed to operate [9.30 is the earliest outside London it seems!]. So I pay up for a change, and resist remarks about London being more emancipated.

The journey to Seaford seems unduly long. Mainly because I am intent, sitting on the top deck of the bus, on looking at detail in terms of walking back to Brighton. I peer at.Kemptown, Rottingdean, Saltdean, Peacehaven, and Newhaven. Am I really going to walk back through all these places today? At Seaford I recognize the newsagent, next door but one to the railway station, where I previously asked about the location of the 12 bus stop after my Beachy Head walk. I disembark at great speed: today's walk begins here.

There is an old heart to Seaford, centred on the church and a cluster of old houses in narrow streets. But they are set back from the efforts of an esplanade, which in turn peters out into a shingle walk that heads for the river Ouse. But part of the pathway indicates that it was once railway track, which is confirmed by its presence in photographs of a Victorian set of flour mills that were powered by tidal flow and an intricate set of sluice gates. Green power, declared obsolete in the early 20th century! How the wheels go round!

Seaford and Newhaven are both smallish connurbations that fit into their coastal landscapes, rather than dominating it as the metropolises of Brighton and Eastbourne did. Both have small, contained, quiet town centres, and a coastline away from the all-pervasive thoroughfare of the A257. From each of them you can see and feel the great chalk white serpent of the South Downs curving its backbone through the countryside and exploding its white fangs, in the form of cliffs, into the sea at Beachy Head.

The approach to Newhaven from the east also goes through industrial estate; but there is a reasonably marked right of way that carves its way through active and inactive sites: even a footbridge over one of the minor tributaries. This brings you to a railway station and to a street of Victorian terrace houses before you cross the Ouse on the A259 bridge.

The west side of Newhaven is altogether 'comfortable smart', and more attractive [unless you are interested in industrial archeology!]. There is a riverside hostelry by which I might have been tempted, were it not 10.00 a.m. A shop sells very fresh looking fish, and there are well kept Edwardian and Victorian houses; but these are offset by decaying timber jetties.

There are even some new town-houses with pointed roofs and timbered facades. All this is riverside. As one moves coastward again the land rises to an old Bronze Age settlement of which there seem but a few traces. Yet the site, with its splendid coastal views, was such a natural defensive site that Henry VIII had a further castle built there – with ruins still remaining; and this was subsequently reinforced for potential Napoleonic invasion; then a final dose of cement came with the second world war. A much used site!

It is a fine sculptured piece of land so close to the town.

I am away cliff walking very quickly, with a friendly wave from a coast guard in his tower that cheers me up. There is a colourful display of wild valerian and yellow trefoils, along with sea cabbages, thyme, and some fading sea pinks. The wild barley on the rough edge of fields is much riper than the cultivated. The cliffs here are partly clay, and very obviously prone to subsidence. I think that the coast guard has more than ships at sea to keep his eye on.

It is scarcely a stretch of the legs before the rather strange development of Peacehaven is reached. There is something like a 20-30 yard grass walkway along the cliff top; but then a very linear layout of a 'new town' built in 1919. A Utopia on the grass lawn of a cliff edge, with an odd note of further surrealism by a feature pointing out that this is where the Greenwich Meridian runs southward into the Atlantic Ocean! I step over it carefully!

I speculate on lunch, but find the illusion of utopia broken by the general deshabillé feel of the A259 as it runs through Peacehaven. The disenchantment is reinforced by the only pub being closed. However, a little out of Peacehaven, and still following the splendid cliff walk, I spot 'the Badger' hostelry, set just off the A259, but with fine coastal views; and worth waiting for.

Suitably refreshed I see that there is a path down to a sort of esplanade, but it seems to be subject to the tide and not accessible at the moment. The wide open space containing the Badger is bounded by the A259, and this road now sweeps close to the cliff edge as one approaches Saltdean. So there is a traffic bound stretch of walking. But I have the privilege of seeing a single hen harrier on the cliff edge. It seems to just drop off the cliff edge and effortlessly glide and hover a few feet away. I am not tempted to imitate it, but am impressed and delighted!

At Saltdean there is mercifully an underwalk esplanade that is safe from the tides and away from the traffic. It runs all the way to Brighton; so the rest of the walk is a rumble, with the thrown in entertainment of a red coloured paraglider, who does attempt to mimic the harrier; but without its grace or flexibility. Still it must be an exciting feeling, suspended so high.

Further on it is possible to descend to the sea's edge, and Rottingdean and Roedean, the famous girl's school, look impressive from below the cliffs, while the walker passes the newly developed marina below, where some of the house owners look as if they might go shopping at the local Asda supermarket by powerboat. The cliffs themselves are as imposing as at Ramsgate, but the thin layers of flint seem to be missing, although there is much reinforcement of the cliffs closer to Brighton in the form of pebble dashed concrete and drilled in metal pole retainers which confuse the natural geology.

Thence it is a pleasant enough walk along the seafront of Brighton, with the grandeur of Kemp Town; and a great mound of shingle attempting to make a naturist stretch of beach discreet. There is the paraphernalia of a popular beach front with ice cream and miniature railways and a whole lower area of shops and restaurant, along with a light railway that trundles along the esplanade.

I am soon back in my hotel room and enjoying a hot shower to rinse away the day's walking.

The second pier at Brighton.

16 June, 2009: Brighton to Worthing.

I depart from Brighton westwards on foot with the town bustling with nine o'clock traffic. The sea front has a heterogeneous collection of architecture. The noble proportions of Kempton and Hove are the epitome of Regency splendour with their spacious elegance and repeated proportions balanced by green openings to the right and sea views to the left. The seafront of Hove also has much to commend it and today is set off against an azure blue sea with gold chipped shingle. But all too soon its classical elegance morphs through Victorian and Edwardian architecture to a rather uninspiring collection of sixties architecture: and the beach huts reappear. However there is some sort of discipline here as the roofs are all a sort of sea green, offset by a liberal sprinkling of primary colours on the doors, giving a kind of rainbow effect, or, less prosaically, the cheerful tartiness of a seaside resort.

There is no break distinguishing the end of Hove from the complex of Portslade-by-sea, Shoreham-by-sea and Southwick. If the coast is strictly followed it is an industrial port; not the coastal walker's terrain. The egress of the river Adur does much to contribute to the strange configuration here as it leaves new Shoreham on a western peninsula, then exits to the sea, but leaves old Shoreham to the north with a working lock and dockland to the east. The dock area does at least seem to be active, with blue gantry developments along with timber and aggregate yards. There is also another, unannounced, naturist beach on the shingle, perhaps protected by its industrial site as much as anything else [but something of a shock to suddenly find oneself accompanied by nude figures strolling along in nothing other than boots!]; and finally, by the entrance to the lock [where it is possible to make a pedestrian crossing to old Shoreham], there is a collection of cafés and deck chairs for an elite group of locals. It is possible to walk to the relatively narrow harbour entrance and promenade. But it simply has the frustration that you can see to the other western side, a hundred or so yards away, but cannot cross it as a pedestrian; so you are bound to walk back to weave your way through the alleyways and footbridges of the locks. All very curious and full of local character, if not scenic in the conventional sense!

I adopt the alternative to the coast path along the industrial area by ploughing along the busy A259 to Old Shoreham, which still has the feel of a small community; although engulfed on all sides. The church of St Mary de Haura has a good exhibition of stained glass and sits well in its small garden/graveyard, with a pleasant cluster of small shops and houses round it: welcome shelter from the wind and sun on the shingle. The Railway Tavern [very adjacent to the railway!], provides a pleasant adjournment for lunch.

Fortunately there is a footbridge over the west branch of the tidal estuary to access the peninsula of the newer Shoreham-by-Sea. This seems to have been built up in the sixties and seventies. Weaving through this estate and heading westward there is a pleasant enough coastal path with the comfortable looking houses that border the path having decent gardens going down to what appears to be a long thin lake; some with their own mooring sites. It is only on the return run on the faithful 700 coastal bus that you see that the same houses actually front onto the busy A259. Not so idyllic!

There is no real break from urbanisation before South Lancing is reached. But there is a fair sized green keeping the A259 at a distance.

Paragliders & Breakwaters at Lancing

There is also a clutch of cafés, a disused building that might have been a theatre and an enthusiastic group of colourful paragliders out at sea. At the west end of the green there is no option but to walk along the A259 on its coastal run to Worthing. But at least it is a bright sunny day with the vision of Worthing pier getting bigger and bigger and across the road there is a fine hedge of tamarisk and willow sheltering a golf course. Then the view runs up to the curling South Downs, with the Gothic architecture of Lancing College now well behind me. On the entry to Worthing there is the usual transition of architectural style, smartening up to a Georgian front where Lady Bracknell and Gwendoline would not seem out of place: or perhaps they would be performing in the theatre on the pier?

This once-genteel resort is now in a fragile state, although boldly attempting to regenerate, pedestrianise and update: but still has too many empty shops. Nevertheless there is a considerable collection of comfortable understated architecture, continuing away from the sea front [i.e. on the way to the railway station]. Our Lady of Sion, as a private school for girls sums it up. Somewhat set back from the sea is a park of bowling greens with plenty of activity from both sexes: serious stuff; 'formidable and solid citizens' springs to mind. Even international matches are held here: quality stuff!

27/28 July 2009 : Worthing to Littlehampton.

It is another month before I find time to pick up the walk from Worthing: the weather blustery for July, not showing the town at its best. I find a slightly dingy-looking hotel on the sea front to the west end of town; but my room is comfortable enough, while the cavernous dining room seems sparsely occupied by business people rather than holiday makers. The town seems rather deserted on a Sunday evening, much of it redeveloped into shopping malls. But there seems to be a rather handsome square with a row of what look like heads by Elizabeth Frink, that does redeem the aspect to the sea.

Monday seems a slightly brighter day and, once breakfasted, I head towards Goring. The beach huts here are all very square, all white, and all angled to face southwest: very regimental. It is almost impossible to tell where the Goring boundary is crossed except that the beach huts now have pointed roofs, are square to the shore and a few colourful rebels have painted the eaves of the white huts in blues, greens, even red: rather fun; a variation in local rules? Is one a conservative seat and the other liberal partnership?

Of course the sun, sea, sand, shingle and seaweed run on as ever, making infinitely more varied patterns as they interact in their banded profile.

Goring seems to be comfortably anonymous with much green space behind the immediate coast. Tamerisk hedges line the coastal walkways, with suitably placed dedicated seats to indicate that much quiet enjoyment has been appreciated here. A wooden café at the end of this stretch boldly flies a Union Jack, summarizing the patriotic ethos.

There is an open green patch as Goring runs into Ferring and here some of the dogs are even walked by ladies in long dresses. Although I am not so sure that wellingtons or trainers quite compliment the rest of the outfit; even when worn with aplomb; even bravura! The openness continues, almost with an illusion of countryside.

62

But then two latch gates interrupt fences that border an un-made road running down to the sand, sea and shingle.

This is singular in two aspects. The first is that where the road opens onto the shingle it is scattered with unchained bicycles whose child owners are distant figures on the beach, speaking of a different age of innocence when such freedom and trust was normality. I am only too aware that I am so much a 21st century city dweller who hesitates to leave a chained bike in the city for fear that it may be stolen.

The second item to note is that on crossing the unmade road I am entering the Kingston Estate. This is a determined piece of civilization. There is a broad walk, a public right of way, that is the width of a football pitch, and most pleasant. I let a black Labrador come through the gate before me and the owner thanks me: civilisation indeed. There are houses at the edge of the grass broadway that seem as substantial as they are remote.

The broadway ends after about three golf tees in length [so obviously the unit of measurement again here] and then I am back to the shingle of Angmering-on-Sea, which runs seamlessly into Rustington. But fortunately the tide seems a mile out; light cirrus cloud and a fair breeze seem to be the things to concentrate on. Not since Lydd to Rye and post Winchelsea have I had such good beach pounding, skirting breakwaters, avoiding blond lurchers, [dogs!], heading at the gallop for a trio of collies. I notice that there is even a higher class of seaweed here: a fine red filigree. There are small clusters of people far out with Labradors: families nearer are shrimping; but all in a large space. Quite exciting to actually see the sandworms pushing their day's excavation out into a neat coil under your shoe. No beach huts!

The fine beach walking keeps me away from the B2140 which, out of Rustington, does run close to the beach, even as it leads into Littlehampton.

Littlehampton is all of a pleasant surprise. Some of it an understated elegance of architecture from a bygone age, set well back from the shore by a capacious green, which now includes a pond for paddle boats. Some of the town is a modern development on the east bank of the river Arun that might have been awarded some EU prize, except that Littlehampton feels quite safe from the EU. But the approach from the east along the beach introduces the walker to the lively pointed beach huts, the bright colours sharp with contrasting eaves, bright blue, bright green and brightest yellow [unconstrained liberalism here!]. There is a strikingly modern 'eco caf' that is rounded, low into the shoreline [I think this did win an architectural award]; and a bus load of children teem onto the sand with buckets and spades.

Eco-caf at Littlehampton.

All that are missing are the patient doe eyed donkeys, waiting to make their two hundred yard trot to and fro along the beach. Perhaps health and safety, or animal rights now forbids them? Or, more hopefully, perhaps it is just not the season yet.

To consolidate my affection for Littlehampton I find that the Crown Inn has concessions for pensioners!

The faithful 700 coastal bus runs from the market square where there are still attractive flint cottages. But the ride back to Worthing confirms that it is good for the walker to stick to the coastal way as much of East and West Preston, along with Rustington and Angmerin-on-Sea, are amorphous suburban infill through which the bus trundles.

29 July 2009: Littlehampton to Bognor Regis.

The sea at Worthing is not blue today; it is green [admittedly aquamarine green]: this in spite of the fact that the sky, scattered only with fledgling smudges of white clouds, is a singular blue. But the sea green is streaked with bands of sludge browns, greys and yellows. How endless this variation is, seen from the beach.

I catch the train from Worthing to Littlehampton as I have done the coastal 700 bus ride several times; and it does dilly and dally a little, taking longer than the rail. The train journey gives you the back view of the conurbations that I passed yesterday, then it swings out in to the country towards Barnham, giving fine views of Arundel, rising on the South Downs, with its large fortress castle almost being outdone by the gothic spires of the catholic cathedral. But this is a mere detour; the rail swings away from Arundel, back along the Arun and into the industrial aspect of Littlehampton; nowhere near as delightful as yesterday's approach along the eastern beach. However the station lands you but a short walk from the town centre, or equally close to an attractive pub that sits next to the foot bridge crossing the Arun to the west bank. It is this latter crossing that I make, grateful, like many of the residents I imagine, that we do not have to slog out to the vehicular bridge a mile further out of town and up river.

The west side of the river also appears to be somewhat industrialized and does not look to be too promising. But the 'Westbeach' is clearly signposted; and turns out to be today's treat.

But first one has to pass an unexpected 'small home' site of what appears to be a variation of prefabs, but all immaculately kept with brightly coloured geraniums, petunias, fuschias, begonias and even tightly mown lawns. This 'Noddyland' on the right is followed by a waterside area on the left of decaying boats which, with the tide out, have the appearance of decaying corpses, the remaining wooden ribs resembling rotting skeletons of ancient sea monsters, their flesh fallen away. But at least this is followed by the modern smarter yachting club next door, which [no great surprise] leads on the land side to a well-supported and prospering golf club, sympathetically laid out.

The shoreline is at last reached and runs through sand dunes into a band of shingle and thence a seamless run of sand. This whole western shoreline is a declared 'nature reserve'; and after the previous clutter is a delightfully tranquil space: only two or three figures visible in the 2-3 miles that I can see: making it well worth persevering with the access.

Now no habitations can be seen, save the Littlehampton harbour to my left. But I turn my back on this for my western walk and my only companions are a scurry of sanderlings, which scamper on a couple of times then finally wing out in a delightful curve to arrive back at their previous base: obviously the pickings were good there. There are three white egrets dipping in the pools and the occasional oyster catcher and godwit. I spot some small white crabs; and plenty of evidence of sand worms. I think I see a solitary figure digging for the worms, but then he prostrates himself on the wet sand and I realize that he is simply a dedicated photographer of waders. It is a nature reserve!

It continues to be a delightful walk for several miles, with cut corn and even deer bordering the shoreline.

But all too soon I am at Elmer and then Middleton where there are expensive houses with a protective band of equally expensive chunks of imported Norwegian granite defending the shoreline; and the smell of rotting seaweed. In the distance I think that I see the shoreline stretching to Bognor Regis with a silhouette that, from a distance, looks to be a large mosque: but when you get closer it turns out to be a Butlin's Holiday Camp and just about all that cheerfully goes with it! It does have the advantage that there is an easy pedestrian walk along the sea front and I am grateful that the tide is still out and I can make most of it on the beach. The centre of old Bognor has some charm with the highlights of Steyne Square and the Royal Norfolk Hotel, but otherwise it seems to be a family, trippery sort of place with inappropriate high rise blocks, as at Margate.

However the Tourist Information Office here is good for forward planning when I need to work out how to deal with the next stage of the walk to Pagham Harbour, firstly by approaching eastwards from Bognor Regis, and subsequently by southern forays from Chichester. They supply bus timetables galore!

An enjoyable lunch at a pub on the front of Steyne Square sees me ready to return to Worthing by the 700 bus. Thank goodness that I had the pleasure of the tide being well out for an idyllic beach walk!

30 July, 2009: Bognor Regis to Pagham.

The return journey to Bognor by train from Worthing involves travelling to Barnham to change trains. Barnham is the Clapham Junction of West Sussex; separate lines go to Littlehampton, Bognor Regis and Worthing, while westward lines go via Chichester to Portsmouth Harbour and Southampton.

But for me today is a walk from Bognor to Pagham Harbour, then back to Bognor via the 60 bus. There is a serious west wind, so much so that it keeps most people off the beach and most of the gulls are sitting, bobbing, on the sea. It is obviously the day to be setting off eastward from Penzance on a bike with sails!

Once outside the confines of the centre of Bognor Regis the shingle bank is high enough [I am walking below on the beach] to hide the houses and bungalowitis. Aldwick merges, behind the pebbles, into Pagham and finally there are only the wide spread of pebbles and the surviving scrub, with the final acreage of shingle an impressive swirling mass that must surely change its footprint with the moon seasons and the heaving power of the tides?

A strong flow of tidal water surges between the shingle of Pagham and that of Selsey Bill. It looks as if it is a short enough distance to wade or swim across, but the swirl and pace of the water tells another story. When you round the corner northwards to see the large expanse of the marsh harbour that you must walk round to get to Selsey it is tempting to think of nipping across the narrow straits. But no!

The consolation is to see the large uninhabited space of the harbour and it is not difficult to imagine that it must have been a natural haven in Saxon and Roman times. While three 'rifes', [a variation of rivulets?] drain into it from the north and west, the harbour is now largely a tidal marsh land, with a special flora and fauna and a designated nature reserve.

After all the urbanization of the last few days it is a tranquil space: the first real acreage of coastal space since the Seven Sisters at Eastbourne.

In this nature reserve there are designated areas for nesting shore birds, along with protected flora. So much of the marsh remains as unassailable, even as the harbour is unsailable; which is to say that land and water have designated rights of way that are quite restricted. But there are well-marked paths and, once round the corner, out of the wind but still in the sun, I have a most enjoyable lunch of cheese sandwiches, grapes and bottled water. Not a soul in sight: bliss!

The harbour path runs on towards Pagham. There is a discreetly hedged out development of non- mobile homes on the edge of Pagham that spawns a few dog walkers on the path, but it is an otherwise quiet and peaceful stretch. Looking across the water a small church can be seen amongst the coastal harbour oaks, which, I later learn, is in the name of St Wilfrid, that well-travelled Northumbrian saint, who founded his first Sussex abbey here before it moved to Chichester [although I think Selsey had even earlier saxon claims to a cathedral]. But at Pagham, on the west side of the harbour, there is also a 'church lane' coming virtually down to the harbour and the majestic spire of the Pagham church is clearly visible. A rather large church for what seems to be a small village [counting only the old houses as authentic village – which have been considerably added to this century]. Sadly the church is locked, but it looks as if it might have had a south cloister and I wonder if it too was an old abbey church. It has a delightful tranquility, sitting in the sun of the erstwhile cloister.

Having been previously well informed by the ladies of the Tourist Information Centre of Bognor, I am able to catch the 60 bus, just round the corner from the church, on its way back to Bognor; whence it is a train back to London. The rest of Pagham Harbour and the Selsey Bill remain to be explored from a Chichester base.

12 October 2009: Pagham Harbour from Chichester.

This was preceded by a Sunday evening escape from a busy cosmopolitan, somewhat scruffy Camden Town into the relatively ghosted town of Chichester on a late Sunday evening. A few people spill off the train, but disperse into the night, leaving me a solitary figure. I ask a fluorescent yellow jacketed unloader where North Street might be. 'Just go north mate and you will find it,' he grins and gesticulates somewhere over his left shoulder. Since it is pitch black apart from some faint street lights, I have no clear idea as to which direction north might be, but proceed in the direction that appears to lead into the town centre, with an attractive looking stone crown in the middle of the cross roads. As I progress it becomes quieter and quieter; the few clicking high heels have faded and as I move round the crown at the cross roads I find that I am indeed in North Street and feel tempted to carry my wheeled case as it seems to make so much noise on the bricked, pedestrianised road of attractive seventeenth and eighteenth century architecture. Is everybody asleep already; will I wake them? Respectability seeps out of the shop windows, spilling across the smooth bricks; the street quite uninhabited at this time of night except for a few youths, desultory in their frolicking round the local pub. Some contrast from crowded Camden! The Ship Inn Hotel provides a civilized welcome with its gracious curving staircase [questionable wall paper?] and welcoming staff.

The next day is bright and cheerful and it is a single decker 60 bus from the bus station [across the road from the railway station] that heads off back down towards Pagham. The driver is unfamiliar with where the handsome Pagham church is, not surprising – as it is hidden from his bus route. But several venerable local ladies, the only

69

other passengers, chirp up and tell him where I need to be dropped off: a variation on the Greek chorus. This is country life! I wave my thanks as they disappear onwards to Bognor Regis.

I re-enter Church Lane to take me back to Pagham Harbour, where a local hut draws attention to the fact that this is an RSPB site. On a grey day and with the tide out I imagine that the harbour could be a depressing sight. But today, with the sun shining and the sea high, there is the spectacle of light shimmering on shallow water, running between what seem to be floating islands of grass, while the silhouettes of birds rise and curl in the wind, crying as they fly and fall, each with its own distinctive markings, bridging the gap between sky and sea in a seemingly effortless manner. Appropriately there is an ancient hut here [might it have been some sort of toll gate?] that is adjacent to an RSPB hut; and a notice that dogs are not allowed. The latter being respected inasmuch as the several dogs are on leads as they cross the walk way that bridges the separation of the saltwater bay from one of the three freshwater 'rifes' that run into the harbour bay. There seems to be a gentler and more civilized tone of dogwalkers than at Broadstairs, for here the walkers exchange greetings, even with a dogless walker!

Further out on the boundary walk there are the solitary figures of the binocular twitchers in their dark greens and blues, merging with the marsh and the sea, hunting for the sign of scuttles between tussocks, or the unexpected low flight away into the swirling of the skies. Solitary frozen herons are too easy prey for binoculars!

The path is clear enough round the perimeter of the harbour; but often marked with tidal detritus and ample samples of the local edible samphire. Once away from Pagham it is a tranquil stretch and I meet nobody until I emerge onto the port end of the very strung-out village of Sidlesham [pronounced Siddlesam, I later learn]. This end of the village has attractive old houses, an inn and a green with seats looking out over the harbour. My map says that there are the ruins of another roman villa; but it is not obvious to the hasty walker; so I prefer to sit in a twentieth century seat, rest my feet, and enjoy the view of the sea marsh harbour!

The route now runs out of the village, continuing round the harbour until it enters another nature reserve with an even larger RSPB centre adjacent to the busy B2145 which runs down to Selsey. This road, along with a separated pathway, crosses the most western rife of the harbour, which, in spite of the traffic, seems to have a considerable collection of the local waterfowl.

The B2145 runs almost directly south to Selsey, but the coastal footpath heads away eastwards before it curves back towards the mouth of Pagham Harbour and thence to Selsey Bill.

This is one of the more delightful stretches of the harbour walk, often raised as a defensive wall to protect the inland ditches and low lying field. It is often lined with gorse and hawthorn, but a good spread of thrift, scabious and, as I am to learn in another season, quite a spread of bluebells and primroses. When it finally does push you onto the coast there are some fine oaks which you feel might have been there in Roman times, or been planted by Druids [or maybe they are the daughters of very similar trees!]. All of which seem to be an appropriate setting for the little ancient church of St Wilfrid. It is a small, simple church that is still lovingly cared for and is worth the small detour from the strictly coastal walk: although it is by no means always open [but the sheltered graveyard, with seats, is].

Portions of the coastal path become quite susceptible to tide here and stretches run on raised railway sleepers, thoughtfully covered in wire netting to minimize slipping. It is now obvious that ahead there is an arm of shingle running out to match the one that ran out from Pagham at the end of my walk from Bognor Regis. This shingle again gives the impression that it has a profile that must change with the tides and the seasons. It also seems to give rise in the harbour to a series of flats of mud or shingle that are also a haven for the sea birds seeking shelter and out of reach of dogs and humans! So here I can stand and view the large circle that I have completed to get round from one lot of shingle to another, but for an hundred metres or so of fast running tidal water! Shingle is not my favourite surface to walk on. But it is a mile or so of crunching before the outer habitations of Selsey are reached. Not to say that there are not some vigorous clumps of sea cabbage to the seaward side and some well bull-rushed inland waters to my right: with the sun shining and the sea sparkling. How dare I complain!

The first buildings tend to be low cabin, wooden holiday homes, with stretches of grass and gorse separating them from the shingle: even the odd converted railway carriage. But there are signs that they are becoming popular and updated.

71

Trees begin to appear, the road becomes made up and brick houses arise, one of them with a blue plaque to the composer Eric Coates; the road separates from a formal concrete walkway which runs virtually all the way to the tip of Selsey Bill, the long pier out to the lifeboat station being the most prominent feature on the horizon. This is an easy and pleasant walk with regular bequested seats, commemorating happy times. There is also a large open green with a fun, humpy, cycle track for the local adolescent testosterone. This open space is followed by the odd wooden house butting on to the walkway and, nearer the pier, several small fishing boats, obviously in active service, with appropriate refrigeration units close by. It seems no more than my duty to retire to the 'Lifeboat' pub for a fresh crab sandwich and an excellent pint of beer. Another excellent walk, picking up the 51 bus back to Chichester at a stop just a little way back along the esplanade, behind the refrigeration units.

Lifeboat at Selsey.

13 October, 2009: Selsey to West Wittering

It is via the 51 bus that I return to Selsey Bill with my freedom pass. After a legion of Selsey bungalows, I clamber out onto the green by the lifeboat pier only to find a group of scuba divers using the shelter of the bus stop to strip off to get into their rubber outfits, littering the surrounding grass with their masks and convoluted tubing as well as discarded clothing. The bus driver raises his eyebrows,

'You sure you want to get off here, mate?'

I manage pursed lips and 'Its OK; not my scene,' and disembark to head for the concrete esplanade, while finding the contortions of the divers somewhat hilarious. Happily the hilarity was shared by the divers, as one Ivor shouted to a half stripped Eric, 'Eric,Smile', as he struggled, wearing only his very fitting grey long johns, with one leg half into his wet suit. The ladies on the bus all blinked; but no cameras flashed: shame.

Looking back along the coast, the view is a remarkable curve; easy to see Bognor Regis, even a hint of Worthing, and Brighton could be a smudge. One of those moments when you stop and think – 'Have I really walked so far?'

From this distance it does not look quite as built up as it is. But, with Selsey Bill being so far south, you are virtually viewing it from the sea.

The concrete pathway on the sea wall leads comfortably right down to the tip of Selsey Bill, with housing generally set well back. But when you turn westwards at the tip of the coast it is a different matter: 'No Access to the Beach' notices appear, where houses are immediately on the sea front. Had the tide been well out I might have been tempted to circumvent. But it was more in than out and I could see that there were also high wooden sea-breakers on this stretch. So I had to plod inland through the faceless landscape of detached houses with too many large four-wheel drives, with lawns cut by contractors! But there is finally a road back to the sea front with a green open space on the coast again. Then there is the strange contrast of a large estate of immobile mobile homes, separated from the sea and protected by a roadway of raised shingle, with enormous machines maintaining its integrity. Further along there is a large glass building which seems like an 'all event' place for the caravan estate i.e, café, restaurant, bar, swimming pool, amusement arcade, as in 'the total experience' for a rainy day at the seaside.

I pound along the shingle highway [there was a tarmac road for access to the entertainment centre] towards East Wittering and the tide begins to turn with the hint of some fine beach lying seaward of the shingle. Inland there is low lying farmland for a while with, surprisingly, one of the rifes that run into Pagham Harbour running parallel to the coast. No surprise that the local farm is called Marsh Farm. [After the severe gales of the 2013 winter I revisited this walk to find that the shingle had been broken apart, with the rife now running out to the sea here: so that you have to make an extensive, but well laid out, circuitous walk running behind the caravan site in a large arc towards Bracklesham: a major project of construction].

But as soon as the tide is down enough I take to the more comfortable walk on the sandy beach, clambering over the regular breakwaters. How much more pleasant to have the coast measured in breakwaters than in golf tees.

Bracklesham appears and runs seamlessly into East Wittering. The sea sighs and the sun shines: no one around; my wet footprints appear and disappear; and this is my coastal walking at its best. Swallows that should already have gone to North Africa dart and dive over the seaweed, picking off the remaining midges in this out-of-season sun.

Pleasantly reaching East Wittering, the Shore Line Pub not only offers a good pint of Palmer's Beer, but half a pint of shrimps, and a smattering of locals. Could life be better?

East Wittering stretches long and thin along the coastline, with several blocks of what look like retirement flats; eventually petering out into a greenish patch with a broad path of part shingle, part sand, part vegetation and functioning as another dog-walking stretch. A row of houses appears, but well set back; and I think this counts as the outlyier of West Wittering, which itself lies as a discrete snug of period houses some distance from the south coast, but close to the Chichester estuary, which is the next day's walk. However I have yet to reach the end of my present stretch which runs into a set of superior beach huts set well back from the general tides, so that the sand is very dry and powdery. Behind these is a well laid out car park, with amenities and an extensive green, populated by kite flyers, and with the village in the distance. The sand runs out to the estuary mouth, with the inevitable swirling currents [flags and notices advising against swimming here] and a view across to Hayling Island. This looks like, and is, another long

74

detour. The first of the Isle of Wight's medusa head of serpentine estuaries [I shall spend much time walking north and south for the next few outings, when I am trying to head west!].

Even immediately there is the strange phenomenon of East Head [to the west of West Wittering; but I suppose the east bank of the estuary?], which is a swirl of sand and shingle held together by various grasses and other flora and duly conserved as a nature reserve for flora and a range of seabirds nesting there. It automatically encloses a sort of shallow bay which is well reeded and a further shelter for the birds.

The path to West Wittering runs on the far side of this bay and is a secluded quiet walk compared with the popularity of the beach and the car park. This delightful estuary path runs past the village and up to Dell Quay and Chichester. But for today I investigate the quiet of St Peter and St Paul in West Wittering, note an adjacent church primary school and find solace in the hospitality of 'the Old House'. When I am suitably refreshed, two local ladies with children inform me that the 52 bus will take me back to Chichester: and so it does.

14 October, 2009: West Wittering to Dell Quay.

So it is that I wait for the 52 next morning on the front side of the Chichester bus station. The bus arrives at 9.27. As I hover, two venerable dowagers instruct me, 'Get on dear and have a seat. He'll give you a ticket when its 9.30.' This to circumnavigate the rule that 'freedom passes' are not valid until 9.30!

Like all venerable ladies, they are unquestionably right, and the eastern European bus driver, in his broken English, confirms, 'Take a seat, sir, and when its time I will bring you a ticket.'

True to his word, at 9.30 promptly, three tickets are printed and the more venerable of the dowagers dispenses them almost as if they were wafers at the communion rail. I wonder if she was a school prefect, or has always just been a kind soul!

I have a feeling that I ought not to have reported the above: but I do so thinking that it reflects better aspects of the human condition; and illustrates the ludicrousness of the rule as we are the only three passengers on the bus!

The tranquility of West Wittering is as blissful as I remember it, although, on the way, the bus driver is obviously not honed to respecting horse riders and slows down with a revving of the engine, with the result that the partially arab horse becomes even more agitated. But the very English lady is in full control, even waving her appropriately gloved hand graciously at our driver; and perhaps at us all. Country life!

I dismount, [from the bus!], opposite yesterday's hostelry, even as I mounted yesterday evening. The coastal path leads out from the corner of the green. It is a pleasant estuary walk, with many of these medium-sized oak trees that first appeared in Pagham harbour and which I find again at the other end of this set of estuaries, round Calshott and Beaulieu. There are tranquil views across to Hayling and Thorney Islands, with a smattering of yachts sailing or motoring to or from the various marinas that are available; Chichester, Bosham, Prinsted, Hayling Island, Emsworth, to say nothing of the small dinghy sailing schools at both Cobnor House and West Thorney: a veritable playground for aspiring sailors; and spoilt for choice.

The footpath hugs the estuary, passing a few comfortable establishments; but at least they are gracious enough to allow rights of way; and there are pleasant views across to Thorney Island and Chidham until one hears the jingle and clinking of masts and by now, knows that another collection of boats will appear round the corner, which is the small village of West Itchenor. There are small dinghies, even canoes, on the northern side so not all is grandiose.

The 'main road' of the village runs right to the water's edge; sadly it is not possible to keep on the estuary walk here without going inland along the only 'main street'. On the shore line there is the Itchenor Sailing Club, which like many other sailing clubs, is anti-public access, or exclusive, according to your point of view. If the tide is high you probably cannot access the club along the water front anyway.

The answer is to turn right, heading up the road, away from the estuary, until the Ship Inn is clearly visible on the right hand side of the road. Immediately opposite the inn there is a sign posted footpath, with the sign rather obscured by vegetation when I was walking.

This path runs straight down to the estuary on the far side of the sailing club. A graveled, raised, footpath runs to the right with a panoramic vista of the estuary restored, along with the considerable grandeur of the various mansions in their grounds: this is affluence! Two or three estates later the path runs into an ancient red brick wall that directs the walker inland for a few hundred yards and then opens on to a wide tarmacked avenue of ostentation: all rather eerie in that these vast mansions seem to be unpopulated and silent on this marooned, trafficless road. Then suddenly two flaxen haired small girls whiz out on a pink bike and a pink tricycle, fiercely competing [although the bike is simply egging the tricycle on!]. They disappear equally rapidly into another one of the silent driveways and the eerie quiet is restored. It all felt quite surreal.

At the end of the avenue the path clearly runs back into farmland, although you are always aware that the estuary is not far away to your left. There is a concrete single track road leading to Westlands Farm, which itself is another grey painted wood and glass palace with views over the estuary.

You need to take care not to just stick on this country lane when it becomes a tarmac surface. There is a nifty left turn into a less ostentatious estate, which is marked by a wooden public right of way sign, but again, set back from the road and partially screened by vegetation. Walking round two sides of the square of the estate brings you to a footpath that leads back down to the estuary, which in no time at all leads into the complex of Birdham Pool and the Chichester Yacht Basin. There are rights of way here; but not always very clear. Birdham Pool seems to be more of a working anchorage and there is a simple straightforward crossing, but then the path, passing through a thicket, comes out on the Chichester canal; with an unexpected series of house boats, variously developed to the extent that they are certainly not moveable, some even three stories high and with obvious picnic facilities in the adjacent woodland.

On the other side of the canal Chichester yacht basin sprawls. A single sign directs you inland; but instinct tells you to hug the water's edge and to head for a large black painted timbered building, which is the gate house for the large lock of the yacht basin. This is indeed anchorage for the well- heeled.

Having negotiated the walkway over the lock gates the path heads for a copse of trees. But here my ordnance survey map is at odds with the signs. There is clearly a charming pathway through the copse, running close to the edge of the estuary, with the rest of the walk to Dell Quay being open farm land with lovely views across to the spire

77

of Chichester cathedral and the South Downs behind. The pleasant view extends to the farmland of Hook Farm on the other side of the estuary; quite free of 'des res' buildings for the first time. It is distinctly the most relaxed and rural part of the walk from West Wittering to Dell Quay.

A white egret scats with a herring gull over spoils in the mud flats exposed by the ebbing tide: a draw is declared. A couple of kittiwakes have a mad half-hour of sprinting low over the water in spurts, then rapidly rising and tumbling and twisting: pure show-off high spirits. The winter corn has sprouted, even as a fresh spring green, contrasting with the sepulchral browns of the trees, not yet fired into their autumn colours. All this puts me in an ideal frame of mind to sample the fares of the Anchor Inn at Dell Quay, an ancient timbered place with fine views over the harbour and well frequented by the grey pound; as to be expected in this part of the world!

However the pleasure of the coastal view for the walker is compromised by the fact that it is a fair walk inland to acccess the 52/53 bus route back to Chichester.

But it is the end of another season.

2010: SUSSEX INTO HAMPSHIRE.

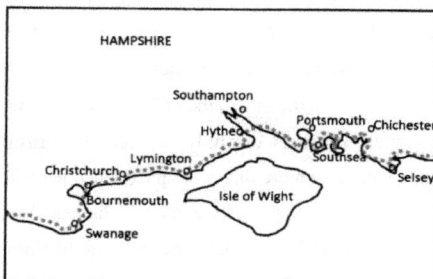

16 March 2010: Dell Quay to Bosham.

I venture out from hibernation; and note that I accomplish less walking this year, largely due to the fact that Chichester has tempted my partner and I to achieve a permanent outpost there: and that in itself takes up quite a chunk of 'free time', – [curious how 'busy' this period called 'retirement' can be!].

This Dell Quay to Bosham is but half a day's walk- if you do not have to get to Dell Quay in the first instance. However, if starting from Chichester then you have the choice of two routes of accessing the splendid pub that is the most significant coastal feature of Dell Quay. The first option is to take the 52/53 bus that goes to East and West Witterings and get off on the A286 where the minor road runs down to Dell Quay; a walk of less than a mile. The second possibility is to go for the 56 bus to Bosham [or the redoubtable 700 coastal!] and get off just before Fishbourne, with a considerably longer walk down to Dell Quay through Apuldram. But it is not advisable to try to walk out of Chichester in this direction. While the immediate architecture outside the west walls has some charming properties, all too soon there are a series of roundabouts for a College, a hypermarket and finally the A259 and A27 bypass. These become progressively pedestrian-unfriendly, while the last, as a 3 lane system is distinctly hazardous, even for driven traffic. There are underpasses for cyclists and pedestrians – but they are not well marked from the Chichester end; but easier to find if coming the other way!

However from the pub at Dell Quay there is a well-marked pleasant estuary path leading northwards to Fishbourne: this is a delightfully tranquil and quiet spread of water, which is probably much busier at the peaks of bird migration; but even now has a flock of wigeon on an island reed bed, the odd sparrow hawk and enough swans around to suggest a swannery. All this all the more astonishing when you know that the juggernauted A 27 and the railway are pulsating on the other side of Fishbourne. However the estuary side of Fishbourne has large meadows and a carefully nurtured fen of rushes. As I approach these, having passed by nothing more than a couple of Jack Russell terriers and a golden labrador with their respective walkers, I see a mass of fluorescent yellow outfits and surmise that there must be a batch of workers maintaining the flora and fauna, or even cleaning out drains and channels. But closer inspection reveals that it is but a junior school outing – all wearing hard hats as well as fluorescent jackets! Ah, those carefree days of childhood that we spent catching frog spawn and sticklebacks from the pond on the common with a stick and some string round the neck of a jam jar with a couple of friends, quite unhindered by hats and fluorescent jackets: a bygone age of innocence! Health and Safety now rules!

The path heads round to head south for Bosham Hoe, heading through a distinctive corner of high reed beds, well preserved and conserved. Then onto the coastal estuary path again with vistas across to Dell Quay. It is possible to cross the first of the rivulets draining into the estuary, but at the second the way turns inland for some distance before the water can be crossed. Henceforth much of the water's edge is on private land. So the walker has to turn right at Hook Farm and head for Bosham on surfaced roads, quiet and virtually single tracked as these are: but picking up more traffic the closer one gets to Bosham Hoe.

Once past the Hoe it is possible to head for the estuary edge and pick up a path to look across the next finger of the estuary to the dinghy sailing round Cobnor House: but the quiet lane also runs north to Bosham. Both these approaches, the coastal and the inland route, show Bosham at its best [although I haven't seen it from the sea!]. Sitting on the bay's edge, the village spreads before you, with the elegant spire rising above clusters of handsome and varied houses on the waterside: probably not so idyllic if the tide is out and it is blowing a gale, but the tide is in and the sun shining on the water. Moreover I have seen the first yellow celandines and tiny violets flowering in a road side bank near Church Farm, while a corner house has hundreds of snowdrops still spreading through the grass. But it is the few spring flowers that really bring the cheer after this all too long winter.

Bosham from the South East.

Lunch at the Anchor in Bosham is another collection of the grey pound; an occasional younger mistress, but perhaps not that sort of territory [or time of day!] for that sort of company: more solid couples eating solidly, in comfortable silence. But some hands twitch, tremble, or strum the table. I am now back in tourist territory.

Replenished, I find the coastal walk to the head of the Bosham branch of the estuary is fairly short, but delightfully tranquil after the bustle of Bosham. The A27 [with the 700 bus route], can be seen, but, thanks to the south westerly wind and my diminished hearing, not heard; and there are no buildings, dogs, dog walkers nor tourists. Quite blissful.

The 700 takes me back to Chichester yet again.

17 March, 2010: The Chidham peninsula to Nutbourne:

Another promising spring day! Two in a row after this drab persistent winter seem like an indulgence. So my day begins as something of an indulgence too; I decide to go hunting for an updated map as I see that on looking at my old map I can only do a walk down to Chidham and back, whereas the updated map proposes a circular coastal walk past Chidham, round Cobnor Point and then back along the west coast, which borders a

81

wider and quieter estuary than that of Bosham; and subsequently is more favoured by the bird wildlife, as I am about to find out. If you are winged it is also more directly on the flight path from the estuary entrance at West Wittering, which must be another good reason for landing there if you have just batted a smallish pair of wings across the Channel, or even from the Bay of Biscay!

But diverting into the tourist office to buy the map and unable to resist sniffing round for any other appropriate illuminations, means that I just miss the 700 coastal bus., so I opt for the local 56 to Bosham, which circumnavigates all the dreaded roundabouts of yesterday [even the bus has a problem crossing the A 27].

Some 400 metres after the Broadbridge stop there is a set of wooden steps going down into the field separating road and estuary, with a well -established right of way across the field. The path along the estuary edge is self- evident, but vulnerable to the state of the tide in parts. This tidal influence is worthy of note here as it also applies at the south-westerly tip of Cobnor Point and if the tide is high there you cannot get round the point, as low scrubby trees protrude into the water, with a high bank and barbed wire fence behind the thicket [I just got round in time!]. Elsewhere on this stretch of coast there is often a man-made embankment which has a variable path on the top of it [sometimes narrow and twisting, sometimes broad and level – much as there was round the west of Pagham Harbour]. I learn that the official description of this structure is a 'bund' on the local notices.' Please keep to the bund', they read; which does presume that you know what a 'bund' is: not exactly in the first 800 words of one's vocabulary [but it does occur in the Shorter English!].

Walking south from the A259 gives a pleasing view across the estuary of the houses and church of Bosham, An inlet takes you to the road leading to Chidham and here the coastal path runs out of the inlet through a private development of houses, who kindly allow pedestrian access through to the main estuary coast again and a continuation of the bund, without which I imagine there would be considerable flooding of the adjacent fields and homes, certainly at the equinox, if not daily.

There is shortly an opportunity to take a right turn inland and to go back to Chidham if a shorter walk was required, or if the church and pub were to be investigated. But I note this for a future occasion and march towards Cobnor House. There are clusters of small boats and dinghies apparent on the water's edge here and it turns out to be a Christian Centre for Youth Sailing. Again a section of 'strictly pedestrians only' on marked paths follows. But this is compensated for by Cobnor Point where the National Trust are setting up a wild life acreage for migrating birds and as a water vole habitat, with a broad bund with disabled access [not for the voles!]. There is a slight feeling that 'Wind in the Willows' could have been written here.

I have the treat of seeing shelducks in their green and orange plumage; a flock of some thirty Brent geese grazing, then, when I am past them, they take off and fly past in ever changing formation. Meanwhile three bomber mute swans fly low over the estuary water to veer into a skid landing in the inlet that I had just coasted round. I spot a single small white egret; this phantom icon of the southern coast.

At the tip of the point is a judiciously placed seat with a beautiful view across to West Itchenor, the tip of West Thorney and down to the estuary mouth, flanked by East Head and Hayling Island. This idyll is completed, apart from my bar of chocolate, by the spectacle of an entrance of Dunlin in their thousands; a myriad of tiny forms, whirling and spiralling; thousands of birds in an energy of dance, like some swarm of bees. I wonder if there is some sort of crowd hysteria, some sort of endorphin surge that activates these gatherings. It seems almost visible, even tangible, in their surging flight.

The sun and lack of wind are kind enough to let me sit here a while to enjoy the glitter on the water and believe that spring is finally thinking of arriving with the flight of Dunlins. There is even a small wooden bird observatory just round the corner. But I hasten on, for this is the corner that is tidal and without the defensive bund; but with a natural steep bank of 'private land'.

Back on the artificial bunds and heading north the estuary I look across to West Thorney of Thorney Island [yet another finger of the estuary!] with more Brent geese, oyster catchers, the odd curlew and, behold, a trinity of the white egrets; so elegant when strutting on their long legs but rather like flattened herons in their flight.

Landward of the bund there is usually a dyke, with the juxtaposing land being a rough type of meadow. It looks as if there is a long term project to let this grassland become sea meadows again, perhaps flooding with some tides, as there seems to be a second line of defence being laid on the far side of the fields with another bund that is currently being faced with large Norwegian granite rocks.

As the traffic on the A259 hoves into view, so a few dog walkers present themselves, escaping from Nutbourne for the fresh air of the coast. There are various paths that lead away from the water to the road, round ponied fields, thence through out-of-season horticultural greenhouses on to the 700 bus route; with 'the Barley Corn', a hospitable pub on the cross roads at Halt, if you are in need of refreshment. I am easily back to Chichester in time for tea!

9 June, 2010: Nutbourne to Emsworth via Thorney Island.

An interlude when I had hoped for two days walking, but heavy rain kept me at home in Chichester, although it meant that I could get on with hanging some pictures.

I remembered ending the Chidham peninsula walk by coming out between two old white cottages, set back from the present A259 on what was probably the old road. I remember also walking eastwards to find respite at 'the Barley Corn'. So it is easy enough to wait until I pass 'the Barley Corn' on the bus before getting off; thus avoiding getting off two stops too early as I did on my last saunter!

It is as well that I did remember the exit between the two cottages as it would be easy to miss if approaching for the first time. The 'public footpath' sign is well down the path between the two cottages-and not easily seen from the road. The hedged path leads through some remnants of commercial glasshouses into some arable land, with fenced-off oblong paddocks on the right, which speak of a nearby riding school, although there are no equines around at the moment. Thorney Island lies to the right and ahead of these paddocks, sweeping out to the south and west, with the tip of the island scarcely visible. I can hear the clinking of masts at Prinsted and, with a cool and refreshing southwesterly breeze, my better foot goes forward.

It is something of a select dog-walking stretch here. A lady with a cross-bred pointer lets him off the lead; he runs past me, over the embankment, straight into the sea and turns to crouch out of sight of his owner, but utterly focused on where she will eventually appear. Breeding certainly shows! Of course I am totally ignored by both.

But I press on round the raised footpath, with the spire of Southbourne church clear between the trees that screen me from the A259. The path leads to a select run of shingle beach, occupied only by one young mother with her toddler and her Labrador. The path then leads past some fairly large, substantial, bungalows. I cannot help but think that the rather portly gentleman whom I meet, apparently exercising an ancient, one-eyed border terrier is the owner of one of the said bungalows.

Then the path swings across to the marina, accessed by two single-file, wooden foot bridges and a stile. It is not the classiest of marinas; but perhaps has more character as a result. There is even a stretch for chaining small dinghies within a few hundred yards of the more substantial boats. It definitely has the feel of a punter's marina.

At this point it is now easy and pleasant to look back across to the Chidham peninsula of the last walk. But suddenly there is a significant inland waterway on my right; obviously a place to revisit when the bird migrations are operating. It has the feel of a tranquil haven. Evidently [after the map is consulted], it is 'the Great Deep', which originally separated the original Thorney Island from the mainland. Now it is bridged on each coast by solid bridges [and a surfaced road bridge inland for the RAF camp on the island] such that the inland waters appear to lie below sea level.

Even as the eastern bridge is crossed the walker is confronted with a formidable mesh fence, along with a distant entry phone system. The other side of the fence is MOD/RAF territory and the electronic system makes contact with the RAF office in the centre of the island, where your intentions [bird watching!] and time of entry are all clocked in. Until I exit some two hours later on the other side, having looped round the island, I meet nobody except a couple of RAF runners, keeping up to scratch. But this is not quite the full picture as West Thorney not only has a fine 10th century church, sympathetically restored and the art interest of a local school outing, but also a Yatching Association Centre of dinghies and windsurfing for teenagers.

Emerging from this focus of activity the path, after tangling with some overgrown hawthorn, competing with the white and pink of hedge dog roses, I suddenly find myself in a tunnel of sloe blackthorn, more hawthorn and expanses of yellow flowering honeysuckle, while everything is kept to shrub height on this exposed [and airfield] site. This network of bushes houses a lively crop of goldfinches, dunnocks and occasional

85

greenfinches. The path finally opens out at Longmere point and the vista of Pilsney Island lies like some raised sand bank. The relatively narrow entry to Chichester Harbour, between the Witterings and Hayling Island, is finally visible again, last seen when walking round West Wittering and East Head.

The west side of Thorney Island is definitely a quiet walk, something of a dog's back leg shape to it; but the lack of activities found at West Thorney mean that most of the larger bird life is here, with gulls and waders in the shallows of the Emsworth Channel. There are a clutch of plovers in the fields and three elegant white egrets.

There is a solitary memorial to one Alan Jones, who died a young man; but virtually no external activity on the RAF station. However they do let me out as I exit over the Great Deep again; and there is a good footpath back over 'the Lesser Deep' on its western side. Then the neck of the island has a cluster of houses and a boat yard, somewhat more upmarket than the Prinsted marina side. A footpath is marked, but I was somewhat foot weary by this time, so headed for the road with a row of terrace houses facing onto fields; with this minor road eventually opening onto the dear old A259.

An old, timbered, 'Sussex Arms' inn lies not far away to the left [towards Emsworth]. Sufficiently refreshed the 700 provides a shortish journey back to Chichester. All these north/south loop walks! This is the most branched of estuaries yet; and more to come!

28 June 2010: Hermitage to Havant

A humid, sticky day. The 700 bus waits patiently outside the Cathedral in West Street, Chichester. I dismount just past yesterday ' Sussex Arms' and head westwards down the road to cross the river Ems, heading towards the town centre of Emsworth. A large and atttractive mill pond, privately owned, straddles the road; and is full of avian wild life, with an enormous swan's egg on their raft like nest, so close to the path, [I fear for its successful hatching!]. For the strict coastal path walker one has to beware of a sign immediately after the pond that says ' public path' as this, while taking you past the swan's egg in the middle of the Em enclosure, keeps you on the eastern bank of the Ems, leading down to the rather convoluted marina. Nor is it easy to find the route down to 'the Wayfarer's Walk' marked on the coast. It is one of those privately-developed areas where the main purpose seems to be to confuse walkers! As the old part of Emsworth is very charming, with both brick and stuccoed period houses, it is easy to see why they wish for this privacy. [The same cannot be said for the modern infills - but doubtless they are pleasant enough to live in]. But some clear sign posting might diminish the number of people wandering around trying to find a way through!

Between the older houses at the end of King Street there are several series of steps down to the edge of the bay but when these are negotiated, rather as on the west side of Bosham, there is no path; just a spread of shingle and mud, mixed with seaweed and algae: and a hope that the tide is in the right phase, out! However, the view of old houses and the restored buildings, relics of what counted as industry from a bygone age, are charming and, once these are reached, a sweeping promenade round another large pond more than compensates for the earlier rather picky squelch of the 'Wayfarer's Walk'. As it is low tide, there is a fairly marshy view of the Chichester estuary to the south and to the west a prospect of Hayling Island with its long bridge connecting it to the mainland. As, on my map, there is a 'PH' next to the bridge, this is my destination for lunch.

The estuary road at Lavant

Once out of old Emsworth there is a string of new mansions, several with sea defences, some sympathetically planted with rugosa roses that seems a most attractive way of conferring privacy. I fear for the few paddocks that still border the path! How long before they are a new plot for building? However there is a clear, pleasant, coastal path here that runs past shrubbery, much of it flowering tamerisks, to Conigar Point. But the 'Wayfarer's Walk' suddenly transforms into 'The Solent Way', which visits the remains of a castle and an intact church. But as a dedicated coastal walker I am not so easily distracted and the walk sweeps round towards Langstone Bridge with fine tamerisks dominating the pathway. Parts of the path are fortified by coconut sized rocks bound in large, wire, mesh cages [gabions?]. But for the one-off walker it seems difficult to see why some areas are chosen while others are left to the forces of nature? Presumably they know where the currents erode: or is it about who can pay?

The arrival at Langstone is via another series of ponds, attractive cottages and a converted lighthouse. The ponds are more hidden, and therefore more charming, than at Emsworth: the Langstone ponds have broods of ducklings and coots scuttling amongst their reeds and waterways.

Having crossed another waterway running into the harbour I am attracted by 'the Royal Oak' for a very early refreshment; only to realise afterwards that is probably a larger pub, ' The Ship', closer to the bridge, that is probably the one marked on the map. However I have a feeling that most of the locals go to 'The Royal Oak' where, when the weather allows sitting outside on the benches, you are both away from the traffic and could not be much closer to the water.

The A3023 to Hayling Island is busy, but opposite 'The Ship' I cross to a more secluded cycle and pedestrian way, with initial clear blue signs indicating 'The Solent Way'. This looks like an encouraging start, appearing to be fairly rural. But I negotiate being on the right [as in west] side of the Langstone inlet via the ordnance survey map rather than any blue signs. There are other walkers here, but they are all either strolling in the shirtsleeves of office outfits or lunch-time joggers in lycra and it is not long before I recognise that the Solent Way is entering the industrial sector of Havant and Langstone, including an electricity station, an oil refinery, gravel and sand stores [aggregate?], sewage works, waste recycling and several others screened behind high fences. Not a walker's paradise. The more so as you have to go inland to use the road that services the industrial estate to cross the river Langstone that outlets here. If you are making a continuous walk, then once you have crossed this bridge there is a pathway on the landward side of the road which leads down to the west bank of the river, is even signposted as a cyclist and pedestrian right of way, and has a good tarmac surface when you get there.

However today I think that I have walked far enough and decide to try and pick up the 700 coastal bus service. This turns out to be an arduous piece of negotiation that leads me to the dreaded mix of the A3[M], the A27, and the A259.Having negotiated a turning to Bedhampton I am advised by a pleasant, but rather overweight lady, that a 23 bus will take me to Havant bus station, where I might pick up the ever-reliable 700 coastal bus. Thankfully this turns out to be true and I am soon back in Chichester, having had an upstairs view of all my previous day's walking. It is only when I review the map that I realise that it might have been more appropriate to turn left when the coastal path emerged onto the industrial road. Then I might have had a shorter walk to Brockhampton, from which I might have bussed to Havant. But that is all part and parcel of working these things out 'spontaneously' and being glad that you have not dragged somebody else round saying 'are you sure that this is the right way.....?'. Quite what I do about picking up the continuation of this walk of the 'Solent Way' remains a problem for another day.

18 August, 2010: Langstone to Southsea.

The driver of the 700 coastal bus advises me that the Tesco stop in Havant is the nearest that I get to Langstone harbour. So I duly dismount with a plethora of roundabouts facing me, the dual carriage way of the A27 racing overhead, and a corresponding confusion of unsignposted pedestrian walkways presenting as bridges, underpasses, and as steps or slopes. I am aware that the sea is to the south, so by the position of the sun I try to head that way through the maze of options until I come to an east west choice, no signs, and the roundabouts and roads all hidden on my ordnance survey by the broad brush of the overbridging dual carriage way. Fortunately a middle-aged local lady is crossing the other way and is not affronted by my request for help. She takes my arm [I am obviously of that age now!], and advises me not to follow any of the main roads but to go down the pedestrian way to the left and to follow the alleyway between two visible rows of houses; to follow the path of the alleys until it runs into two fields, to cross these, and then I will be on the coast. It sounds too good to be true; but she is obviously my fairy godmother or guardian angel in disguise, because it is just so, even though it does not show on my map at all! While this is an excellent omen for the day the

89

disadvantage is that it brings me out at the east side of Langstone Bridge, which runs across to Hayling Island. I am glad to rediscover this old collection of houses and pubs, but it is an hour's walk from my last destination on the estuary of the River Langstone [see above]. The bridge to Hayling Island in August carries almost non-stop traffic, but once that is crossed I am able to complete the previous walk without hesitation or deviation and to scuttle down on to the west bank of the river onto a tarmac-surfaced cycle-pedestrian track forming the Solent Way which runs round Langstone Harbour into Portsmouth. Indeed it is possible to see Portsmouth's tall white millenium effigy as a goal to head for, even if it seems a somewhat daunting distance away at the moment.

The tide is out, with only trickling tributaries of water winding between the mud flats, strewn with flopped, stranded seaweed. Reeds and grasses in muted greens thrust upwards, trying to give a vertical component to the flat landscape. But the whole is a strange composition of sombre green and browns, with the strange little marooned Baker and Biness Islands, sporting a cluster of low trees on the larger of the two, as if hiding a hermitage? The anchor shaped Hayling Island seems to merge with Southsea and Portsmouth from this distance, the narrow gap between them being hidden by the angle of viewing; and so they form the backdrop of the horizon, surmounted by a massive skyscape, with some gathering, grey, cumulus clouds looking as if they have a few buckets of rain to dispense. But they are to the north, and the wind a south westerly, so I am optimistic.

This all is a pleasing landscape to the south, but ignores the fact that at this stretch of the coast the A27 and M3 merge and run within 100 metres of the coastline: thus the good tarmac alternative for cyclists and pedestrians! For some of the way hedgerow, and even bullrushes, separate the walker from the motorised traffic; but for stretches they are very close. The change comes with the advent of the Farlington Marshes, a peninsula that is a designated nature reserve. Here it is pedestrians only; dogs on leashes, and a southern deflection. If you are keen to get to Southsea you could cut this loop out by continuing on the cycle path in a westerly direction, paralleling the motorway. But the marshes are a haven, even if the hub-hum of the motorway is never entirely lost. Visually it is tranquility enclosed in a walled barrier on which walkers patrol; you could even drive a coach and horses [or a Land Rover]. It is dotted with couples or solitaries carrying

90

tripods, telephoto lenses, and cameras, gently sauntering round. Obviously dedicated twitchers on the bird sanctuary; I seem to be the only determined walker.

The enclosed marsh is a collection of summer grazing for young stock along with dykes and static waterways, well reeded for natural habitat. Although there are instructive notices telling me what birdlife I might expect to spot here, there does not seem to be much to see at the moment [but see the river estuary below!]. However rounding a corner just past the most southerly tip I have the treat of seeing three six inch long stoat kits, sidling into the long grass. Their mother must be somewhere near; but I don't hear her calling. Of course I am too slow to capture them with my camera, but am amazed to see two more only ten yards down the path looking quite lost but staying close to each other for comfort.

They look quite trusting and make no attempt to disappear into the grass. I wonder if this is their first outing. While I manage to photograph this pair, I leave them to their ways; but warn a young lady with an exuberant spaniel on a lead when I pass her some 500 yards further along. Such an unusual sighting suddenly makes the whole Farlington detour more than worthwhile.

The Farlington diversion completed it is back to accompanying the M3/A27, now compounded by the fact that the A2030 runs southwards under the motorway and down along the coast to Southsea and has to cross the Broom estuary to do so: plus there are road works! Fortunately the pedestrian and cycle trackers are still catered for with clear rights of way; but there is a thunder of commercial traffic along with the tourists' and locals' cars. The conundrum is that the wildlife on the estuary, pretty close to all this activity, is more rewarding than the whole of the Farlington marshes. It may just be the state of the tide, but here are the dippers and waders as illustrated on the notice boards of the marsh reserves! Godwits, shanks and sandpipers, some solitary, some in small flocks. It seems such a contradiction to stand on a bridge of roaring traffic with a plethora of bird life below; and there were all those dedicated bird watchers on the marshes with scarcely a pair of interesting wings to be seen! I think that it is the food source in the estuary mud that attracts?

Fortunately, immediately after the blue railings of the bridge end there is a direction to an estuary walk away from the A2030, now calling itself the Langstone Harbour Walk. From the bridge it looks as if it might be something of an industrial archaeological landscape. But it is pleasant enough, even if the sound of the A2030 is rarely absent. Just when the path seems about to go into a gravel and sand works it diverts into a coppice of fir trees; which ends abruptly at the entrance where all the lorries access the site. However, once across this, the path follows the waterside and leads past the local sailing club and playing fields, with an altogether more civilised feel: although do be careful of cyclists whizzing along on this fairly narrow path [when there is a good tarmac surface for them in a separate lane on the A2030 !].There is a hostelry on the estuary side where the road branches to the industrial estate and Northend. But I push on, in spite of beginning to feel a little sunburnt and foot weary, as I can see the marina at Southsea. There follows a broad path, accommodating all comers [pedestrians, skate boarders, cyclists, prams!], while the main road has turned inland from the coast. There is a well-cared for tribute to the armed forces to mark this run in to Southsea. Here are blackberries a-plenty, with several serious and not so serious pickers [I fall into the latter group – but do indulge!]. Several tranquil inland waterways parallel this stretch, and I am pleased to see that they support a group of breeding swans. There are at least three cygnets; whereas the cluster of nine swans at Langstone were all adults, with no apparent offspring.

I arrive at the marina and find a pleasant well-populated Wetherspoon's pub, 'The Thatched House' [that does not comply with the trade descriptions act!]; and catch the 13 bus back through suburbia into Portsmouth; and thence to Chichester via the faithful 700 at 5.00pm rush hour, full of noisy adolescents on their way home..

92

31 August, 2010: Southsea Marina to Portsmouth Harbour.

This highlights what was a problem in the last walk and may increasingly become a problem, which is the time it takes to get back to the point at which you left off in the last walk. If you are back-packing and stay where you finish, then this is no problem. But completing this collection of estuaries from Pagham to Southampton, all from a base in Chichester, is not only a major exercise in trekking north and south when I am trying to head westwards, but also takes a good part of the morning getting to my starting point!

So today's journey means that I have to go all the way to Portsmouth Harbour [on the 700!] and find, from the Tourist Information Office [near the majestic 'Mary Rose'], that I need to catch the, once an hour, number15 bus to get to the ferry for Hayling Island at the tip of Southsea Marina peninsular. This means that it is 11.30 before I start on what is certainly less than half a day's walk.

The ferry is a smallish boat that waits to collect any passengers from the bus. But I sit and watch it as it pushes its way across to Hayling Island against what is obviously quite a strong incoming tide, channelling through the relatively narrow gap of water. It is a lovely day and, with seats and a mobile café next to the Lifeboat station, it is tempting to just sit and watch the day go by. Single-line fisherman obviously know this to be a good time and place to spend the day. They and a couple of resting cyclists seem to be the only people left once the ferry has departed. After the hassle of travel it is pleasant to just sit and absorb!

But I consult my map and apply myself to the walk back to Portsmouth.

The 'Solent Way' cuts out the marina peninsula. This is understandable as the inlet that houses Southsea Marina is marsh and mud, without a path or road boundary. So after the 'Thatched House' where I ended my last walk, the prescribed Solent Way cuts through suburban roads and Bransbury Park to the formal esplanade that starts to the east of the impressive architecture of the Royal Marines' Museum, and runs all the way into Portsmouth Harbour. It is also difficult to complete a walk along the northern side of this peninsular as it is either new blocks of flats, or the enclosed private marina [rattling with the clinking of masts] or a very narrow road that hardly takes traffic both ways, and with no pathway, is a pedestrian hazard.

93

But I am glad to have come to the tip, to see the ferry and the Hayling Island close too. I set off on the shingle, trying not to disturb the fishermen too much. At this stage I am walking due south and cannot see whether I can clearly get round to the west running esplanade. There is a very military looking pier that looks to be fenced off, and I begin to appreciate why there are only solitary fishermen here; and no 'Solent Way'. The map does also say 'Fort Cumberland' and I see high fencing with barbed wire, with a hefty high concrete wall, with some large man-made slabs at the base, variously covered in green slime in parts. Not encouraging.

However one of the fisherman, who is just getting his gear together from the boot of his car, says that it is not difficult to get round the military base if the tide is out; and if I do get round this corner, then there is a wider beach. So, always reluctant to give up and go back, I cross over the pier and start to negotiate the rocks; realising fairly quickly that I am not as nimble as I was ten years ago! It suddenly feels rather solitary and a bit scary, and, while having no hesitation about hanging on to any useful bits of fortification, I begin to wonder if I should have really tackled this. Then a local dog comes bounding up behind me and overtakes; followed by a much tattooed owner, casually lolloping over the rocks [but forty years younger than me]! I reassure myself that the water is not deep anyway [but rather full of seaweed] and hope that the beach must be round the corner from the final twenty yards.

So it turns out to be; and my heart rate starts to return to normal, the beach looks decidedly beautiful and I notice again how blue the sky is today as the looming dominance of the radar scanning fortress passes out of sight. As relief seeps in I also notice that there are very few people at this end of the beach; they are all male, and seem to have all their clothes tucked away in tidy bags; everything hangs out! Certainly a change in architecture, and possibly yet another reason why the 'Solent Way' cuts the corner here!?

But it is some time since I walked on a good stretch of beach and I am very happy to walk on without any worries, and in a somewhat uplifted form of mind. The beach has its share of shingle, but it runs along, interrupted by two piers, all the way into Old Portsmouth and disappears into Portsmouth Harbour, only to become part of a well-marked millenium walk that even crosses over into Gosport. But this is to get ahead of myself.

My present walk passes, after a discreet interval, on to the terrain of families, buckets and spades, the rejoining of the 'Solent Way', and the impressive and contrasting architecture of the Royal Marines' Museum. For some time I simply enjoy the pleasure of walking along the beach with the view of South Parade Pier; a distinct prospect for lunch. However, as the density of families on the beach increases I decide to increase my pace of walking by moving onto the more solid surface of the esplanade. It also gives me a clear view of the pleasant immediate hinterland of Southsea, with plenty of green spaces, floral displays, pools in which to paddle boats in the rather gross shape of large white swans; and even miniature golf courses. In a word, so like the seaside holidays of childhood. But I do notice that there are no donkeys on the beach [memories of Bridlington and Scarborough from my own childhood!].

In no time I am at the pier; but select a little café on the edge of the beach for an egg sandwich and a diet coke. The idyllic setting of azure sea and sky while sitting under a large red and white umbrella is somewhat upset by two sweet young girls who get fairly hysterical about a wasp that fancies their spilt strawberry milk shake; and a younger lad, with very thick spectacles, who is virtually equally hysterical as he is sure that his elder sister has eaten half his portion of chips. I guess that you can choose the setting: but the company reflects the rich variety of the morning's walk!

The esplanade continues towards the remains of Southsea Castle, which have been landscaped to provide walkways and seating with fine views across to the Isle of Wight. On the east side of the castle there is a new pyramidal shaped 'Aqua Centre' in construction; while the west side has 'the Blue Reef Aquarium'. Southsea is obviously keeping up!

A Cleopatra's Needle of a war memorial dominates the spacious Southsea Common that separates the rest of the walk from the various hotels and houses. Clarence Pier is more of a promenade, largely hidden by the terminal for hovercraft which scud across to the Isle of Wight. It is also an area of amusement arcades, ice cream and candy floss, even local sticks of rock, along with roundabouts and swings: the full works of the seaside resort.

Shortly after this a sequence of small squares, set in to the pathway, each with a subscriber's name, and with overlapping j-shapes, mark the beginning of a millennium walk which, in due course will lead the walker over to Gosport. But here the path leads past the ruins of the Royal Garrison Church, through the Square and Round Towers of the fortification of Old Portsmouth, which protects the unusual [yet well worth a visit] Anglican Cathedral, a mixture of old and new. Then the path loops round the extensive new developments of the shopping and hotel mall of the old docklands, with its dramatic Spinnaker tower: all very trendy. It has probably also gutted trade in the centre of town. But that is not my problem today. However I decide to end my walking day with a drink in 'The Victory' which is one of the pubs opposite the bus and rail stations: and it does seem to have been deserted by the new attractions round the corner. The 700 takes me back to Chichester; but there will not be many more trips on this '700 coaster route'. It has been a walker's mainstay from Brighton to Portsmouth. No mean stretch: and all free transport for the aged!

1 September 2010: Portsmouth Harbour to Stubbington.

I think that I have made my last official ride on the 700 bus from Chichester. For today I am to cross over Portsmouth Harbour and head for the Solent and Southampton. So it is the faster train journey that I take; and straight out of the station onto the Gosport ferry, not much more than a 10minute journey it seems. Purists might say that I should have walked round Portsmouth Harbour; and I do realise that I have missed the castle and the Kingsway. But much of this side of Portsmouth is either ferry terminals, motorway, or Navy base: so not really pedestrian friendly. Besides, my home rules state that as soon as you can ferry across an estuary – do so!

In Gosport the millennium stones lead straight out of the ferry down to the marina and across what looks like a fairly new bridge into what looks like a naval base; but the magic stones lead in here and do go through to the esplanade that becomes the Solent Way. But for some reason it looks a little too military and so I follow the road past the Royal Naval hospital along a very red-bricked-in road, with the walls topped with barbed wire. Not very jolly. Anyway the esplanade has to deviate round Fort Monckton. So the Solent Way is picked up again as it crosses a golf course [a long time since I commented on their coastal frequency] and leads to the ruin of some older military base at Gilicker Point. I am directed by a gentleman somewhat younger than myself, who tells me that he is walking a circuit while his son is being treated, at the Military Hospital that I have just passed, for brain damage as a result of being out in Afghanistan. The lovely day suddenly has a more sober perspective.

But there is a fine Nature Reserve walk along the coast, mixing shingle, sand and grass, with fine views over to the western end of the Isle of White, and for a while almost a feel of being in the country, until the houses of Lee-on-Solent start to appear and the B3333 runs parallel to the coastal walk. This runs almost continuously to Hill Head and Stubbington. There is a slightly less built-up stretch, with a coastguard station and where a seemingly unused airfield comes pretty near the coast. However it is all very quietly civilised after the closeness of the A27 and A3 and their heavy traffic approaching Southsea. On this part of the Solent it is only random local traffic, and no heavy goods. There is a local hostelry on the coast at the beginning of Hill Head which seems to be fairly packed out with the grey pound; and I cannot recall seeing quite so many recovering male stroke patients tottering off to the gents in the whole of my coastal walk! Perhaps there is something about the sea air of the Solent that is strongly recommended for recoveries? It reinforces my gratitude at being in good health and being able to tackle the coast in my own good time!

I set off with some relief towards Hill Head, with the first set of beach huts that I have seen for some miles; and all very tastefully painted a dark green to merge with the local background vegetation. The habitation all ends at Titchfield Haven which is a mixture of a nature reserve, a small local fishing harbour, and a smattering of a marina, along with a discreet spread of cafés and ice cream places. But if I am to get back to Chichester today I decide that I must make my way inland to Stubbington to catch the 72 [or 34 – a little local lady tells me] to get back to Gosport and Portsmouth Harbour. After a fair trek through leafy suburban Stubbington this is all accomplished; with the same lady explaining the complications of the one-way system that the bus negotiates in Stubbington: which never really shows on maps.

The coast to Warsash,Hamble Rice and Southampton await another day.

2011: MORE OF HAMPSHIRE

16 August, 2011: Hill Head to Southampton.

Nearly a year has passed by, in which I did some winter, bird watching, walks around the Chichester estuary, but on another day, hastily pushing on a tight-fitting shoe after playing badminton, I injured my right Achilles tendon. Recovery from Achilles injury is slow, particularly if you try to run for a bus before recovery has really happened, [as I did]!

So I think that I shall achieve even less of the coastal walk than last year. Hey-ho. This is not a competition I remind myself. But, when the tendon has healed, it does make for a real feeling of privilege to be back on the walk. How we all assume the walking action, until a bit of it goes wrong. Then the whole process has to be re-learnt!

This will be the last walk that I make from my Chichester base. I arrive at the 34 bus from the adjacent bus station to Gosport. The young bus driver is more than kind in dropping me off as near to Hill Head as he can [not an official stop: the bus driver's kindness makes a real difference from city life!].

The smart dark green beach huts at Hill Head seem surprisingly closed up for this time of year.

Round the outflow of Titchfield Haven, which holds water for a series of well-reeded inner water ways, a haven for water fowl, there is a tarmac road for a short while, with numerous parking spaces, but a concrete sculpted footpath on its seaward edge. Then, as the road swings inland, the 'Solent Way' [poorly signposted throughout this area] becomes a natural footpath heading up to the top of some sandstone and earth cliffs of modest height; and distinctly crumbly in parts. A solitary figure is out windsurfing, or at least trying; more a lesson in making the observer appreciate that it is quite a skill, as he repeatedly capsizes. Hard work!

On the beach a few clusters of people follow the safer art of flying kites.

Parts of the cliff top are meshed with thickets of blackthorn and hawthorn, so that the path occasionally wends though wind protected tunnels of shrubbery, which also draws my attention to the fact that it might be a good year for making sloe gin: a bountiful crop here! But I am grateful for the protection that the bushes form as the forecast sunny day has turned into one with a chilly strong south-easterly, necessitating a zipped up jacket rather than a short-sleeved shirt.

Landward there is the stubble of reaped corn; a lone kestrel hovers over the fields and the gorse. Then a flock of plovers swoops up from the shore and mixes with a flock of smaller birds, which, without my binoculars, I cannot identify. It seems strange to see a flock of mixed birds. Perhaps a response to the kestrel?

The shingle supports sea cabbage and the odd escaped rosa rugosa; while on the cliff top there is sea parsley and small yellow snap dragons, along with ragwort. But some of these, and the grasses, have already set seed: with the greyness of the day there is suddenly a touch of autumn in the air.

The Solent is certainly the Rubicon of this walk. Never before has there been so much north and south walking when you are trying to go west! The Isle of Wight is beginning to disappear behind me, so that I can see a gap between it and the Calshott peninsula on the other side of the Solent, with its industrial drama of power stations and oil refineries.

But on my side there is a stretch of open country walking until suddenly you are in a 'Holiday Home Estate', 'from as little as £19,995' the hoarding says, but with no clear indication as to where the Solent Way goes! Or was I day dreaming again?

I did see a group of walkers across the stubbled field; perhaps they were marking the boundary of the estate? I could possibly have scurried down onto the shingle, and passed the estate front by that route: but I am in the extensive development and spend an unstimulating fifteen minutes finding an authorised way out, as much of it is ring fenced. But, having walked along a road with speed humps I find a track that leads back down to the Solent, passing a large substation on the way.

The coastal path is now close to sea level, but alternates between a firm path and shingle crunching [my least favourite medium] along the edge of Hook Park, a pleasing open space. But a word of warning as you approach Warsash and another set of clinking masts [the equivalent of cow bells in the Swiss Alps?]. There is a long, reeded, finger of inland water to your right, while the shingle curves forward, even sporting a few fishermen, with the illusion that there might be a pedestrian bridge at the end to take you to Warsash. But not so; it is a blind end, and you need to take the first right crossing over

99

the water. Fortunately I meet a family, equipped with shrimping nets, coming the other way that gives me this clear indication! Happy days for the family outing; completed by a wet, chocolate coloured, labrador and an even soggier, but similarly coloured, spaniel.

Warsash suburbs now loom and it is not long before you are in the mast clanging marina. There is a well-placed 'Rising Sun' pub, but it unfortunately looks oversubscribed by all the locals who have arrived in their cars. I push on. My bar of Cadbury's fruit and nut, plus my bottle of water will have to suffice for the next stretch. I walk on looking for the berth of the little pink Hambleton ferry.

Two elderly gentlemen, with bespoke walking sticks and the Daily Telegraph under an arm [who must surely have reserved seats at the Rising Sun], advise me that the ferry terminal is obvious once I have disappeared down a path that runs down the side of the rather large car park [serving both the marina and the Rising Sun]. Like the white rabbit, I scurry down this pathway and, emerging from the vegetation, spy a bright pink, small, concrete hut, with a long wooden walkway going into the estuary of the River Hamble. On the far side I spy an equally small, and equally bright pink tub, putt-putting across the waters, weaving its way through the numerous moored and active sailing boats, with the ferry looking rather like a marine version of Thomas the tank engine.

It is but minutes before the twinkle eyed skipper, somewhere between Rip van Winkle and a hobbit, bumps his boat into the walkway, disgorges his three passengers, and, in return, I and a family of five, plus a whippet, all scantily clad for the fine day that was forecast, tumble into the boat and pay our modest toll. I do think of the nursery rhyme 'three men in a tub, the butcher, the baker, the candle stick maker', but cannot remember what political situation it referred to? It sounds pre-trade union? Nevertheless I wonder if they were as goose-pimpled as my present companions were by the time they reached the safe harbour of Hamble.

Hamble is not quite what I expected; the estuary front here seems to lack any charm, although the rather grey weather certainly does not help. It does not improve when sailing clubs and docks stop the pedestrian walking round: so one is driven to walking up the hill into Hamble.

I think of lunch again, but the waterside café is fairly packed out and I fail to find a welcoming inn at this stage. On the map the Solent way has various unconnected red dots leading into town, and when you get to a T junction it is instinctive to turn left, hopefully seawards. This is confirmed by a cohort of kids, mothers, prams, and even grandmothers, struggling and straggling up the slight hill.

Fortunately the narrow tarmac road soon has a separate footpath through trees that at least comes out on the Southampton side of yet another sailing club [sailing clubs seem to have taken over from golf courses as a measurement of the coastal walk!]. I appreciate that, still without lunch, I have the greater part of my walk ahead. But I could easily have worked on finding a pleasant hostelry and then caught a bus from Hythe to Southampton; so it is of my own choosing!

However my legs, thankfully, seem to feel like walking – so I proceed. After a couple of open fields the water's edge suddenly becomes a narrow concrete path, bordered by a high mesh security fence, protecting what look like large oil storage tanks. In the middle of this stretch a long jetty stretches out, but at least the footpath has steps down, and under, the overhead jetty. It does also mean that fast progress can be made on this surface. Whereas once back to the 'rural idyll', it is back to shifting shingle. I am full of admiration for the one or two runners [even the odd cyclist!] who travel in the opposite direction on this most wearing of surfaces.

It is possible to stick on the shingle, but a path curves through some woodland and is too tempting: a single-track tarmac road leads to an imposingly situated period 'Hamble Cliff House'; distinctly private, but, fortunately the owners away and there is a boat- run back down to the shore.

It is not too long before another boat club appears; but as a couple of cyclists come up behind me and charge through it, I am emboldened to follow suit at a somewhat more sedate pace. The road behind the club runs seamlessly into the Royal Victoria Country Park, in the middle of whose copious acres stands a very large, seemingly deconsecrated, red-bricked church. I wonder as to whether it might have been a convent? But my feet seem to be in automaton mode and make good ground over this pleasant stretch of parkland. So that I begin to think that I will not have to chicken out at Netley and catch a train or bus in to Southampton!

But Netley has more 'private' frontage. So you have to follow the road parallel to the water's edge, up past the temptation of the 'Prince Consort' Inn [I think at this stage I might not get out if I go in!], after which the houses on the left disappear and another open space/parkland appears, running down to the water's edge and the ruins of an abbey and a castle. However the feeling of making it to Southampton are now unstoppable and carry me on to the well maintained shores of Weston and Woolston. Even the grass is mowed here. It is back to shoreline suburbia me-thinks; but pleasantly so.

As you round the corner of the river Itchen, Southampton is across the water. Yet another marina appears, and I spy a bus that says 'City Centre'. I also see a chain of buses crossing the very fine, high rising Itchen bridge. At the next bus stop I hop on and in the town another bus takes me to the rail station, whence a train back to Chichester.

6 & 7 September, 2011: Ocean Marine Village to Hythe and Calshot

I have the feeling that this might be my last outing for this summer. There is a distinct autumnal feel to the air, and the weather forecast is not good for the next few days. I am now sufficiently far away to have booked into an hotel on the edge of Hythe; but first I have to get there. A train to Southampton Central station, where there is a city bus that goes to the ferry terminal at the new development of 'Ocean Marine Village'. The principal ferry here is for the Isle of Wight, but at the same terminal there is a smaller gangplank to the left hand side, with a machine or an operator offering tickets for the crossing of the Solent to Hythe: something like a half-hourly service according to the season; and a jolly trip amidst all the big traffic of the Solent.

the Ferry to Hythe.

The approach to Hythe by ferry shows a rather pleasant old town frontage with a long wooden pier, with new developments either side [one full of clinking masts!] while seawards there are the hulks of oil storage and the towers of E.ON, power suppliers, stretching along the coast. The boat docks at the tip of the pier giving the option of walking the length of the pier, or a ride in a miniature train that times itself to the arrival and departures of the ferry and drops you at the bus station and the charm of the old Town.

The official Solent Way heads down the ancient main street, past a new Waitrose and along Shore Road and Frost Lane, with the former having good views of the Solent to Netley and Victoria Park from the last walk. But the authorised route then cuts back to Dibden Purlieu to plough across Hatford Heath on the rather busy B3054, heading for Beaulieu like a homing device. By doing this it cuts out the whole of the Calshot peninsula. Although much of the Solent west coast looks to be industrialised, I think that the east side of the river Beaulieu and the Calshot peninsula do warrant investigation. So I have booked three nights at my curious Indian-run hotel on Frost Lane. There is little accommodation in Hythe, so the hotel serves as the place for business men of the local industry, along with local imbibers.The large rooms speak of it once having been a very comfortable Edwardian residence.

My first task is to try and sort out the reality of the local bus service; and the stop at the end of the pier, along with the ever friendly and helpful bus drivers, indicates that the 9 and the H3 might take me south to Fawley and Calshot; while the 112 might take me to Beaulieu [and on to Lymington for another stage?] but there seems to be no service to Exbury or Lepe on the east coast of the Beaulieu river. I begin to see why the Solent way skates straight across the Heath!

So I head for Calshot on the H3: which runs only a few times a day; and not all of them go as far as Calshot. This is perhaps not too surprising as Calshot, apart from the ruins of a castle, is a very long row of beach huts with a handful of houses. Even the beach huts are very much 'them and us' inasmuch as those running westwards are on a private estate, while those running eastwards to the cluster of 'Activities Centre' [some fairly heroic wind-surfing going on], castle ruins and life boat station, are in the public domain. This latter stretch has something of the feel of the immobile-mobile-home developments! But there is a fairly extensive sea marsh nature reserve to the left, with

103

plovers and a pair of unusual, juvenile, yellow wagtails . The view across the Solent is pleasant enough, but the remainder of the horizon is dominated by the futuristic look of the E.ON building with its high security ring of mesh fencing, and rolls of barbed wire inside. Inside there is a large circular building, resembling a flying saucer, and a highly militarised system to regulate the water outlet. All quite Sci –Fi in appearance; or a set waiting for the next Bond film?

The water outlet is fortunately crossed by an enclosed metal bridge, gated at both ends. However, after this there is a bramble walk where ladies from Fawley, with green wellies, big floppy sun hats and plastic bags, are busy reaping the rather squishy harvest. Blackberry scrub merges into copsed woodland, with intermittent views over the Solent until you stumble out into the delight of Fawley Harbour, whose old, large, brick building may have had industrial use, but now looks like the yacht club; accompanied by a very spruce, 'The Jolly Sailor' pub. There is also quite an attractive green with the odd seat; but the tide being well out, the ensuing spread of estuary mud does not enhance the picture!

There is a short uphill walk into Fawley where you come out into the village square by a wedding dress shop [this useful, and unexpected, piece of information in case you decide to walk in a clockwise direction – and start at Fawley, i.e., turn down by the wedding dress shop!]. There is another suitable hostelry in the square, but as it is beginning to rain and a rare No 9 bus [to Southampton via Hythe] is imminent, I catch the bus and plot my next day in Hythe.

8 September 2011: Chalcot to Exbury

This is another walk that I do in reverse, simply because I know where the bus stop is in Chalcot and the infrequency of the bus that I am heading for. Also, while it shows as Chalcot to Exbury on the map, by public transport it is by bus to Blackfield, then by foot across Blackwell Common and head onwards to Exbury, from where I can investigate the coastal route back to Calshot. So much for plans.

I actually have the choice of a 9 or an H3 to Blackfield and dismount at the cross roads with a large pub on the corner, well set back; and head for the common. I might mention that it was pouring down, with driving rain at a good 45 degrees, so that I am

soon drenched and admiring the few new forest ponies that are standing behind gorse
shelter with their back to the wind and rain. I persevere.

Blackwell Common Ponies.

At least it is open countryside and I am heading westwards. The road, having
crossed the heath, runs into oak woodland which provides some protection; but I am
bombarded by lichen-covered twigs and a spattering of early acorns. I do have a distinct
feeling that I could have had a comfortable day in the hotel doing sudoku in the Times!

I stay on this quiet road [who would come out on such a day?] until it reaches a T
junction, where a right turn gives a view of a collection of buildings which I take to be
Exbury. And so it is: a classic approach – with the cricket ground and community hall on
the left, with modest old and new houses leading to the boundary of the extensive Exbury
Estate and its gardens, running down to the river, making much of the estuary out of
bounds, but at least housing a fine collection of rhododendrons and open for inspection at
certain times of the year. However, I am consoled by the quiet shelter of the church
dedicated to St Katherine. The interior has a poignant, if somewhat theatrically draped,
WW1 side chapel memorial to John and Alfred, whose lives were wasted in the travesty
of that warfare. Life-size effigies, like 20th century knights, are moving tributes and the
stillness of the chapel contrasts with the buffeting of the weather outside.

As if in some sort of sympathy the weather had slackened when I emerged and I
head south to Lower Exbury along the edge of the estate. The road turns right towards
Inchmery House and suddenly there is a good coastal path behind breakwaters! But,

because of the wind and driving rain, I choose to follow the narrow winding road with its protective high hedge and row of trees. Oval rose hips and round hawthorn berries glisten a bright, wet, red in the hedges, and even the blackberries are lustrous in the rain: but it is not the weather to stop and pick them!

The estuary mouth with its low shrub-clad islands and mud flats is devoid of habitation, appearing as a true wilderness/nature reserve. It looks a beast of a navigation by boat!

The road rejoins the coastal path near a dwarf lighthouse and a row of terraced cottages with slated facades, make up the village of Lepe. The wind is approaching gale force and I feel vulnerable to being blown over. Needless to say there are no other walkers; a few people sit in cars at the large car park on the sea front of 'Lepe Country Park', which on a fine day must be a pleasing local attraction. It certainly has a welcoming large café where a few of the car owners are watching the weather lash at the view across to the Isle of Wight.

A decently wide pathway does go eastwards towards Calshott, with some inner ponds and marshy waterways. There is an extensive abandoned defensive sea wall towards the end of this path, with faded wreaths of poppies commemorating that this was the site of a launch of the D Day landings, and even of a planned pipe line to take fuel across to the Isle of Wight. It has a somewhat haunted feel on a rainy, grey, day, as if uniformed ghosts are all around, but otherwise it is deserted. Apart from the weather, this is not surprising, as the path dead ends a little further on. Barbed wire fencing is accompanied by notices of 'strictly private'; and the cover of 'nature reserve'. It is another stretch of privately-owned coast that stops the walker making it through to Calshott. So the only legitimate option is to return to the road down to Lepe and turn left towards Stanswood farms until the road runs into woodland. Then, after the gatehouse to Eaglehurst it is possible to follow paths into the wood that will come out near the garage in Calshott, whence an H3 bus back to Hythe.

I will confess that, because of the inclement weather, I did follow a shorter route through to Stone Farm. For most of it I saw nobody, but then espied a major group of men doing serious land/drainage restructuring, at which my heart fell, thinking that I was trespassing and would be instructed to return whence I came. The foreman came forward and raised his hand in an authoritarian manner. But, lo and behold, it was to stop his troops working the heavy machinery while I walked [squelched!] my way through! What unlooked for kindness [I think that I cut a fairly bedraggled figure]! Even the rain no longer seemed so bad: and by the time I had passed Stanswood Farm and reached the woods the rain had, for the first time, actually stopped.

This is a tricky peninsula to complete, particularly by public transport, but the bleakness of the neglected war memorial at Lepe, the strange silted wildness of the mouth of the Beaulieu River, and the effigies in St Katherine's Church justified the tramping through rain and wind. But it is easy to understand why this corner is cut out of the 'Solent Way' walk; which is further endorsed by tomorrow's walk!

9 September, 2011: Exbury to Beaulieu.

This is the last stretch of this cul de sac; and for one depending on public transport, it remains perhaps the most difficult. I choose to go to Exbury from Hythe as yesterday, but this time head northwards towards Otterwood Gate and Beaulieu. Had I known that which I now know, it would have been possible to walk from Calshot to Beaulieu in a day. But you would have to know that you have to cut through the backwoods and road to Lepe as the intermediate coastline is privatised. Similarly, private ownership of the river's edge dictates that in today's walk there is none of it open to the public. So from St Katherine's at Exbury it is a case of following the very pleasantly wooded northern minor road to Otterwood Gate were the scene opens out to the heathland of grazing territory and a distant vision of traffic hurtling along the B3054; a much busier road than the quiet woods that I have just meandered through. The Otterwood road passes some fine residences which overlook the heath with an 'Oaktree' pub on the corner as you join the B road, along which you have no alternative but to tread the verges into Beaulieu. This has a gracious entry into the village green running down to the wide river, with the road bordered by the walls of the abbey and manor house. There are seats under trees on the green, and the forest livestock graze and ruminate in some comfort; the seeming pastoral idyll. But drivers beware on the narrow bends in the charming village: you may well have a dribble of donkeys, or a heave of cattle, ambling in the opposite direction; all of them quite sure that they have right of way. Me thinks the local council have no problem keeping the green or the verges well mown here! The Solent Way is signposted again here.The signpost indicates that it runs immediately down by the side of the prominent Montague Hotel. But that is for another visit.

While the abbey and house are highly visible from the village, their pedestrian access is a good mile away. I think that it is assumed that everybody comes by car or bus. It has something to learn from Petworth, where there is pedestrian access to the House from the village, but vehicles are sent round to the trades entrance! But then Beaulieu is a car museum!

I am fortunate enough to catch a bus which has come from Lymington to return to Hythe from Beaulieu [more of this in the next trip!].

After a summer or two of north/south estuaries, I look forward to heading west again in an undiverted manner!

2012: HAMPSHIRE INTO DORSET.

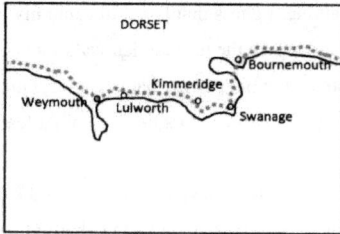

16 April 2012: Arrival at Lymington.

How time flies as you age! Another winter has passed.

My first base is Lymington for three days' walking, and the Angel Inn on the High Street proves to be a comfortable and central choice. A fine traditional, small town, inn that has been up dated without losing much of its old world charm [though I do feel rather as if I am on a boat from the way the floor lurches in the corridor leading to my attic bedroom; making me think that I have perhaps had too much to drink when I have not!]. Lymington is a charming coastal town, with two stations since it also serves as a ferry access to the Isle of Wight. But you do have to change at Brockhampton, on the main Victoria to Weymouth line, to get to either of these stations.

So far my web site information has been accurate for accommodation and transport. But cutbacks are about to manifest. First, the tourist information office has been amalgamated with the museum office; and the well-meaning ladies are not yet in full control. For instance they warm to me mentioning the 'Solent Way'; but only have knowledge of its westward direction from Lymington to Milford [where it ends] and know nothing of the stretch from Beaulieu to Lymington, which I hope to complete tomorrow.

But the second victim of cut-backs is the 112 bus that I used from Hythe to Lymington, passing through Beaulieu, which ran several times a day and still did on their website. Fortunately, at the Lymington bus station one of the local bus drivers, depping as information officer [more cut backs?] with a large left earing and an engaging smile, updated me; and I learnt that such buses only run on Tuesday and Thursday, and the

109

10.10. is the first one that I can catch [London web planning had left me with the illusion that I could catch buses around 7.00 or 8.00!]..While this means that a third of the day will have gone before I can start walking, I guess that I should count my blessings that tomorrow is a Tuesday, [and that I did my Hythe to Beaulieu walking last year!]! There is also no chance of me catching a connection on the way back from Lymington; and rain is forecast for tomorrow. Hey ho!: My programme is toughening up! At least I now know what to expect.

Having arrived on a sunny day, I at least have time to inspect the charming Lymington High Street which seems to have more than its fair share of couture shops for the not-so-young, mixed with the usual spread of small town high street shops, in which real butchers, fishmongers and greengrocers are an increasing rarity. Chain brands rule the day.

St Thomas and All Saints has an unexpected interior of Early English rather dominated by a Georgian Balcony; along with a lady chapel dedicated to St Ubaldesca [to whom I have considerable difficulty finding any references!] and, stuck on a wall in the entrance hall, a saved, curious and colourful, collection of medieval bosses consisting of red-winged angels in green frilly frocks, mixed with local dignitaries: very medieval!

Lamb shank and a couple of glasses of passable Merlot do me well in the evening.

17 April 2012: Beaulieu to Lymington

I wake at 7.00 to hear the rain pounding down and, staggering to my ablutions, I see a thunderously grey, heavy, sky. I decide that I can safely lie until 8.00, by which time the sky is still grey, but it is not pouring down. Two coffees, a bowl of muesli and a croissant later, it is fine enough to slip across the road to stock up and to sit in watery sunshine to await the 112 bus to Beaulieu Garage. Apart from one old dear [should I insert 'another', I wonder?], who goes through the panic of 'Oh I have lost my freedom pass;' pause: 'I had it a minute ago', followed by much scrabbling in various bags, plastic and otherwise: then 'Oh, here it is; in my pocket all the time!': well apart from her, to whom I cluck in genuine sympathy, I am the only other passenger. Since she, after various diversions for current road works, alights at Lymington Hospital [I do hope that she managed to find the right ward!] I have the privilege of solitary transport to Beaulieu via very narrow roads, through Norley Wood, East End and East Boldre; with the only excitement being where a water main has burst with a local car parked on one side and the repairer's lorry, some further three metres away, on the other. There is an interesting comparison in tactics between the bus driver [professional and patient], a young lady in a four by four [automatically assuming right of way], two elderly ladies [cautious even beyond expectation] and two guys in a white van [get through at all costs!]. But it does all resolve amicably: that is country life for you.

The bus edges along the border of Hatchet Moor and I again notice how closely grazed the land is and the stock rather thin. Then there is a diversionary free visit by the bus to the doorstep of the Beaulieu motor museum; but everybody seems to come here by private transport, car or hired charabanc. So I finally end up at my final destination outside the garage in the village, where a solitary lady, of a similar age to myself, is patiently waiting to take the bus back to Lymington. I feel that it justifies my journey out; but do think of her problem of this perhaps being her only option of a weekly trip? There must be a greater issue here of restricted bus services sounding their own death knell; and I hear the harsh clang of the bell of statistics tolling.

But, now on foot, I head round the sharp corner on the narrow village footpath to meet five donkeys coming the other way; all in file on the footpath! I have no alternative but to step into the road and fortunately all the oncoming traffic does slow down. Donkeys really do have right of way here!

I do note that they are rather thin donkeys, confirming my earlier observations from the bus. The winter must have been harder here; or there is serious over-stocking on the heath-like moorland. This is borne out in the rest of my walk where I notice that the verges on the narrow lanes of the Solent Way are all very closely cropped, more closely than any mower could go and there are none of the violets, primroses, or celandines that I see in the gated woods. Harsh statistics again!

However I pick up the Solent Way easily enough, having identified it as running beside the Montague Hotel on my last visit. It runs through some recent affluent developments on the riverside to open at last into fields and a tranquil view of the river; but still definitely green welly territory, along with King Charles spaniels or sleek black labradors. But this does not stop an appreciation of the rural idyll, the placidly flowing

111

river with half of the trees still in winter's form, while the rest are tinged with spring's fresh green. Further on I realise that part of this tranquillity is because there are no white boats [of various status] to clutter the vision; even as London squares recover their architectural dignity and tranquillity when cars are removed!

The path soon dives into woodland and there is the first of a series of remnants of the old trades of the river, linked to both baking bricks, and building ships at Bailey's and Buckler's Hard; the latter being the most prominent. It is now a row of two attractive terrace houses separated by a green, a museum, and a hotel: although in its day there were four tightly-packed rows of houses, and from these came the workers to build one of Nelson's ships [the museum is worth a visit!].

But I run ahead of myself. The path has two options; a straight walk through the forest, coniferous on one side, and deciduous on the other, or a meandering path that runs along the river bank. As I am somewhat late starting I choose the former. But I have the entertainment of being accompanied by a family of four on a cycling day out. They are actively led by the young brother, who hares off along the riverside path. Dad dutifully follows; big sister shows that she is quite capable of keeping up without losing her cool, or showing too much enthusiasm; while mum distinctly struggles and occasionally gets off and walks. So it is something of a hare and tortoise exercise, with their advance troops frequently having to stop and wait for poor, not so old, mum. I feel for her; but I actually arrive at the approach to Buckler's Hard ahead of them. The first of my 'hare and tortoise' encounters, where, in this case, the tortoise wins! It will not always be so in the rest of my walking!

The approach to Buckler's Hard, mentioned above, is not a welcome one, as it is via a fairly large private sailing club blocking the riverside. So walkers and cyclist have to turn right and go up the hill. Of course I am overtaken by young brother, father, and lanky sister in turn: but I instinctively know that mother is staggering up the hill behind me; and having to push her bike as well! At the top of the incline they do all gather together, and go off in the direction of Beaulieu, while I turn left to pass Buckler's Hard and note that the whole of this peninsula of the river is private, so the walker has to follow the Solent Way on the narrow road going towards St Leonards Grange. At least there is a comfortable seat at the cross roads where I have a quick swig of water, a bite of chocolate, and admire the view down into Buckler's Hard.

The narrow lanes to St Leonards were where I met fattish and highly pregnant Hereford cattle [or crosses thereof] who are the local mowing machines for the verges. Occasionally, in gaps of the, mainly high, hawthorn hedges, there is a vista of the Solent estuary and the distant hills of the Isle of Wight. I suffer a splattering of hail for some three minutes; but given the sombre weather forecast I count my blessings.

St Leonards is marked as a Grange and indeed there is a largish handsome house but there is also a hamlet; its 'chapel' and 'tithe barn' are surely the remains of an abbey of some considerable size? With a stream coming through Cooper's Wood and the Beaulieu estuary so near, surely this is a site that no itinerant monk would have overlooked! Amidst the considerable craggy ruins it is as if the monks have been reincarnated as a cloister of rooks-and not a silent order; but binoculars suggest that there is at least a choir stall of jackdaws amongst them! Different uniforms!

There is a small triangular green with another welcome wooden seat where I eat a quick cheese sandwich [I being prepared for there being no inn on this walk] and enjoy the accompanying version of avian plainsong and their fun acrobatics in the abbey ruins.

More 'Private' notices tell me that I am not going to get down to see the mouth of the estuary at Needs Ore Point; my memory from a wet walk on the other bank when passing lower Exbury will have to suffice. A shame.

The next stretch of road does have lower hedges and some quite glorious views across the Solent, sharpened by bright yellow fields of flowering rape, and the sun struggling to come out: but still decidedly windy and changeable. A left turn hides me from the strong westerly wind and heads me along the southern aspect of Sowley Pond, which by anybody's measure is a small lake engulfed in woodland. My presence stimulates a buzzard to hop out of his tree and laconically flap away while my glasses spot a solitary great crested grebe. Two nearer fowl are mallard drakes [civil partnerships are obviously rife!]. But then, where I think I see the grebe's partner sitting on a nest in the reeds, I see a mother mallard emerge from the reed with six newly fledged ducklings bobbing round her, sometimes ahead, sometimes behind. She goes further and further into the empty space of the lake: and I am grateful that I startled the buzzard out of his perch. I walk on feeling privileged for this glimpse of life on the lake; but not wanting to

113

stay to see my imagined sequence with the ducklings and the buzzard.

Some five hundred yards after the private woodland of Sowley estate some kind farmer has allowed the Solent Way to go round his/her fields: and the way is clearly signposted. The signs lead you past the fringes of Pyewell house and I am taken out of my appreciation of the spread of primroses, celandines, violets and white wood anemones by the unmistakable sharp sound of leather coated cork on willow. Cricket on the Solent Way? I think that Pyewell house must now be a public school? It seems that it is; and there are two lads on their school holidays, practising in the nets. I am jolted back to civilisation by this apparition, and by a very formal avenue of trees, leading to a field with a 'beware the bull' sign. Fortunately there is only a diminutive, Thelwellian, Shetland pony in the paddock: and no indication that a sudden metamorphosis is likely!

The 'Solent Way' signs continue and lead through South Baddesley. Then there is a sharp right turn to head for Snook's Farm, and suddenly you are crossing a long wide run of grassland that very much has the appearance of a private airfield; but I missed the 'danger' notices, if there were any! Snook's Farm looks like a pirate's storage for freezers full of lobsters and crabs; rather unexpected!

Somewhere round here the narrow path takes you past a golf course. This one slightly makes me think I am hallucinating, as the number of golf balls lying around make me first think that there has been a mad spawning of mushrooms in the field. Then I see a group of hunched figures, who I deem to be golfers, chipping and putting under tuition: thus a hailstorm of golf balls in progress!

A narrow lane leads down to the estuary road and past the Lymington ferry terminal to the Isle of Wight. I feel tempted to hop on the bus back to town [the train is not crossing the river at the moment]; but nobly plod on to the vehicular and pedestrian bridge someway upstream. I am rewarded with a flock of black-tailed godwits, handsome in their black, white, and buff markings as they pick in the mud of the tidal estuary. It is interesting to see how they are unmoved by the noisy traffic zooming past. But as soon as a pedestrian stops to raise binoculars – they are off, scudding en -masse over the estuary water.

The bridge is almost worth the detour, as to the north there is a harbour of stagnant fens; with notices on the bridge road, 'danger – otters crossing'! No lady with a lollipop to help them! But well done to the people of Lymington: and it starts to rain again.

Dressed crab, with cherry tomatoes and beetroot, accompanied by a glass or two of Pinot Grigio round off the day in a most civilised way.

18 April: Lymington to Barton-on-Sea

'Rain before seven, fine before eleven' the saying goes and sort of held true today. It was certainly teaming down when I opened an eyelid around seven o'clock. The problem was that I really wanted to be out walking at an earlier hour than yesterday. So I did set off at 9.20 between downpours, only to have to lean against one of the terrace houses to put on waterproof over-trousers on my way down to the mouth of the river as it began to pour again. However the downpour does tend to keep people off the streets!

Having done part of this route on the Monday of my arrival, I know that turning right at the estuary end of the High Street, then persevering until a left turn into 'Solent Way' will take you down to a green on the river's edge and thence a pavementless stretch of road [care on the turn], will let you slip into King's Edge Lane, which immediately feels quietly countrified, even as gentrified. This lane runs down to the main marina, with its collection of chandlers, outfitters, and cafés. But there is a clear signpost for a public footpath across the front of these buildings. This path leads into a quiet lane which, with right-angle bends, misses out the coastal path round the 'Normandy' nature reserve. I suspect that there may have been access to this reserve down the side of, or through, the marina. But since it is still rather wet, and the wind is close to force six, I persevere with my chosen route. All rights of access [or not!] are clearly signposted in this area and my diverted route allows the pleasure of seeing a solitary young stag roe deer grazing in an open field; brazen enough not to immediately dash for cover. I am also consoled by a notice stating that the Normandy Reserve is out of bounds as it is breeding territory, as well as a haven, for migratory birds. I am also rewarded by another gaggle of twenty or so godwits [most likely the same flock as yesterday; different location?] busy dibbing and dabbing in the shallow waters.

Arriving at the sea front, I see a good raised sea wall capped by a well-gravelled path for the walker, which must, with its fine views of the Solent and the Isle of Wight, make it an idyllic walk on a fine day. But, although the rain is abating, the force six south westerly wind is a head-on battle, with each breath feeling like a double dose of oxygen.

The Solent Way is well signposted, but is not quite as direct as my ordnance survey map suggests and even the more-detailed version from the tourist information office does need some interpretation. There are various dykes and inlets and it is as well to make sure that you cross 'Denham's Dyke' before you cut back to the coastal path.

The birds are battling with the wind too: a tern heading in my direction beats hard and scarcely moves at a quicker pace than I do; while those that give up and turn eastwards hurtle off, caught up by the wind, at an alarming pace. The sensible majority of sea birds are bobbing it out, sitting on the water; or they even hide in the marshy hinterland, where there seems to be a collection of the large, multi-coloured, shell ducks amongst mute swans, along with darting, black, water hens and some sea plovers. Some of each of these are nesting.

There are very few walkers braving these rather wild conditions, but as I approach the fine sweep up to Keyhaven I do see two couples, all with binoculars trained on a multicoloured duck sitting on a tussock in the marshland as if there might be eggs underneath.

'Ah – twitchers', I think.

I approach, and am asked, 'So what is it?'

'A duck' is my opening move, with some aplomb [it is quite large] and I continue, 'Yes, dark head, red beak, orange-russet breast and black stripe on white wings?'

'Yes, yes', they chorus, 'what is it?'

I see that I am not to be enlightened.

I begin, 'I don't know but....', yet before I can qualify my comment,

'Well you're not much use', comes from one of the plumper ladies.

'Well, I think that it is a shell duck – but the head is rather dark; should be greener. I need to check when I get home' I utter, trying to regain some ground.

There are some that you don't win!

Well at least Keyhaven is round the corner and a welcome shelter from the wind for a while. It would be easy to follow the minor road down to Saltgrass, or to follow the raised walkway if the weather is kinder. There is a ferry from Keyhaven out to the very narrow curving peninsula of Hurst Castle. But this is a summer offering only; and so is not available. In view of the prevailing wind and looming dark grey clouds I eschew the privilege of trekking out to the castle and back. It must feel singularly close to the Isle of Wight and very worthwhile on a fine day!

So I head over the footbridge over the outlet of Sturt Pond and scoot into New Milton, managing to find the Needles Café, [with splendid views of the 'Needles', chalk rocks sticking out of the most westerly point of the Isle of Wight] and have a welcome tuna baguette just before the Needles disappear from sight in an absolutely torrential downpour. Thank goodness I was not halfway to Hurst Castle! It might well have been 'a singular experience'!

Refreshed, and the weather clearer, but still ridiculously windy, I tackle the walk along the sandstone cliffs to Barton-on-Sea. The sea pinks are out in force, but even they seem a little battered by the force seven blow. The white lace patterns of the crashing, ebbing waves pile up to seem like a plague of scurrying, white mice [even rats!] pouring out of the waves' edge. The buffeting wind and cliff combined are somewhat scary, so much so that I actually cling to the barbed wire fence that borders the path, and almost fail to notice that I am going past another golf course! Needless to say I do not meet any fellow walkers on what might be a most pleasant stretch in good weather.

Barton-on-Sea has a fairly comfortable-looking sea front. But I am only too pleased to catch the X1 bus back to Lymington, having struggled to find somebody who knows which is the correct side of the road on which to stand [I distinctly do not wish to go onwards to Bournemouth in this weather!]. Even the double-decker bus rocks slightly

117

in the gale force wind and rain; but the coastline looks quite magnificent from upstairs on the inside of the bus! On the way back I can see the Isle of Wight Needles being lashed by rain again and sun streaming through the scudding clouds a little further on: very dramatic from the right side of the rapidly steaming windows of the bus!

19 April 2012: Barton-on-Sea to Christchurch

Another rainy start: a wet April making up for a warm dry March.

Both the X1 and X2 make the Lymington – Bournemouth run, with 80% of the route identical; but to arrive at Barton-on-Sea one needs the X1. The bus that I would prefer leaves at 9.28, all of 2 minutes before the freedom pass kicks in. The information officer, another jovial bus driver doubling up, advises a walk down to the post office to beat the time limit; but this accomplished the official timetable for the bus is only 9.29. So I walk to the next stop which also says 9.29. However, a wily veteran with a twinkle in her eye, says 'Oh, they are always late by the time that they get here: and they let you on. Don't worry, dear'. It is good to be looked after sometimes!

Whereupon the bus duly turns up; and I duly follow in her wake.

Eventually I recognise the street heading for the front of Barton-on-Sea and, once dismounted, I scoot down to the large green on top of the crumbling sandy cliffs. There is something of a quandary here. A fast walk on the top green leads to a dead end fence of a large estate of immobile-mobile homes; still shut for the winter. A lower path looks like a good option; but at the end of Barton-on-Sea, where the 'mobile homes' begin, the pathway is crumbling – and does not look safe. The third possible option is to walk along the beach and, tide permitting, scoot through to Highcliff. But you would still have to cross the outlet of the Chewton Bunny rivulet. Anyway the tide is in.

As it is raining slightly, I make the mistake of being a 'visitor' to the holiday homes [I should have learnt by now!]. They are ghoulish places out of season, and, without either a ball of string or a compass, the jumble of look-a-like avenues in every direction becomes something like walking through a hall of mirrors at one of the old fun fairs: very disorientating. You begin to doubt your own identity and to wonder where you are really going. In this instance it is compounded by the official escape road to the beach being 'temporarily unavailable' due to more slippage of the cliffs, I suspect. I finally do find an exit onto the A35 and by a restored sense of direction, and the fall of the land, I head down Chewton Bunny into Highcliffe, where a kind lady, having consoled my shock at having negotiated the estate, directs me to the sea front. This immediately looks more promising and civilised, with another choice of high or low paths, but a clear view that there is a run, via various 'groynes', towards Christchurch: and some pleasant beach to go with the route. Part of this route is steeply wooded down to the beach with some daunting sets of steps soaring up the hill. I imagine that these go to Highcliffe Castle; but it could be that they just go to a car park!

It is an easy walk into Christchurch, passing a smaller 'Holiday Park' and running on to the esplanade flanking the very narrow outlet of Christchurch Harbour. With this gusty wet weather I am only too pleased to dive into the small pub, set amongst the other cafés and fish and chip providers. Over another crab sandwich and a good local pint the daily sudoku is completed and I am ready to cross to Hengitsbury Head to complete my circuit into Christchurch. This entails taking a neat little ferry [sailing every 12 minutes] that fights its way across this narrow, but fast flowing, stretch of water. The lagoon-like harbour seems to be a haven for swans, there being some twenty seven in various states of furious paddling [i.e mainstream] or stately floating [i.e.out of the tidal current]. But none is even thinking of flying in this windy weather.

The peninsula on the other side has beach huts back-to-back, some facing out to sea and some into the harbour lagoon. In the summer it looks as if you can catch another ferry that will take you across the lagoon up to the present moorings in the heart of Christchurch. But at the moment it is a case of walking along the western side of the harbour along the Stour Valley Way. In fact this is a well-surfaced road and, although it is out of season, there is a small, green tractor engine with mini coaches to match, which looks like something out of Disneyland and is driven by an elderly, flat-capped driver with a prominent hooked nose, rather sad eyes and a large handkerchief which he uses to mop at the rain dripping off his nose. I am tempted to cadge a lift; but there is nobody else about, and it is not a day for hovering. So I set off on foot.

I am quite pleased when I am overtaken by the same Walt Disney contraption in about five minutes, with two young mums and four bucket and spaded children enjoying the ride. The driver gives me an almost cheerful nod. I hated to think of him sitting there,

119

unpropositioned, all day long!

The walk is quite delightfully wooded and quiet once the 'train' has passed.

A song thrush bathes itself in a puddle, scarcely three feet away and as I stop to savour the moment [thrushes being quite rare in London these days] two sedge warblers flit across the path and disappear into the thorny hedge, chirping at each other and far too interested in matrimonial matters to notice me standing there. The walk is justified; more of a St Francis moment than a Walt Disney moment. Further on I pass a slightly sad man walking an even sadder dog with arthritis in its right fore-leg: but then meet a rather jolly young man coming the other way in tow to a large rotweiler bitch. I only hope that everything is under control when the two walkers meet!

The route eventually leads to pleasant riverside paths, with pleasing properties, some with moorings on the far side. Unfortunately you cannot cross the river until you reach the B 3059. There is a dormant 'Wich ferry', still holed up for the winter, which really would have provided a short cut. So I plod up to the bridge. But before going into town and catching the X2 back to Lymington I have the unexpected treat of visiting the Priory Church of Christchurch, which is as a small cathedral, and in a very pleasant close. The church nave is ponderous, handsome, Norman, with icing cake, early-English, on top. An organist is practising a gentle adagio and the vergers obviously love their treasure. It seems a suitable peacefully, resolving, cadence to what has, otherwise, been a very blustery day.

23 July 2012: Christchurch to Bournemouth.

A blissfully sunny summer's day, following two very wet months, during which I seemed so busy that I could never get away for coastal walking: and following a weekend when there was almost too much music-making. But a few days of recuperation at Chichester sorted that out, with two windy days at Pagham Harbour and the Chidham Peninsula blowing away all the cobwebs with equal proportions of ozone and vistas; including spotting two mergansers who have stayed for the summer.

So the next break begins again with the Weymouth train from Waterloo; but this time heading for the 10.05 to Bournemouth. Happenstance makes me in time to catch the 9.35 [remember senior concessions start at 9.30?]. But then the guard/conductor/factotum announces to the one tenth full train at 9.32 that concessionary tickets are not allowed on this train. I remind myself that I am on holiday and disembark [but make a mental note to right an indignant letter to Southern Trains when I return to base!]. I do part of a sudoku before catching the 10.05 as originally planned: and it works out in my favour as this train does stop at Christchurch [by midday], so, having booked a hotel in Bournemouth for three nights near to the station, I choose to dismount at Christchurch and walk, with my small amount of luggage, to Bournemouth Central.

The station is a little way out of the town centre, but an attractive young lady, with a distinctly east European accent, indicates the right road to head for the town centre and the riverside leading to the harbour. The shopping centre is packed with market day stalls which, sadly, seem to be crammed full of things that I would never want, except perhaps some of the garden plants [not very practical when on a longish walk!]. The hurly-burly gives way to the tranquillity of the priory precinct and I then follow the road to the quayside which, on this sunny day broadens out into a popular green; families everywhere. Heading off to the river, past the Captain's Hotel, I find that the Wich Ferry is now pottering back and forth across the relatively narrow stretch of river, while other trips go up or down the river. Delighted to find that I get so much ahead for 90p, I retrace my steps from the last walk; but with considerable more pedestrians joining me; and now two Disneyland trains running, burping along with buckets and spades, footballs, coloured plastic bags full of everything and obvious picnic carriers. The same driver is brimming with sun tan and smiles!

On arriving at the end of the Stour Valley Way it is easy enough to cut behind the rows of beach huts onto the beach running westwards to Southbourne and Bournemouth. There is a path going up what might be described as cliffs, but they seem to resemble mud banks and, walking along the beach, I give them a decent berth,[a very wet summer, with recently reported deaths in a mud-slide, flashes before my eyes].

Due to the tide being moderately low I am able to make good progress on the border between firm sand and shingle; although the odd shoe-full of seawater reminds me that I need to keep pretty close to the shingle.

The cliffs gradually get some stony stratification and to look a little more like sandstone than sand. From the top of them there are fine views back to the priory in

Christchurch harbour while the fallow grassland is full of hare's ear mustard and charlock in the seeded grasses, along with spreads of evening primrose. From this high-ish point the beach below is splattered with Lowry-like figures, spread between the groynes, and the few, brave enough to splash in the steady, Mediterranean- blue, of the sea. It is a day when you do think 'Why go anywhere else: why am I doing all this walking!?'

While the first part of this stretch is wild grassland [car parks in the distance!] there are regular seats for the range of walkers [some obviously have no intention of going very far!] to enjoy the views. Each to his own.

The walk runs into Southbourne [East Bournemouth!] and as the beach is so busy I stay up on the hard surface footpath with its less traffic, so making for good foot speed.

Summer Beach from the Cliffs.

As the cliffs run into Boscombe the high walker will suddenly come upon Boscombe Cliff Gardens: a quiet oasis of a few formal beds of herbaceous planting, rather than corporation annuals; and all enclosed by mature trees: an oasis indeed. After this staying up on the cliff does feel a little too much like walking through suburbia, so I descend to the beach at Boscombe pier where there is a substantial promenade, with beach huts; and I enjoy all the shapes and sizes that an English summer beach presents;

122

bumps, lumps, and designer bodies all in one conglomeration: white, red, peeling, and immaculately tanned, under similar headings.

I feel decidedly overdressed in jeans and a long sleeved shirt: but I do not wish to burn!

About halfway between Boscombe and Bournemouth piers I reclimb the cliff, now quite a substantial walk up a tarmacked zig-zag, with resting seats on the way! But I do regain a good view of the sweep of the bay. This reclimbing I do as I have booked accommodation near the station, it being peak holiday time and I reckon to be on target to head directly into town.

I wander from the front through tree-lined roads of spacious flats, hotels, and residential homes, with the inevitable decline in grandeur as the station is approached. My hotel is an adapted Victorian house overlooking a park. But nothing quite prepares me for the colour dyslexia inside! Joseph's coat with many patterns of clashing colours would describe walls and furnishings!

24 July 2012: East Cliff Bournemouth to Poole

Another amazing blue-sky day: people piling to the beach. A first detour to find the tourist office near the Pavilion [but always check, the location of 'i' does have a habit of wandering or merging with other buildings!]. The first thing was to find the frequency of the ferries across the neck of Poole harbour [not kept by the office!] and secondly the time of buses from Swanage to Bournemouth [not on the Bournemouth web site!]. But the Office has bus timetables not only to Swanage but also to Weymouth; so that future journeys are also sorted: real forward planning… if not for present projections!

From the Pavilion grounds there is a lovely cool walk down through pine trees, in the shade of which a collection of local artist display their varied wares. I arrive at the pier fair ground, thence to the rapidly filling beach, whence I head upwards for the cliff walk. Ascending is somewhat like the man going to St Ives, with everything but the kitchen sink, distributed fairly unequally between various family members, coming down to the beach. It is always curious to see which parent is the prevailing beast of burden: and if it is the male, whether it is done with bravado, or because the hen is pecking and does not want nail varnish cracked!

But even here the cliff face is covered with tall, yellow evening primrose and offers expanses of sea views as an immediate contrast to the downward heading hordes. At the top of the cliff, a regular distribution of sea-view-seats are already occupied by the grey pound [probably not wanting to walk up and down the cliff in this weather]. It is a pleasant and easy walk westwards, with the open grassland often dipping into conifer-wooded sections, which, delightfully, provide welcome shade, also hiding expensive houses and blocks of flats, some gated, all in their own grounds.

The only disadvantage to this high walk is that the frequent gullies through the cliffs mean that the walker zig-zags north and south like repeated Ms, at the same time often going half way down and up the cliff height. While all this is pleasant enough, Poole does not seem to get much closer. So, at somewhere near Branscombe, I descend through tropical gardens to face the beach crowd.

I hardly dare to mention beach huts, but here they come in all colours shapes and formats. Plurality rules. There are not only double decker huts, but some are actually stepped up, with their own forecourt, and in ranks, three or fourfold, into the foot of the cliffs. Beach huts are a serious industry here!

The density of people pulses with the distance from the various gullies, which generally also give road access, or at least have a car park at the top. Perambulators, ready inflated coloured tyres, ice boxes, tents, towels and wind screens all process down to the beach. I can't help but be reminded of BBC films of ants carrying all and sundry to and from their nests. Had I heard David Attenborough on the loud speakers warning the bathers to use sun screen, I would not have blinked an eyelid.

In contradiction to expectation, the quietest spot on the beach [and where I stop for water and a bite of chocolate] is where there are two back-to-back football pitches in the soft, beach sand, with bright yellow metallic goal posts. But I imagine that beach football must be as different from grass football as beach volleyball is from indoor volleyball. It might also be that they are placed at the foot of Canford Cliffs and there is no easy way down here! However the cliffs do begin to subside here as Poole is approached. Finally the tarmac walk stops following the beach and, along with the shared cycle track [supposedly banned in July and August – thus giving excuse to various youths to delight in illegal skirmishes] flicks right to join the road going round the inside of the

Poole basin: and some pool it is!

Much of this inland harbour seems to be shallow, and to attract a different profile of interests. Youngsters fish with simple rods, or even catch small fry in nets on sticks. Young couples stand and paddle on what look like plain or windsurfing boards, while rubber-suited groups indulge in non-motorised aquasports - canoeing, windsurfing. But this idyll is against a backdrop of a steady stream of cars heading for the ferry; so much so that the plain pedestrian arrives at the ferry boarding area more quickly than families stuck, quietly cooking, in cars. It is the school holidays!

It seems that at this time of the year the ferry crosses as soon as it loads and unloads; always a full load of vehicles: but the number 50 double decker bus, in the midst of the cars, does stand out, and, fortunately, has a designated bus lane, whereby it can skip the car queues once it is in the stretch of suburbia leading to the ferry. The ferryman at the ticket office tells me that the 50 bus is every 20 minutes at this time of the year, while the timetable on the bus stop says every hour: another example of checking on local knowledge!

I treat myself to a sandwich and a diet coke at the ferry café and am pleased to catch the next 50 bus back to Bournemouth, after it has lumbered off the ferry. Today has been but a short excursion compared with yesterday and, arriving at the Bournemouth bus station, which is adjacent to the railway station, I am pleased to retire to sit in the shade of Kyneston Gardens and, while perusing the Times, watch two eastern european youths, stripped to their black and red shorts, play tennis on the park courts with great enthusiasm, if not skill. The coastal views were crowded and dramatic: but this seems a gentler, more civilised end to the day.

25 July 2012: Poole to Swanage

I am now starting the official "South-West Coast Walk", admirably described in two booklets, one going in an anti-clockwise direction, starting at Minehead, in Somerset, while the other starts at Poole and goes clockwise, as I am about to do. So all my contacts lie in the first of these books, while all my directions lie in the second: both compulsory guides for my trip, potentially heading as far west as my legs will take me!

I might be more than half-way: perhaps Faversham was a strange place to start!?

But first to get on the 50 bus. It is the first 'freedom pass' bus, [9.30 exactly], and there is already a grey pound queue by the time that I get there 15 minutes early! By the time it has stopped a few times in central Bournemouth it is full and whizzes past waiting grey pounders, who will have at least a twenty minute wait for the next no 50. I realize that in all my sojourns so far, this is the first time that I have struck the 'rush hour' of the school holidays!

Arriving at Poole within half an hour good use is made of the privileged bus lane, scooting past the already queuing cars. A double-decker bus on a relatively small ferry does seems something of an anomaly, and I wondered if it needed to place itself for ballast balance. But yesterday's observations, while I scoffed a sandwich in the café, said that it went wherever.

The gap across the neck of the bay seems to be no more than four hundred metres making it surprising that there is neither a bridge nor a tunnel. But maybe the locals, particularly the sailing fraternity, prefer it that way?

Once we have crossed I am the only person to disembark at the first bus stop for Studland Bay, with a full busload going on to Swanage. It is easy, from the bus stop, to access the small beach of Shell Bay that looks back to Bournemouth, then, round the corner, lies the long curve of Studland Bay. It is good that the tide is more out than in and I have to worry more about buckets and spades and the holes that they have dug, [or are digging!], than getting a shoeful of water. Carloads of people have already arrived before me and seem to increase in density towards Studland itself, where there is a café and other facilities. At the beginning of my walk the families are all clothed in varying degrees, but in the middle stretch, mainly adult, people are without any inhibitions, and, generally very brown all over; then towards Studland they become clothed again. I had been warned about this variability of flesh exposure, but I am far too busy avoiding castles and holes to notice much, except that those who have worked hard enough to be brown all over do have a certain 'je ne sais quoi' about them. However, given the intensity of the sun, and a fairish complexion, I am quite glad of my long-sleeved cotton shirt, jeans, and baseball cap. I got burnt walking from Christchurch on Monday with my shirt-sleeves rolled up! It is midsummer.

The café at the end of the beach is most welcome for the shade, fluid replacement, and a fresh crab sandwich; and I beat the lunchtime rush.

I am grateful for the guide indicating that you must look out for the left turn of the coastal footpath just before the barrier on the tarmac road leading up from the beach. The post has lost its sign! But follow the path and you are immediately away from the beach crowds with an initial walk through a shady copse: and I take a further breather from beach pounding.

Leaving this tranquility behind, with the seagull-like cries of children on the beach fading, a sombre defence shelter appears and commemorates those lost from the dragoon guards in the war, and the part played by locals in the great D-day rescue of troops at another date: an appropriately sobering moment: in stark contrast to the present clamour of buckets and spades!

A little further on there is the option of either going left down to the South Beach or right into the village of Studland. Having had enough exposure to the beach, and as the tide is now coming in and pushing the crowd back to the shoreline, no surprise that I opt for the village, manage to walk past the pub without need for refreshment, and follow the road down the hill until there is a very clear National Trust sign to 'Old Harry Rock'; even to Swanage.

Thank goodness for the National Trust and this being a listed site. You could drive a tank along this wide open grassland walk and, as the land rises, a vista looking back as far as Milford unfolds; even Pendlesham Castle with binoculars. Apart from the sheer beauty it is one of those moments [as at Selsey Bill], when you can look back at the long curve of the coast and think 'have I really walked all that way?.'

In this generous expanse of headland, 'the Foreland ', there are but a few walkers and cyclists and they serve to give perspective to the drama of the free-standing isolated chalk pillars of 'Harry's Rocks' which must be equally impressive from the perspective of the boats bobbing round them.

We are diminutive, and mostly resting from the combination of the exertions of getting to the top, but also absorbing the expanse of the sweeping views. All well worth the effort, and such a far cry from the crowded beaches at Studland [which might be a very impressive sweep on a fresh November morning – with only a few dog walkers, possibly the occasional horse rider - as in a local postcard!].

But the path over to Swanage goes still higher than Harry's Rocks, and after a brief enjoyment of the vista I continue up the broad slope of ungrazed and uncultivated pasture, but possibly resown with wild flowers at some time, for it is a mass of colour.

Amongst the tall seeding grasses, shades of purple and lavender from thistles stand boldly, white and purple clover nestle between pale pink leguminosae; while there are yellows and whites in daisies and cruciform flowers: a very carpet of colour. All enhanced by the fluttering of several chalk hill blue butterflies and a rarer little pearl fritillary. But all these are easy to miss when the grand scenery is so spectacular. Perhaps walking uphill helps – as the eyes are naturally cast down. A lady and her partner, descending and taking in the grand perspective of the view, smile their approval as they see me stop to contemplate the detailed joys of the field's flora and fauna.

The view becomes even more distractingly impressive when the peak of the ordnance points are reached; here the views stretch in all directions. Not Mount Everest or even Mont Blanc; but you do see why this area has justified World Heritage Site status. It is not just that you can easily see the whole of Poole harbour, but it looks as if you can see most of Salisbury Plain as well; perhaps even the South Downs as a blue trace? I am distracted to closer sights by the fluttering of butterflies, mainly marbled whites, but also rather distant copper-coloured flights that I can't see distinctly enough to identify. But they are fluttering and dancing in pairs – so hopefully breeding.

As I sit to take all this in, a group of some six or seven middle-aged ladies amble past in a state of some hilarity, seemingly caught up in their happy gossip more than the splendour of their surroundings: but I am sure that the environment must work by osmosis; and they are happy anyway. They are followed by a large, slightly lame, man and his son, the latter must hover somewhere near double figures in age. I overtook them at the start of the walk, and we seem to have been doing a hare-and-tortoise movement ever since. They pass me by again, and as the path, if you keep up to the right along Ballards Down, has a clear run into the distance, I see them getting smaller and smaller: the boy darting round his father, who yet, with his size and lameness, moves with considerable lightness. This time they are the tortoise, I would be the hare; and they are the first to arrive.

Eventually I follow them, eschewing the rapid and steeper descent, which I think is the official South Coast Path. The southern part of Swanage harbour is clearly visible. The high pathway of Ballards Down continues as a comfortable walk, but there is a clear crossway, with the left-hand turn going down to Swanage by a fairly steep descent, turning into quite a narrow path with part of it in steps. I meet two cyclists coming up carrying their bikes. The wife is a good five minutes behind her husband. I try to encourage her that the views from the top are worth it and the riding on the downland to Studland a little easier! She does not look too convinced: but such devotion!

Soon the path is hedged in again and Whitecliffe farm is reached. The coastal path is well signposted in blue. But I choose to follow a yellow coloured sign into Swanage, which delightfully brings me out at a corner shop with the usual range of refrigerated liquid refreshment. Moreover I see a bus stop for the 50 bus back to Bournemouth! I have completed today's objectives most pleasantly. But, refreshed, I walk into Swanage to do a little homework for my next visit.

The beach at Swanage is also in full, August, swing of bodies, over-exposed in more than ways than one; but the helpful tourist information on the seafront has a useful list of accommodation, and I pick up various other bus timetables before finding the public bus station next to the private, volunteer-run remnant of the railway station. The 50 bus home is late [probably a jam at the ferry?] and is nearly full as soon as we start. It is August on the English South Coast!

3 September, 2012: return to Swanage

I arrive with some mileage already under the belt from a golden wedding celebration in Scarborough, celebrating a wedding at which I had been best man. Although none of us any longer resembled the original photographs it still does not seem like half a century ago; back with friends the time had flown in reminiscing.

As it was a day return to Scarborough from Kings Cross; and now onwards on the Waterloo train to Weymouth, destination Swanage, I have covered some train miles. But not all the way to Swanage by train, as Wareham or Poole are the nearest railway stations with bus connections [40 and 50 respectively]. I choose Wareham, and am delighted by the charm of the old town, with the additional detail that it is a double decker bus that goes to Swanage via Corfe and Kingston, with much more dramatic views of the castle at Corfe, followed by the high run between Kingston and Langton Mattravers looking over the Purbeck Island, Poole Harbour and beyond. Long live the Freedom Pass! But it does involve some low gears and hazardous passing for a double-decker bus.

All of the villages round here have period charm, stone buildings, and narrow steep streets: chocolate box charm; even period drama locations.

Swanage is still in the memory bank from the last visit, so I nip off the bus at the railway station [a limited rail service is run by volunteers to Corfe] and scoot down the High Street to the White Swan, which seems a central point for an overnight stay and, more immediately, a place to recover from the miles travelled.

A feature of my latest meanderings is that planning ahead is paramount in this vista of relatively uninhabited cliff walk. So, while I already have B&Bs booked for Worth Mattravers and Kimmeridge, I also have to think of strategies for getting back to Wareham for my trains. Although the well-organised person might well be ploughing on and have accommodation booked at Lullworth and Ormington, and onwards to Weymouth, I am being cautious in the new scope of my travelling!

As I did not find a Tourist Information Office in Wareham, but know the one at

130

Swanage, it is to this that I return. I find that I might catch the once-a-week 274 from Kimmeridge on Thursday; but that the valuable X43 that goes to Lulworth has already finished its summer season [yet a more glorious September day you could not have!]. But it is as well to know these things before you travel; and not to arrive hoping; web sites do not always give you the most accurate details!

Since the guide book admits that signs for the coastal path are somewhat sparse in Swanage I use the afternoon to do a bit of homework. It is quite simple to follow the seafront round to Peveril Point and then curve round up the rising cliffs, although you can easily cut across the open sloping green once you see two imitation classical pillars and a car park. The exit from the green is at the apex of this triangular space; and it is worth turning back to admire the idyllic views, with the last views of the white 'needles' of the Isle of Wight. How long ago it seems since I first saw the Isle of Wight! Here, higher up at Peveril point there is the end of a run of woodland, and then a much smaller open space where there are seats to admire the view. These seats give me time to enjoy the afternoon sun, and think of the five chalk fingers of the southern coast, how they rise out, grasping towards [or against!] the French coast: the thumb being Ramsgate of the Isle of Thanet, then Dover and Folkestone, followed by Beachy Head above Eastbourne, now the Isle of Wight; and the little finger yet to come at Lyme Regis?

Meanwhile, sitting on my secluded seat, I am obviously at the right time for the rush hour of early evening dog walking. If I mention a pair of portly daschunds; a seemingly legless, plump, pekinese; a very sprightly red setter; a golden retriever which comes to see if I am eating anything; a wire-haired terrier desperate for ball-throwing; then you can supply the matching owners. The dog traffic abates; I enjoy the tranquility for a few more minutes, and wander back to the White Swan. An evening meal at a local Italian restaurant, and a night cap pint at the Inn see me ready for the morrow.

4 September 2012: Swanage to Worth Mattravers.

Breakfast is not officially served until 9.00 at the White Swan, but as I am ready [and packed!] by 8.30 I wander down at 8.45 and am offered, in the midst of the cleaning, a cup of tea by the landlord, who is waiting for the chef to turn up. He also offers me the choice of the Sun, Mirror, or Times [no marks for guessing which I take]; while bacon, mushroom, and tomato soon appear, along with a welcome coffee.

Having made my reconnoitre yesterday, I am soon up through the cliff woods and into the secluded triangle again. Leaving the grass behind there are signposts on the first bit of street, but then you have to look out for acorns on lampposts at the next junction, turning left, downhill, into an urban road; but as soon as there is woodland on your left there is a signpost for your walk. The woodland has a network of paths without very clear signs. The guide suggests going as near to the lower cliff as possible, but I favour staying up in the woodland and eventually strike a good open flat pedestrian route, 'The Isle of Wight Road', which is very pleasant, and has fine views across the bay. It runs past Durlston Castle, and tumbles back into the wood as a meandering path coming out at a car park, and a narrow tarmac lane curving down to the lighthouse at Durlston Head. This lane has the advantage of a bridge crossing the steep gully [whereas the strict coastal path has steps up and down this gully!]. A pleasant walk ensues through open heathland with panoramic views. There are also the preserved relics of a masonry mine, with the turning wheel for the donkey, the narrow opening, and the rail track going down into the mining cavern: a very vivid reminder of how a hard and dangerous living was made for many years.

The ease of the tarmac path also allows me to appreciate the small blue, the white and the peacock butterflies that are reported to be down in number this year: although I am very aware, as I am just reading a biography of Alfred Wallace [who nearly pipped Darwin to the post with his recognition of evolutionary forces] that he and his friend, Bates, managed to find more than a thousand variations of beetles in a single field. But then, I am supposed to be walking and enjoying the views! A clack of jackdaws on the cliff keep me company; almost like an omen: while the pasture here is grazed, mainly by beef cattle and so is not quite as rampant with wild flowers as the open land was at Studland.

Now I follow the guide's suggestions and, turning before reaching the lighthouse, follow the path nearest the cliff edge, rather than the higher path running along the ridge. The weather is idyllic, blue skies and a gentle breeze; the buoys marking lobster and crab cages bob, red and yellow, in a sparkling sea; and for half an hour I see nobody but the cacophony of jackdaws. Then when I stop at a stile for refreshment [and to savour the view] three young ladies overtake me, going westwards. When I restart I am overtaken by a tallish man, with only sandals as his foot gear, and wishing to have a pint in Worth Mattravers before catching the lunch time bus back to Swanage: obviously a local man!

He questions me on the nature of two thrush-like birds that each alights on a separate fence post then, as we approach the nearest it flies on to the next empty post, overtaking its partner. We decide that the flashing white of the tail in flight and the behaviour must make them wheatears. It is a strange and charming habit of accompanying; but as my co-walker strides off ahead, he takes them with him.

The stone of the cliff has been much quarried in this area, which has enhanced structures such as 'Dancer's Ledge', where the only form of dancing seems to be in the form of climbers well roped. I see that I am easily going to make this walk [as I have completed walking round St Aldhelm's Head on a previous weekend with friends from Cranbourne!] so I stop to eat my lunch sandwiches on the west side of the gully at Seacombe Cliff; and am now passed by small groups of walkers going in each direction, including the three young ladies who previously overtook me: perhaps they spent time at 'Dancer's Ledge', watching the climbers? I am not sure that we are not both being hares today? The Seacombe Cliff also seems to have been another well-mined source of stone, with the ruins of buildings reminding one that small communities once lived there.

The subsequent walk round to Worth Mattravers is straightforward, with an unavoidable descent into the Winspit gully, and the remains of another mining area on the opposite cliff, with the coastal path rising steeply on its landward edge to Aldhelm's Head, but, since I completed this circuit previously I am able to head straight for my accommodation in Worth Mattravers. There is a pleasant pathway with a couple of charming cottages tucked away; and quite a lot of red, unripe, blackberries on the way up. As I branch left to a footpath that meanders across a meadow the three young Rhine maidens pass me again. In this case I know that they will arrive in Worth Mattravers before me: they are just faster hares!

The heat of the day makes me pleased that I have not had to go round St Aldhelm's chapel, and I am pleased to cool down in the delightful parish church of St Nicholas, which has a very fine late Norman chancel arch; and a gravestone, accompanied by a relevant pamphlet in the church giving an account of the local farmer who used cow pox to vaccinate his family against small pox, shortly before Jenner did his more famous vaccinations. While the farmer's children were well protected without incident, his dear wife had an unfortunate reaction to the vaccine and nearly died. The locals were not impressed; but several of them did die of smallpox that year. Such is the path of science!

The local inn is on the meeting of three roads, going under the unusual name of 'Square and Compass' [possibly stone mason's tools?], and also serves as the local museum, while its front space, with splendid views down to the sea, is a mixture of a sculpture studio and a grave yard, with seating in stone and wood: but fine local ales anyway. A comfortable, quiet B & B in a cul-de-sac completes a fine day of coastal cliff walking; but it is worth including a description the St Aldhelm's corner while I am at this point.

The path to St Aldhelm's Head entails going across the Winspit gully [see above] possibly inspecting the extensive ruins of buildings and excavated caves of the old mining site, but eventually going up via a railed stairway along the northern border of the site. This is quite a climb, and quite close to the edge. Thereafter it is a fine clifftop walk with the lookout point and the chapel soon visible. I think that the lookout was an important radar point in WW2, but now seems to be run by volunteers, of which there seemed to be quite a family gathering when we passed it on a weekend in August.

The small square chapel is something like a thick walled fortress with a Norman feel to it; and I remember that we had sandwiches against one of its walls, grateful for the protection that it gave from the prevailing wind. I imagine that this could be an exposed place in inclement weather. Refreshed, we hastened on and there really is a long distance vista as you round the corner and see the hump of Houns Tout with the coastal cliff walk stretching out to Portland Bill: all that a series of walks yet to come: more consoling to see them when they are completed!

Shortly after rounding the corner there is a stepped descent into a gully with an immediate stairway back to a similar height. A tedious way of progression: not so much the going north and south in estuaries when you want to go west, but here going up and down when it would be rather more pleasant to amble along the cliff top. The gully does, at its base, have a path cutting back to Worth Mattravers if you so wish; but we rose up again to Emmet's Hill and on the top path stopped at the small remembrance garden enclosed in a dry stone wall, dedicated to the Royal Marines; delightfully maintained. From this walk the hulk of Houns Tout overshadows the small beach of Chapmans pool, and the two or three figures seem to be but small specks of colour on the sand. It is not until you round West Hill that you see that there is low level access from the Worth Mattraver's road. Further along the cliff top there is an early well sign posted walk across fields to an official car park [this road continues to run down to a row of houses near the chapel and radar station that we recently left]..But we crossed this road into another field that led into a farm lane and thence onto the road running into Worth Mattravers.

5 September, 2012: Worth Mattravers to Kimmeridge.

So it is over this road that I retrace my steps the next day, having overnighted in a very comfortable B &B in Worth Mattravers. There were only two of us staying there, with the other guy being a somewhat overactive and overweight [but on statins!] semi-retired police officer, who was already up and gone before I emerged for breakfast at 8.00am! He rather unnerved my pottering as he had told me yesterday that he was going to make Lullington today, which is at least twice as far as I hoped to make; moreover it was the third time that he had done this in the last two years , and he was carrying 4 litres of water! I remind myself that my walking is not a competition and that pacing the day so that you enjoy the whole experience, butterflies and buttercups included, is now my inclination [besides he was a good twenty five years younger than I!].

At 8.30 the day has an azure cloudless sky, a stillness and a mantle of silence; quite eerie: nothing stirs round the houses. I am some way out of the village before I am passed by any sign of life; a car with a grey haired lady seemingly about to take the dog, which is bouncing against the car window, for its coastal walk.

After the right hand turn at the redeveloped Renscombe Farm the road is but a single track, descending into a copse and emerging into a row of cottages with a clearly signposted left turn for the walker. Once clear of this enclave the staircase going up the side of Houns Tout is clearly visible and the track swings round, passing the footpath going down to the bay of Chapman's Pool; but then the walker needs to look for the turning left through the gate of a grass field to head for the foot of the Houns Tout staircase. My clack of jackdaws seem to rejoin me here. I wish that I could understand their language; and that I could use their thermals and a few flaps to get over the top of the hill!

It is a well-maintained staircase and a straight climb, but somewhat unnervingly close to the cliff edge for me. It is definitely a case of keeping eyes focused on each step and not looking at more than three steps at a time. Time to admire the view at the top when you have earned it [I do begin to wonder if I am cut out for serious cliff-climbing, having a moderate sense of vertigo!]. But at the top the view justifies the climb; back to Aldhelm Head and forward to Portland Bill is a run of craggy cliffs capped with the shorn gold of stubbled corn fields and the speckled colours of rough pasture: no habitation visible. There is even a well-placed seat on which to recuperate; to absorb and admire the view. I toy with the idea of staying up on this contour and walking to the attractive village of Kingston. But no; this is a coastal walk, so it is onwards and downwards, with the steps not all quite so near the edge, but neither so well maintained.

From the heady heights of Houns Tout it looked as if the rest of the coastal path to Kimmeridge was a wide sweeping path at a constant lower level. But once I have flitted through the wooded gully at the base of Houns Tout I find that my hopes were an illusion, for the broad sweep turns out to be the farmer's strategy for conforming to an EU regulation for leaving a broad strip fallow at the edge of every cultivated field.

Illusions of a coastal path

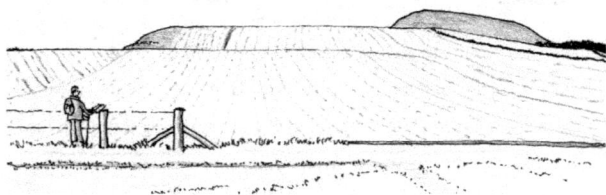

So the reality is that the coastal path is still a narrow way, separated by barbed wire from this broad strip of fallow land! Also, at closer quarters, there are several streams and gullies running though the walk and, although there are very welcome wooden bridges across most of these, the fact that one of the bridges informs you that 'this bridge was moved inland 20 metres in 2006 due to cliff slippage', does nothing to boost my confidence in this stretch of cliff walking! While the sea and the sky are quite mediterranean in their colours, when I do dare to look at the fabric of this stretch of cliff it does look rather more like packed mud than the hard rock of yesterday's walk. Later on at Kimmeridge Cove, where oil is commercially extracted, I realise that much of the cliff is probably impacted shale!

But meantime I scuttle along, and when there is enough space, sit, recoup, refresh, and soak in everything but the structure of the cliff. I have never seen quite so many red admirals, and they are but the dominant butterfly amongst chalk blues, small whites, the odd peacock, and some dusky moths that ought not to be out at this time of day? Equally entrancing are another pair of wheatears that repeat their charming pattern of accompanying me by flitting from post to post, always just ahead of me; delightful companions. I can scarcely believe that it is the pair that travelled with me yesterday; but if it is just that they are preparing for migration, it is interesting that they stay in pairs, and not in a flock.

These pleasant companions stay with me right until I meet somebody coming the other way; then the birds disappear into the field of shorn corn, where they are quite invisible. Swallows cascade over the cliff's edge, presumably catching the remains of summer insects, blown by the wind. Soon both will be gone.

The approach to Kimmeridge Bay is heralded by the appearance of a Victorian looking tower-cum-folly, which is what it turns out to be: Clavedon Folly, built by a wealthy, bachelor, reverend; and his folly subsequently moved back from the crumbling cliffs at great expense by the Landmark Trust and rentable for holidays. This part of the walk is popular as the bay has a largish car park; and not much else other than a hidden row of cottages – presumably, originally, for a small fishing community; now probably for oil workers or second-home owners?

The bay itself is calm and sheltered with snorkellers gently splashing around, out from the local 'marine centre'. The shoreline is a stone beach [the artefacts too large to call pebbles?] interspersed with slabs of shale-like stone. It seems to attract a certain following, and some fishing. But as there are regular, small, spontaneous trickles of shale and earth from the cliffs, I am not encouraged to spend too long in the sun on this 'beach'.

As the path comes down to the 'beach' there is a diversion through shrubs to the cottages, and this path leads out on to the road that runs to the oil well, west of the bay, and to the rest of the coastal path. But I back track slightly and pick up a footpath that crosses across farmland to Kimmeridge, easy enough to follow if you have binoculars to read the sign post at the far side of the second field! This path brings you into the top of the chocolate-box village [with some newly thatched cottages!] passing an old farm where most of the outbuildings have been converted into expensive looking 'des res' accommodation; not for local workers I think! The small church again has a Norman arch, as at Worth Mattravers, but this time only at the south entry door. However there also is a sun catching graveyard, with a very welcome seat to while away an hour or so – as I am early for my comfortable B& B at the old manor farmhouse. There is also a very good café/restaurant made out of the old post office. A village adapting to commercial survival!

Kimmeridge: post office + manor house.

Fortuitously, in the morning, well rested, I am able to catch the weekly [yes-weekly!] 274 bus, [oddly the same number as my local bus in London- but rather different local scenery!], to Wareham. The present bus is a small sixteen-seater vehicle, with a friendly local driver, who seems to pick up his local collection of 'elderly dears', who would otherwise be marooned, as would the odd, elderly tourist; to which latter category I belong! After half an hour of scenic driving, I reinforce my impression, ambling previously along the high street, that Wareham is a pleasant place: but in no time I catch a train back to London, Waterloo.

Kimmeridge to Lulworth Cove is a military stretch of coast, generally out of bounds; but with some latitude in the summer holidays. However as I have had forced circumventions of army bases so far [Hythe and Lydd?] I decide that in my walk they may to be avoided: even as river estuaries are to be crossed by ferries as soon as one is available. Both extremely sensible approaches I decide, even, as in this instance, it means missing some impressive scenery!

So my next outing will commence at Lulworth Cove, hopefully.

22 October, 2012: Waterloo to Lulworth Cove.

Definitely autumn: trees in London flaming yellow and red; leaves falling almost as fast as they fade.

The Weymouth train heads out from Waterloo at 10.05 prompt and seems to have a fair sprinkling of young male immigrants, either heading for tertiary education courses, or for employment in care homes in Bournemouth; or possibly both.

By the time that the daily 'easy' Sudoku has been completed the view from the train is of newly ploughed fields; but fewer autumn colours in the hedgerows here: a patchwork of variously shaped striped browns, some greens; both edged in the darker greens of copse and hedgerows. But overall a mist prevails; it is my first misty day this year, and no more than four or five fields are visible either side of the train: no distant vistas today.

It is not until the train reaches Southampton [and I grow a little impatient] that I remind myself that I have actually walked this far [with quite a bit of walking north and south, and up and down, rather than west and flat esplanade!]. Subsequently, in the train journey, I am impressed by how much inland coastal estuary lies so close to the railway line between here and Wareham.

The purpose of Wareham, with its curious 'St Martins on the wall' dominating the High Street, is to catch the X53 bus, a veritable 'Jurassic Coast' bus running all the way to Exmouth, which might drop me at the pub at Portway, whence I can walk down to

Lulworth Cove in order to continue my westward walk.

But first I take refreshment in Wareham in a hostelry with an old exterior, but inside all bare boards, pristine screens, and a large pool table; obviously the 'sports centre' hostelry!

The X53 bus emerges from the mist and accommodates my other two waiting companions. The older, even more portly, gentleman is obviously a regular as the bus seems to stop exactly outside his house, without any bell having been rung: while the other passenger, a dapper lady, carrying off grey cropped hair, smart black trousers and trendy trainers, outstayed me on the journey; and I thought might be destined for somewhere bijou in Weymouth. The bus driver is also sufficiently on the ball to remember to drop me at the Red Lion at Portway. But the pub is not quite where it was marked on my map, with the result that, on this misty morning, I head off in the wrong direction. However, rapidly realizing my error, I take the first signposted footpath heading south, which leads through a field of still standing maize; my sudden presence startles the local pheasant population, who are feasting on fallen cobs of sweet corn. The path eventually does lead me along the back of the pleasant village of Winfrith, coming out close to the post office, and to the turning that I was seeking for my rural walk towards West Lulworth via Fields Farm and Vine Down. The former is a vast commercial dairy farm of friesians, with everything done in tanker size, including piles of black plastic covered silage bails looming out of the mist: while the latter, Vine Down, I can only assume, is an anti-walker establishment, as the broad track suddenly has a bold 'Private' notice, while the alleged dotted red footpath leads into a harvested field of maize which is a quagmire of water-filled tractor marks, large and deep. Just as well that I do have good walking boots on today, and a stick to prop myself against falling into the tracks. Sadly for the farmer, many of the cobs of corn remain on the ground in the mud, and it is the pheasants who are busy gleaning , with rabbits also hopping in and out of the mist; then away into the hedgerow.

The path squeezes between overgrown hedges, with planks over ditches and into ploughed fields, I find that the furrows have taken up most of the path, with the general feeling of hostility emphasized by the yapping of dogs emanating from the mist-shrouded buildings of Vine Down. The general spookiness is increased by my plodding setting off a large barn owl from a nearby stretch of hedge; silently flapping to within a few yards, then gliding away into the mist, nothing else in sight: very eerie.

But then when the path reaches the boundary of Vine Down there is a lane from two other farms. The sense of an ancient right of way is restored by the appearance at the roadside of a rounded old stone marker, with engraved mileages. Moreover the footpath becomes an enclosed right of way with a border of shrubs and small trees on either side; eventually running downhill into West Lulworth. On a fine day this might have had fine views: but today there is but a field and a half of visibility, with an enveloping shroud of soft, damp, mysterious grey.

I am pleased to arrive at West Lulworth and, not having taken my map out more than absolutely necessary in these damp conditions, it is only then that I realize that West Lulworth is quite separate from Lulworth Cove; the latter being the location of my accommodation for the night. But I do note that there is a 102 or 103 bus from time to time, and it does go through Wareham. My antennae [web site searching] had missed this! I also note that there are several places still offering B & B at this time of the year; but am more than pleased with the comfort of Lulworth Cove Inn when I finally arrive. Moreover my bedroom overlooks the exit up the cliffs of the South Coast Path. So I am back on circuit! Even more so when the manager kindly books me in for the next night at the Smuggler's Inn in Osmington Mills [which happens to belong to the same owners and provides a similarly excellent standard of hospitality!]. Lobster bisque and pinot grigio seem a due reward for a somewhat damp day of ups and downs [in the mind as well as under the boots!] even a log fire: and all is well.

After all, I say to myself, at my age it may be that I will not come this way twice! Whereupon I have another glass of wine in front of the fire.

23 October 2012: Lulworth Cove to Osmington Mills

The waking day seems singularly still, although overcast; no rain, but a pale patch of blue sky towards Portland Bill in the west: and I can see the broad-stepped coastal path rising up the cliff from behind the new bold Heritage Centre, curving up towards Hambury Tout, [I wonder if the local occurrence of Touts is from the middle English 'tute' – which seems to mean a lookout, or something that sticks out – they are certainly used for high places!?].

Having settled bills, I cross over the car park onto the broad white-stoned pathway. This is certainly completely different from the narrow cliff footpaths between Worth Mattravers and Kimmeridge. I set off a solitary figure, but half way up, as I turn to admire the view of the nestling Lulworth Cove [and to catch my breath] I see that two, green-wellingtoned, local young ladies are using the same route to exercise an energetic young, black, labrador, that dashes hither and thither over the rising and falling grassland.

I reach the coastal summit of Hambury Tout to find that the new coastal vista includes a solitary, shaven head, fairly well-tattooed figure, fag in one hand, and a white pit bull terrier straining on its leash in the other. Curious company for the inspiring tranquility of the Jurassic coast; but then I espy an extensive non-mobile home site in a dip to my right: so my surprise is moderated.

The shaven head is, in fact, both affable and even deferential. I do, having reached a concensus on the likely weather, point out that a free ranging, under-age, labrador is just about to come over the hill. I receive a grunt, a rapid stamping on the remains of the cigarette, a gruff 'thanks guv' and the already straining leash is yanked hard in the direction of the caravan site. I proceed moderately rapidly away from the scene; but as I hear no subsequent yelps or shouts I assume that a class war, temporarily, has been avoided. Would that the Middle East factions could be so easily persuaded!

Mist after Lulworth

There are dramatic cliff formations in this stretch of the walk. Durdle Door seems to be one such, with its chalk arch jutting out into the sea, joined to the mainland by a narrow neck, which in turn has a cascading stairway down to the cove of St Oswald [who I always think of as a Northumbrian saint?]. The dramatic arch is seen on many postcards, even as it is the purpose of a visit from a covey of blue-uniformed students. Fortunately, by the time that they appear, I am half way up the next assault and the mist is beginning to descend again.

The map tells me that I am in for a sequence of steep ups and downs, rather like a more isolated version of the Seven Sisters at Eastbourne, except that here the orientation of the chalk seems to go through ninety degrees. In one place the stripes are vertical [and I wonder if they are induced by draining water] but then they are diagonal and finally horizontal: reviewed, it is probable that they represent a frozen-in-time, rolling of an erupting wave of chalk. But in practice they all remain as steepish hills, and I am more than pleased by the company of my stalwart ash walking stick to aid my ascent and to prevent too rapid a descent: and more than pleased that I took the trouble to wedge an inch and a half of stainless steel tubing on to the tip: it bites into the turf admirably on some of the slippery slopes. At least there is the choice of several paths, away from the cliff edge. But Hambury Tout, Dungy Head, and Swyre and Bats Head all indicate a switchback of climbs; all this is a mostly solitary escapade in the static, cloaking mist; the pale patch of blue seen in the early morning long gone. It is a strange experience, climbing into a very limited vision, where the barbed wire fence and the tufts of grass separating the muddy steps become the horizon. No birds seem be flying; there is no sound; just the shroud of mist: which makes it all the more eerie when a single black silhouette emerges, coming in the opposite direction. It is on a strange stretch on the top of Swyre, where there is a choice of four narrow paths running in parallel to each other. We both change lanes, but then, intuitively converge as we pass; perhaps in relief against the isolating claustrophobia of the mist. He, heading for Lulworth, has already come from Weymouth [but he did start at 7.15 am-and is at least thirty years younger!]. Yet he is also peeved that in this weather he will not really see the architecture of the Durdle Door arch, to which he had been looking forward. Although, when he does get close, I think that it might look particularly atmospheric: picture post card sunshine isn't everything! But I have to admit that I could not resist saying that I had captured several rather good shots earlier in the morning when the light was 'better'!

143

After all these mist-shrouded ups and downs, there is a longish walk at some height with the uncanny interlude of the mist beginning to clear out at sea so that the sun illuminated first one patch of silver sea, and then a sequence of more distant ones of shifting shapes, as if opening up a way to a far and distant land: quite magical; all the more mysterious because I could not actually see the breaks in the sky.

Over the next mile or so, round the White Nothe, [= a nose of chalk cliffs], to the seaward side of the path, there is a land of half-fallen cliff, given over to an extensive wilderness, where a silent, soaring, spread of jackdaws reigns, with smaller birds fluttering between brambles and gorse, visibility too murky to allow identification. Out of the swirling mist a cluster of seemingly deserted coastguard's cottages emerges, with no apparent vehicular access: and did I see a headless rider gallop by: did I cross myself and mutter a prayer: or was I just getting tired?

Coastguard in mist

But then I am brought back to reality by the call and sight of the black-headed stonechats, scolding each other on the gorse, and flying down ahead of me on the path down to the village of Ringstead. Descending quite rapidly, the chalk path heads through a copse, where a small wooden bridge crosses a stream that is quite hidden from sight by brambles and ferns, but audibly gurgles and chatters. It is followed by a series of dells decked with hart's tongue and ladyfern, while the lichen-coated hawthorns have middle red berries, and the ivy their pale green flowers. As the path descends the trees change to small ash and sycamore, giving way to wooden and brick houses in various configurations. The partly made-up road runs along the seafront and I find a spot on the near-deserted shingle beach to lunch on sandwiches from Wareham, along with half of a bar of chocolate. Parents with two children descend behind me, and the young boy dry skis down the steep slopes of shingle that the sea pushes up. The mist is clearing and the parents are happy just to sit on the higher steps of shingle and see the bay emerging into hazy sunlight.

A young, fair-haired, man follows with a short legged miniature schnauzer, and both have obviously relished a muddy walk. His owner, bare footed, tries to persuade his pet to join him in a sea paddle, to clean off the mud: but this has been done before, and the dog sits firmly on the shingle: not wagging its tail. Giving up on the cajoling, the hound is seized by the scruff of his neck and unceremoniously dumped in the seawater, where a good dunking ensues. Released, the dog has his revenge in splattering his owner with the vigorous shaking of his coat, and manfully rubs his splendid grey whiskers in the bit of sand where the shingle gives out. But I am impressed that the owner has a towel that he does share between his feet and the dog, in that order: although I am not quite so sure about the hygiene. The freedom of being a young bachelor! Thankfully, no health and safety rules here!

From the tranquility of the beach it is but a short, but presently muddy, walk along a wooded, low, cliff, with alternating views of sea and enclosed wood, until the walker suddenly emerges next to the Smugglers Cove Inn at Osmington Mills. Moreover, as well as being my booked accommodation for the night, it seems to have an authentic history of smuggling, as well as being very comfortable.

24 October, 2012: Osmington Mills to Weymouth

Another cloudy day awaits me, but visibility is somewhat better. A solitary breakfast as, although popular with diners from Weymouth [I presume], I seem to be the only person staying over; and the staff are very hospitable for their single guest.

The official guide fortunately points out that the coastal route follows the dead end coastal road upwards through the lower village. The narrow footpath branches off to the left; but you do have to keep your eyes skinned to see it [I had checked it out yesterday afternoon!]. There is no serious climbing here, although it is seriously muddy and waterlogged; a different sort of hazard. There is a left fork to head for the back of Black Head rather than going to Osmington; then there is an extensive outdoor activities centre for children between Black Head and Redcliff Point. The centre is all behind high security fencing these days; but does seem to be well used with some exciting and challenging sets of climbs and swinging lifts.

The footpath leads back to the cliff, but we are back to areas of slippage and mud shale, with wild areas of bramble and hawthorn: ideal for undisturbed and isolated wild life, but not the walker! Redcliff itself is a more open spread of headland with fine seaward vistas to Weymouth and beyond; splattered with clumps of walkers from Weymouth. It is also, somewhat inland, home to ranks of holiday homes, all in orderly patterns. I almost begin to wish that it was misty again!

The walk down Bowleaze Cove still seems possible along the coastal side, leading directly on to the beach, and the river Jordan [!] is negotiable in good walking boots, but not in trainers! A simple scramble over a suggestion of a pier then allows a shingle beach walk, with firmer sand where the low tide is breaking: and I am very visibly heading for Weymouth. Inevitably there is the emergence of the fast track esplanade near the first café and the legs are allowed to swing into casual overdrive; no need to watch out for slipping mud, catching brambles, or hard-work shingle.

Before striking the suburbs of Weymouth there is the interlude of Lodmoor Country Park where the beach bird life shows a scatter of sea plovers and the unusual scenario of rooks cracking open mussels [the intelligence of the crow family is not to be underestimated!]. There is a single pied wagtail, and a flock of fieldfares plucking up courage for the next big migration.

The shingle has been stacked up quite steeply here, and a plumpish lady with two lively retrievers has to go on her hands and knees to surmount the upward shingle slope; two steps forward, one backwards is slow progress! It somehow contrasts with yesterday's lad at Ringstead, who repeatedly, gaily skied down the shingle, and easily ran back up. Ah, sweet youth!

Next I see signs for the 'Aquarium' and the 'Skate Board Arena'. I am obviously back in town! Old Weymouth has an attractive seafront of various grades of hotels, of varying magnificence and homeliness; but all looking on to the impressive curve of the beach, with the harbour and Portland Bill to the west. The prominent clock tower heralds the Georgian part of the town; and the splendid statue of George himself. The tourist information office has relocated to the new Pavilion near the harbour. But the good news, once I find it, is that there is an X53 bus which is a coast liner to Exmouth: the next stretch of transport problems sorted! A quieter pint and sandwich away from the sea front, and a train takes me back to London. I suspect the next batch of walking will be in spring 2013! But I do think that I am in for a flatter stretch!

2013: DORSET INTO DEVON

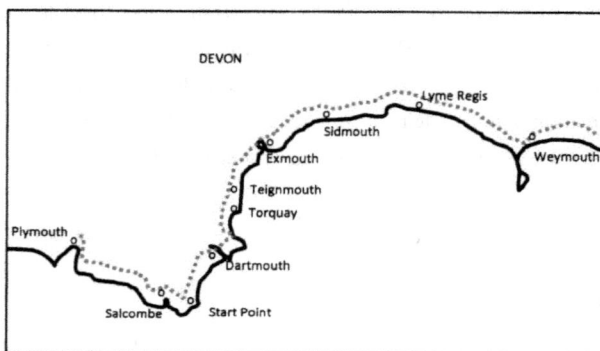

22 April 2013: Weymouth conundrum

Part of the conundrum is that spring has not really arrived, and we are heading for May: a long drawn out winter, and I am into my fifth year of walking! The rest of the conundrum is that as I am getting considerably further from London, and thereby needing more expensive train tickets; I really should pack in more days walking per visit before getting back for orchestra and string quartet on a Friday evening!

This time last year I was wearing short sleeve shirts and it was the nearest we got to a feel of summer until around September. This year has seen snow drifts in the west and north with lambs and ewes buried dead in the snow covered fields, never mind on the moors: and the land has scarcely recovered from extensive flooding; winter sown crops failing to germinate. How dare we urbanites complain of chill winds and grey skies compared with the sufferings of country folk! But we do; and a late April weekend of blue skies rushes the white cherry and the blue lungwort into blossom, along with the bright yellow shout of celandines, while the earlier primroses have been singularly valiant in defying the wintery conditions.

But here I am back in Weymouth, the train fast to Winchester and from

148

Dorchester South, but pedantic round Bournemouth and Poole. Unfortunately there is a biting wind on the beach at Weymouth, making it cold and grey, and more out of season in feel than the inhabitants, depending on tourists for income, would like. The static donkeys seem to be counting their blessings, and only the residents, with their old age and their scooters, huddle on the esplanade, clustering with their folding walking sticks on some of the many seats. I note that Weymouth is the first place where I notice a shop with vintage [meaning secondhand!] mobility scooters for hire in the High Street!

But the beach and its esplanade do form an impressive sweeping curve, while the large, post–Olympic harbour nestles in the inner curve of Portland Bill. This sweeping vista in both directions somehow masks the old harbour and town, with its charm of narrow alleyways and houses, both large and small, that have bay windows on the first floor, a particular variation of the piano-nobile? Characteristically of an old port, there are pubs of all sorts on every corner as well as halfway down the street or harbour-side. Holy Trinity church is also a striking edifice on the old harbor-side with a fine marble pulpit and font evidence of its Oxford movement origins, also reflected in the fine reredos and unusual mosaic in the Lady Chapel [an attractive relief Annunciation on the wall]. But I somehow think that the pink-coloured walls are not authentic; on the other hand they do not compromise unduly the sense of space and stillness that the architecture creates. I am intrigued to notice that the rotas on the notice board not only include flower arrangers and acolytes, but also 'shadows'. I wonder if this is something I didn't know about the Oxford Movement?

I also walk along the western side of the old harbour to find the Nothke Gardens with its castle and fine views. Had it been warmer and less windy I might well have dallied here a while. But I hasten back to the shelter of the hotel to plan my three days of walking.

Weymouth Old Harbour.

If, in sequence, I should do Portland Bill, then head along Chesil Beach to Abbotsbury on the second day, then I might aim for Bridport [or West Bay] on my final day. But with the weather forecast suggesting that the week might deteriorate, I decide to leave Portland Bill until the last day.

23 April 2013: Ferry Bridge to Abbotsbury: St George's Day

Breakfast is something of an event at my seafront hotel. At first there are just five solitary figures, a mixture of business people and aged tourists such as myself. But then a coach load of portly figures from Yorkshire appear, showing evidence of having indulged in all the variations of a 'full English breakfast' over a number of years. The interest arises when they try to fulfill their present ambitions through the medium of the three Spanish waiters.

An elderly, bespectacled, doyen, of considerable proportions leads,

"Full English, luv, with two poached eggs, please"

"Poached eggs; with brown or white bread?" is the Spanish counter move.

"No luv; no toast: just poached eggs."

"Poached eggs, madam; with brown or white bread, please?" – is the continuing theme.

"Albert, you have a go at 'im". The forces were increased.

150

"She wants, bacon, beans, tomatoes, and sausage. But not fried eggs: poached eggs, lad".

"Yes, I understand. Poached eggs with brown or white bread?"

It went on, and I studied the headlines in the Times closely; thankful that already I had an achieved delivery of a pair of poached eggs on brown toast without any complications before any of the above happened.

Finally escaping in to the fresh air and the task of today's walk, the guide to the SW Coast walk perhaps needs to clarify that 'Ferry Bridge', in Weymouth, refers to a large, rather marooned inn on the neck of Portland Bill, on the out skirts of Weymouth, as there are ferries and bridges elsewhere in Weymouth [more of this when walking to, and round Portland Bill]. Since I sorted this out yesterday I am able to leap on a no. 1 bus near the statue of George IV on his roundabout, [from which most buses depart or at which they call]. A helpful lady driver knows exactly where to drop me next to the Ferry Bridge Inn to begin the Chesil Beach walk. So I have but to scuttle across the road to go down beside the inn on what is a short length of tarmac and then a foot path. This is well sign-posted. The tarmac lead to another conglomeration of immobile homes – designated a 'holiday camp' here: and the path runs nearby for a while. It is to be explained that this is the recommended inland walk along the border of East and West Fleet, a narrow and shallow inland water some ten miles in length, that is separated from the sea by the massive straight run of Chesil Beach; although this should really be called 'the Chesil Shingle', as it is just that: a huge up-throw of fine shingle with ups and downs of a size that make people and boats look tinyly Lowryesque. I have had enough experience of shingle crunching to take the guide's recommendation - and to follow the inland route here: besides the 'beach'/shingle is currently closed to protect nesting birds during the breeding season.

The reward of the inland walk is to see two wheatears, a crush of celandines shouting their gold; and a cluster of whimbrels and terns, busy at the water's edge. I suspect that there may be rich pickings of crustaceans, weeds and worms here?

After the 'holiday homes' camp is passed, the path opens on to a common, spattered with various matches of dog walkers at this time of day [and it is a lovely day so far]. The path runs round the first bay, but then strikes another camp; this time

151

military, and surrounded by chain-link fencing, with barbed wire on top. Clusters of camouflage fatigues and heavy, polished black boots seem a strange contrast to a large spread of green grass peppered with bright, white, dainty, daisy heads. The 'coastal' path hugs the perimeter fence right round the enclosure, then goes along the bottom of a field to enter a gully over a stile, followed by one of a series of tunnels of closely woven thorn trees, where patches of the path are slithery mud and water that might top boots, never mind the strong walking shoes that I have. This is where the walking stick is useful for putting in the middle of the puddle and leaning on it so that I can scoot round the not so muddy edge! I meet a family of five in one of these tunnels further on; open sandals not being very encouraging for the mother, while the father and son skate round the muddy patches in trainers with some agility. I can only encourage them that the path does get better in a little while, and that subsequently they can catch the no 1 bus into Weymouth [this to balance the statement from two ladies, impressively attired for walking in the Himalayas, who march straight through the mud and inform them that it is at least 5 miles to Weymouth – the intrepid pair having already done the full coastal path through Nothke Park et al!]. The wife and daughters thank me for the encouragement and offer me a hand across one of the larger puddles. I realise that the age of chivalry is not yet dead: but does come with many variations!

While the Fleet waters look a bright blue in the sunlight, the fields show the scars of the hard winter with the bare earth showing where crops have failed to germinate, either through cold or flooding; and even the grass fields look dull, without the bright green of growing grass that should be around at this time of year.

I finally reach the spot where the river Fleet emerges into the inland lake. Named Fleet Rodden, it is a bird sanctuary that deviates the path away from the water's edge. But not without providing a good viewing seat where I both have my lunch and am able to enjoy, through binoculars, the sight of a small flock of shell ducks, with their handsome very dark green heads, orange breasts, and white necks and bodies: one of the most colourful, handsome, as well as largest, of our ducks. Numerous waders and, the now well accepted, small white egrets complete the company attracted to the pickings where the fresh water runs into salt water.

A close of trees clothes the river mouth, along with a scrub of bright yellow gorse, so that the walker has to skirt along the edge of this, after which there is an immediate stile with a sign to Abbotsbury, even if the field the other side is rather muddy. I mention this as some maps do seem to suggest that you go further up the hill before turning towards Abbotsbury. It is good to see better pasture here, and Dorset ewes with twin or triplet lambs who are scuttling, suckling, even sun bathing: a cheery sight.

After some more muddy gateways and stream crossings, the path goes up the side of Wyke wood, turns sharp left and over a stile that still has gate hinges on the far side. My bag catches in one of these, and I make something of a parachute landing on the other, considerably lower, side, [I must always remember to carry my mobile with me – a wrenched knee or a sprained ankle here would have been a problem! After the military camp it is a fairly isolated stretch of walking]. I recover composure, and my bag: thankfully no serious damage to either.

The signs are clear over the nearby narrow road, with a sharp right turn before the next woodland enclosure, and the path runs up hill to give a view over the swannery of Abbotsford with a pleasing vista along the edge of the ridge until it descends to the swannery car park, with various routes up into the abbey village. Apart from the pleasure of the vistas of farmland and sea, there are some very handsome stone stiles along this stretch: no danger of catching bags or feet here!

I have to say that two pints of orange and lemonade at the very pleasant Ilchester Arms make me realize that I had somewhat dehydrated on this warm and breezy day: this in spite of carrying water with me. Abbotsbury a charmingly preserved Dorset village, with the old abbey ruins converted to be enjoyed by families. But, with its narrow, curvy lanes, not really a place for two-way through traffic!

A proper stile.

A further volume of refreshment follows, with some alcohol content, back in
Weymouth [via the X53 coastliner] in the Duke of Cornwall, which is celebrating St
George's Day in a colourful manner. Jolly, portly, figures draped in large red and white
flags, some wearing curly red and white wigs, and obviously having been to other
previous venues, help to round off a pleasing day: as does half a pint of shrimps with a
glass of pinot grigio at the Kings Arms on the harbour side, some-time later.

24 April 2013: Abbotsbury to Bridport/West Bay.

Fortunately breakfast is without event this morning. But yesterday's bright blue
and gold has reverted to a grey and hybrid cloudy mist, with temperatures low enough to
turn hands purple and white without gloves [where is the spring – ah, fickle April?!].

While waiting for the X53 bus I chat to a local lady who is going to see her
daughter in Exeter; and is impressed that I am intending to walk from Abbotsbury to
West Bay. I feel encouraged and emboldened to say that, many moons ago, I set out from
Faversham; which elicits the reply, " O, have you gone past the Isle of Wight then,
darlin'?"; which makes me think that, in spite of television, there are those who are
geographically somewhat constrained. Perhaps predictably, she stays downstairs on the
bus; but the view from upstairs is limited by the mist. Nevertheless Abbotsbury arrives,
and the Ilchester Arms recognized, the bus having negotiated with a large on-coming
lorry, a narrow right angle bend, bordered by cottages and stone walls. Me thinks

Abbotsbury is overdue a bypass!

The coastal guide is helpful in saying that there is a path off to the left just after the post office-stores, which is a tranquil track with a vista of St Catherine's Chapel on the hill ahead. But the path swings right to lead down through pasture and along a stream onto the Chesil Shingle. I do manage twenty minutes of heavy shingle walking before returning to the land's edge, where, somewhere near Lawrence's cottages, there is a rough track to sanely walk on. But it is worth a foray onto the mountain of shingle, semi-frozen into piled waves, as it reveals a sea shore dotted with dedicated fishermen, more or less at 400 yard intervals, with serious sets of apparatus, some with two or three rods, and most of them with small sheltering tents or screens. It smacks of a dedicated escape mechanism: each to their own solace; including a thermos of coffee and a sandwich. But for the westward heading walker negotiating each one is innovative. Do you totally walk land side of them, thereby going into a shingle trough; or do you stoop under the fairly high fishing lines; or do you weave in and out between the virtually vertical tall rods? These decisions are arrived at by trying to pick up the vibes that are, or are not, emanating from each of the shelters.

I also ponder the possibility of developing 'shingle walking shoes', that might be tennis raquet like, as in snow shoes: or possibly even 'shingle skis', as in cross country skis. Do I see a new Olympic sport? Such musings help to get through the sinking plod of shingle walking!

Walking on the land track [possibly made for a 4-wheel vehicle to the cottages?] is perhaps less stimulating; but rather faster and less exhausting, even including negotiating the water-filled ruts. The seaward shingle has the maritime flora of purple, curly leafed, sea cabbage; the sea pink waiting to flower; and a white bell like flower that I fail to identify in these weather conditions: while Swyre Mere has a smattering of tufted ducks along with coots. Half of the mere seems to be full of reeds with channels cut through, as if they might still be harvested for thatching? There is a fairly modern, stile and wooden bridge which, with all the previous rain, stops precipitously in what is now the middle of the mere: very Kafkesque; a bridge descending and disappearing into the middle of a lake; or is it Arthurian! Will a hand emerge waving a sword?

The land path proceeds via fields, closely grazed by sheep, to run behind Burton

155

mere, where, very guttural, second alto, croaks, suggest that there might even be corn crakes; most of this area, rightly and thankfully, being a bird sanctuary.

The shingle is still piled so high that, on returning to the 'beach' after the meres, it is virtually no climb to ascend on to the sandstone cliff that leads to another squadron of non- mobile homes. I pass these and am grateful to find a bench seat with fine westward views, possibly to Charmouth or Lyme Regis; it being difficult to tell through the mist. However it is a welcome parking place for a lunch snack; and from here it is but a short descending walk to Burton Bradstock, which has a restaurant, car park, beach and quite a host of visitors.

I had the illusion from my lunch stop that I was well in sight of West Bay [my day's objective]. But not so! Not only has the cliff climb out of Burton completely crumbled, but there are notices on the beach saying that there have been further serious cliff falls further along and that the beach is closed too!

However I do notice two figures further down the beach who are standing with what look like surveying instruments, facing the fallen stone. So I think that, as the tide is well out and away from the cliff slippage, I might consult them. However on arriving I find that their 'apparatus' consists of artist's easels, with the owners recording their impressions of the dramatic cliff slippage. [It seems to be a somewhat antiquated mode in this digital age [even for me] – but there we go]. I look at the view of fallen rock that they are painting and notice, some distance away, amongst the fallen rock that there is a knarled piece of tree, seemingly blowing in the wind. But this has yet another surprise in store for me. When I arrive, keeping well clear of the slide, I see that it is a lone geologist/ fossil hunter who is sitting there, merrily chipping away at the fallen stones in the middle of the fall. He gives me a hearty 'hello', and continues to chip away with his hammer among the recently fallen debris. Each to their own!

Yet more difficulties are to come as the river Bride at Burton Freshwater only has a bridge the other side of the non-negotiable cliff. While the river, on the curve of the very steep shingle, is about fifteen feet wide and at least two feet deep, yet where it runs in to the sea at low tide it flattens out to spread through the lower shingle. Hobson's choice dictates that I walk through this low spread and get wet feet, as it is not much further to squelch to West Bay along the 'beach' of shingle!

156

It is very welcome to hit the harbour and terra firma: definitely not my favourite day's walking.

[In retrospect I see that the appearance of an apparent coastal path up the cliff, albeit destroyed, at West Burton, was a diversion. I could/should have walked inland towards the village, then taken a left turn down a street which would have led to the bridge that crosses the river Bride inland, even though this leads to yet another cluster of holiday homes, hiding behind the great mound of shingle. Once over the river and through the site, the pathway goes along the cliffs into West Bay. It does epitomize the variability of the coastal walk in these parts].

The harbour has been recently redeveloped and modernised; a tad touristy. The X53 bus is not yet due and anyway is late in the misty weather; giving me time for a quiet pint of shandy at the Bridport Arms, rhythmically accompanied by a child who constantly beats on a table with his plastic mug, while his parents have the slightly stony glaze that say that this is an accepted phase of development that is to be endured. Ah – the joys of parenthood, I think; amongst other thoughts.

The prevailing mist ensures that the potentially scenic ride back is more like a November outing than April's spring.

25 April 2013: Portland Bill in the mist.

Technically this is the walk that I should have done first out of Weymouth, but as the weather forecast was for progressive deterioration I had decided to get the Chesil shingle and the cliff walk to West Bay under my belt while the weather held. And the forecasters are all too right. The rising curve of Portland Bill cannot be seen from the esplanade of Weymouth this morning; but fortunately I did something of a reconoitre when I first arrived on Monday. So I cross the bridge of the old harbour and turn left along the charming painted terrace house on the quayside, most with their first floor bay windows. The path eventually passes boatyards and adventure facilities when steps up to Nothke Park appear on your right. This large open space houses the castle at its tip, and should give you vistas of Weymouth and Portland Bill; but not today. Only dog walkers emerge out of the mist: nobody else being foolish enough to venture out.

There is a footbridge over the lower road on the west aspect of the park, but then

157

follow any signs to the Rodwell Walk – which is the old railway line - adapted as a walkway and cycle track. Beware of thinking to take short cuts through streets here as several of them are cul de sacs! The walkway, as befits an ex-railway track, is flat and fast, but the gorse and brambles are so high that there is little to see, with a clump of bluebells being the peak of excitement. But then it opens out and the enormity of the Chesil shingle is there for you to see, looming bleakly out of the mist. An old viaduct carried the train across this neck of the peninsula, but it is long gone. I have read that the 'Bill' houses a prison and a remand home and decide that this is not the day for scrambling round cliffs, so I catch the no 1 bus, and am carried in parallel to the pedestrian way, through an industrial estate with a visibility of less than 100 yards. Henry VIII evidently built a castle -, but I stay on the bus to Easton, [which is as near the tip as the bus goes]. Easton has the feel of a small market town with a central green; a contrast to the spread of Weymouth.

It is now raining, so I head for the local church – a towerless 'All Saints' of conservative 1930s architecture; only open because a trio of venerable, welcoming, volunteers are preparing for a funeral later in the morning [a cheerful sort of day it is turning out to be!]. I noticed the attractive internal decorations, particularly of the chancel roof, but they draw my attention to the fact that the figures represent the twelve signs of the zodiac rather than the usual cluster of apostles and saints, or even of biblical stories. Their story goes that the commissioned artist left his students to complete the decorations while he went for lunch; and found this zodiac version of the creation of the universe on his return! But you do have to say that they are beautifully executed.

As it has returned to just the dampness of mist outside, I progress out of my shelter to find one of the quarries of the famous Portland stone; deserted and quite eerie in these conditions, but footprint evidence that they are used by pony riders [footprints being about all that I can see in the mist]. The cliff-edged coast seems dangerous and treacherous in the thickening mist and rain.

I come to the conclusion that this is a day to write off; and sit behind a blind man on the returning bus. An elderly lady with a stylish haircut comes to sit next to him and he initiates conversation. She smiles in response; and I wonder if he knows that she has smiled: he certainly continues. When he finally gets off he walks near the edge of the kerb, running his stick along its curve, obviously a more reliable sensor than the inner vegetation and irregular house entrances.

I check out of the hotel early and catch a train to Waterloo, deciding that it will be better to get ahead of myself at home rather than persist in this inclemency.

13 May 2013: Arriving at Lyme Regis.

Half way through May, not far from midsummer, and still the feel of winter has not left us; spring just did not happen in terms of weather. But I feel an urgency about trying to complete my walk; particularly in an increasing stiffness of the knees! This is no longer the young sixty nine year old who started the walk!

This outing's strategy is to head for the attraction of Lyme Regis as a mid-way point in the process, deposit the light luggage that I travel with in the hotel, and be free to go back to West Bay and then forwards to Seaton, and even Sidmouth, depending on both the weather and my knees! I get to Lyme Regis by my last Waterloo to Weymouth train and the ever faithful X53 to my destination, with a changeover in Bridport. The wait in Weymouth is long enough for me to slip into M&S for their latest offer of a 'New' seafood sandwich – which even has a whisper of crab in it.

I have booked in 'The Mariner', a comfortable thatched hotel on the hill [Lyme Regis is all hills] with stunning views over the bay at the back. The ladies in the Tourist Office [entered via the theatre!] are very helpful and not only come up with an East Devon bus timetable [critical two days later] but are obviously personally familiar with the coastal walk. They emphasise that the cliff walk between Charmouth and Lyme Regis has completely subsided, and that the beach walk is only safe on certain low tides, none of which occur on my three days here. There is also a fine of £400 for attempting the beach walk inappropriately [= at high tide!]. I promise to review my strategy.

I also review my strategy in the light of the weather forecast. When I booked the hotel and cleared my diary there was a reasonable forecast for this week. But now it is pretty wet for Tuesday [tomorrow] but with the chance of clearing up Wednesday and Thursday. So I opt for the undercliff walk to Seaton as my plan for tomorrow; a walk I performed many years ago when I spent a memorable New Year in Lyme Regis, not long after John Fowles had written 'the French Lieutenant's Woman'. But first I eat in the

159

hotel; a very fresh and delicious grilled plaice. An even more elderly couple sit in the window seat and share a bowl of the carrot and coriander soup. Their slightly bowed figures turning in towards each other and the silent dipping of spoons into the same bowl has a rather touching domestic aspect; and is fostered by the cheery waitress. Something that I cannot help but think that I would not see in the metropolis.

I look at the weather forecast again on the television in my bedroom; it has worsened to gale strength winds and even snow in the north. I begin to wonder when determination becomes obstinacy!

14 May 2013: Lyme Regis to Seaton.

Well at least no bus to catch this morning; and while it is ominously grey it is not seriously raining when I start out after breakfast. But as soon as I reach the sea front the wind hits me and the rain is driving. So over-trousers go on immediately, sheltering behind some boarding and scaffolding to do so: even the builders are inside sheltering.

The SWCW guide instructs that you follow the front until you arrive at the municipal bowling green, passing old shops and a pub close to the harbor, all firmly shut in this weather. On the western side of the green the route is clearly signposted, with initial concrete steps leading to what looks like a row of municipal chalets, then the steps sneak between two of the chalets, changing to uneven rustic wooden ones. Immediately the vegetation changes to lush, Victorian, overgrowth with gnarling trees making a canopied avenue over fronding ferns, and a spread of white flowering wild garlic, mixed with a scattering of still flowering bluebells - and these are the deep blue of the delicate English bluebell: even the odd cluster of primroses persists in this sheltered environment. This would be a most glorious view [although you do have to be careful of protruding roots from the labyrinth of trees] on a sunny day. Further on, midst the slippery film of rain that has dripped from the lime green leaves of late spring onto the protruding chalk stones, there are emerging clusters of lady fern, looking like a gathering of junior bishop's croziers, or a minor conference of sea horses.

While a diversity of paths is supposed to be available, slippage has cut off all of the sea cliff walks, even as the limestone land cliff rises to the right. Needless to say there

160

is scarcely a soul to be seen in this weather, that is until I am about to navigate some knotty roots on a twisting, blind, corner; when a red tee shirted, runner bursts round the corner like a mobile set of traffic lights; and, with a half grin, is gone like the white rabbit in Alice in Wonderland. I recover my equilibrium and pick my way forward. What strange things people get up to! Walking in this weather is dubious enough: but running!

The enclosed walk does occasionally open out in to a glade of beech trees, often with a restricted view of the sea, or at least towards it. Even more rarely there are the ruins of habitation, old cottages, possibly an old kiln, along with short intervals of made up track that might have taken carts. But now slippage has caused steps and fissures that make it look singularly hazardous. I come across six pale brown eggs, all broken, and cleaned out, about the size of quail eggs. They remain unidentified in origin, but I hear magpies in the wood!

Further on I see what, as I plough on, I think might be an early ajuga, but, in spite of the rain, I revisit it and decide that it is a single purple orchid – and feel rewarded.

After one very narrow passage of single track, with a significant drop seaward, I meet another cheery lady walker coming the otherway, who has set off early from Sidmouth. We exchange pleasantries as to what idiots we are to be walking on such a day, 'the mad english', and as to how much of the coastal walk we have each made in different directions; then I descend down a long run of steps [which gave me a break as I saw her beginning to ascend – so dutifully waited!]. At the bottom of the descent a well-surfaced track leads to a road; and I think that I miss a sign post here as I re-ascend and end up on the Rousdon Estate, which is rather grand [in parts], somewhat art nouveau, and which, I later learn, was built as a replacement for Honiton boys' grammar school. There are a cluster of large austere formal buildings, their own St Pancras chapel, with numerous newer buildings dispersed in acres of landscape. However from my point of view these extensive grounds make it very exposed, and the wind and rain are driving head on, giving me very pink, cold, hands, and a Goretex jacket that doesn't feel as waterproof as it should be. Moreover there is nobody about, and a detour to the direction of the sea ends up as a circuit through woodland with no exit: all part of the grounds! But heading along a bridle path to West farm, through a gate house conurbation, does lead onto a lane that has a fast walking surface and hedgerows that are full of yellow flowering nettles, the early delicate white of cow parsley ['Queen Anne's lace' is a somewhat more poetic name],the magenta of ragged robin and the small white stars of goose grass. I encounter no traffic; and if the sun were out I might be singing; but as it is I am squelching along as fast as I can swing. Although Seaton had not been signposted I see a bridle path signposted to my left and in pursuing this cart track suddenly pass a sign post to a narrow footpath saying 'coastal path'. So I am back on track again!

It is not too long before I cross the completely deserted golf course, past the club house and down the steep road to the main harbour road, crossing the river by a new wide bridge, with the old bridge remaining some twenty yards down- stream as a pedestrian feature. It is still pouring and blowing in equal proportion, so that Seaton has virtually no pedestrians and only traffic squishing through the puddles with windscreen wipers going at twenty to the dozen. In the shelter of a bus stop a kind local directs me to where the X 53 picks up travellers, while the P & J social club on the front is a most welcome respite, especially for a warm mug of coffee at a most reasonable price. I slowly begin to recover from the morning's battering!

The journey back is at least warm in the X53 bus, even if the windows are misted up. In Lyme Regis the water is still running down the hill in torrents as it falls, and when I appear in the Tourist Information Office as a pretty good version of a drowned rat, the several ladies on duty simply burst out laughing! Who would be such an idiot as to go walking on such a day! Moreover they don't have bus timetables for West Devon; too out of range! Their opinion of me, however, is endorsed when I enter a local hostlery for further sustenance, and the bar lady comments, 'you look as if somebody's just thrown a bucket of water over you'. I manage a wan smile, and resist the comment 'I feel as if somebody has thrown several buckets of water over me'. I retire to find solace near a radiator and to contemplate a rather damp Sudoku, a packet of crisps, and a well-earned pint.

15 May 2013: Seaton to Sidmouth

At least better weather and an early start. The receptionist at the hotel, who lives in Sidmouth, has already warned me that the 'old road' to Beer, which was part of the prescribed SWCP walk, has recently slipped. Surely enough, having sped along the seafront and up various steps for a route that was somewhat greener than the main road, I end up on the main road at the old road to Beer, with a detour in operation via suburban lawns and woodland, curving down towards Seaton Hole: the slip now bypassed. The recompense for this detour is the climb out of Seaton Hole on the marked cliff walk with fine views of the bay of Beer. The steep path up has marks of its habitation, with escaped teleman and valerian, from local gardens, mixing with cowslips. The celandines are half open today, something of an improvement on yesterday!

There are a variety of descents into Beer, with and without steps. Is this another nest of cloned, immobile homes I see on the opposite hill? Surely enough, as I start to walk up past the flint cottages at 10.15 I meet I meet the dribs and drabs of home owners, plus or minus various sizes and shapes of dogs, coming down into Beer for their morning coffee, or other beverage.

The path sweeps past the turning to the homes into an open field, reminding me of the spread at Studland, and I choose to go onto the South Down Common of Hussell that reveals glorious views in May sunshine, sweeping back to Portland Bill, and onward to a distant curve that fills me with some hesitation as I think 'Do I have that far to go?' But it is a good stretch on the top; even exhilarating today.

There are a fairly good set of serious stairs down into Branscombe; their seriousness indicated by the fact that a couple, considerably younger than myself, are lying flat out at the top, having just made the ascent. At least I am going the right way for once! Branscombe seems a pleasant cove, and attracts visitors, with a fairly well-attended café. The coastal path sign is rather ambiguous out of Bransombe; but as I saw that the sea ahead looked to be rather blood red [sandstone slippage – rather than remains of an anglo saxon battle?], I decide to opt for a well-gravelled walk to the inland village of Branscombe, and am rewarded by seeing a blacksmith in a thatched smithy doing rather modern repairs, with another small café attached. The road out is very narrow, leading past St Winifred's and, while there are several sign postings across the narrow valley, my map suggests a turning into Pilton copse, which is another carpet of white flowering garlic, pungent in the warmer day. As I stagger up, two young, scantily-clad, male harriers whip past, bounding as fast and nimbly as the odd deer that I spy in this off-the-beaten-track diversion. I arrive back on the coastal path more by intuition and a sense of direction than by signposts. But at least I am able to advise two other walkers, going in the opposite direction, that the muddy stretch that I have just negotiated, is not the official path: and to warn them of new cliff slippage before Branscombe! However I am now safely back on open fields heading westwards, with a further pleasant walk until more steps descend to Weston. Before the steps down there is a large stone set by a stream, with violets and white shepherd's purse still flowering in its shade. It seems an idyllic spot to take lunch: and so I do.

Almost immediately after the steep steps down to Weston there are equally steep steps up on the other side. This is certainly an up and down stretch of coast. I develop a strategy of going up twenty counted steps, and then pausing to admire the view.

Again it is a pleasant walk on the top; but all too soon the drop into Salcombe appears. As I have stayed in Sidmouth previously and done the Salcombe dip more than once; and as I also know that slippage no longer allows access via the original cliff path into Sidmouth, I opt for a detour. So from Dunscombe Cliff I head for Salcombe Regis on a gently descending path, passing a donkey sanctuary on the way, and seeing very few people other than a plumply romantic couple, who disappear towards the donkey sanctuary, which seems to suit their general disposition. In Salcombe there is an interesting old house with dedications to St Cutberga, an under-acknowledged lady, while the actual church seems untitled from the outside. I stay on the minor road running from Salcombe to Sidmouth, ignoring sign posts to the coastal path as I feel these will only end at unpredictable slippage diversions.

My chosen diversion is pleasant enough as, once through the colourful hedgerows outside the village, it runs along the edge of a fine spread of beech woodland with numerous bridle paths indicated. I imagine that the younger cognoscenti of Sidmouth know this quiet retreat all too well. There is also the curiosity of an observatory on the right hand side of the road. Star gazing at Sidmouth is something I had not thought of! Then the woodland switches to the right of the road as, following the landward slope of the cliff, the road drops at a fairly steep incline into the bay that holds Sidmouth; with fine views as I momentarily 'stop and stare' at the switch-over. The church of St Giles and St Nicholas is an easy reference point in the town; and Sidmouth turns out to be as splendidly genteel as I remember it, perhaps with more pedestrianisation round the market place?

It is now that the East Devon bus timetable comes into its own, as the X53 [my bus back to Lyme Regis], only drives through Sidford, which is some way inland from Sidmouth. I had carefully worked out that I would catch a 52B to Sidford Spar [a grocery store – not a geological feature]. But, having patiently waited while various buses zoom in and out, I find, when it arrives, that this 52B is not stopping at Sidford Spar [just as well that I asked!]. However I had also noted the local 899 bus is still standing at the adjacent stop. Galvanising a pair of rather stiffening knees, I am in luck: problem solved: albeit that, when I finally arrive at the 'Spar' bus stop on the main road, the X53 is, unusually, 15 minutes late; I was really beginning to think transport plans were against me today!

Refreshment at Lyme Regis I deem well-earned and more than welcome.

16 May 2013: West Bay to Lyme Regis

At last the weather is as every walker hopes for. Although I must admit to feeling so tired after the Sidmouth to Seaton switch back that I nearly postponed this walk. But a fine pale blue sky and a sweet breeze drew me on. So much so that I rise early, pay my bill ahead of the crowd and catch the 8.37 version of the 31 to Bridport bus terminus. Unfortunately this version does not go down to West Bay and without waiting for a local bus I foot it down to West Bay. Old Bridport is characterful enough, with rows of period houses, but the rest is something of a plod, with gratitude for the underpass avoiding traffic on the busy roundabout that allows the A35 to cross. Then it is important to take the low road to West Bay, and not the signposted high road with its traffic.

As you progress into West Bay it is easy to see the cliffs [and a good path] sweeping up to the west, with a splattering of dog walkers at this time of day; and the inevitable cluster of caravans.

The west turning from the harbour is easy to find and well- marked, with a reasonable, warming, climb in the cool of the morning. There are fine sea views up here and a pleasing walk to Eyemouth, with well-made steps facilitating the descent: and such steps are a constant feature of this day's walking.

There is a small shingle beach at Eyemouth, with a narrow outlet between the cliffs. Having circumvented the outflowing stream, the steps ascend the other side in an equally steep format. It might be yesterday's exertions, or just old age, but I pause for breath after the first sixty steps, and thereafter, I revert to twenty at a time, admiring the view in between! On the third stop I notice a snail with a delightful pale yellow shell, slowly, O so slowly, crawling along a heart shaped leaf. This does reassure me that everything is relative; and that really I am making astoundingly impressive progress. Thank you snail!

The path now proceeds to Thorncombe Beacon, with much of it going through open pasture and being away from the cliff edge. Cultivated pasture means a restricted range of flora, but a wider range of visible fauna: more a question of Dorset ewes and their lambs, or Angus cross beef cattle, some dry Friesian cows, while the young following stock are in yet another field. Perhaps the livestock reflects that the path is away from the cliff edge, but it is quite a relief not to be reminded about cliff slippage in this stretch!

The steep, but stepped, descent into Seamouth is to a wider beach with the temptation of the Anchor Inn. All too familiarly the egress coastal path has subsided and it is necessary to follow the single road inland some four hundred metres where there is a clear sign post to the left, with the path crossing the middle of a field and then heading through a copse coming out into the open to begin a serious ascent to the Golden Gap, allegedly the highest point of this part of the Jurassic Coast. This feature seems to attract a wider spectrum of walkers, along with the good weather. There is a young couple with a lolloping hound, not on a leash. It turns out that the dog is quite afraid of the young stock in the field – as the girl tries to introduce him. But this is still sentiment above animal behavior, as even the dog's rushing away might excite these young animals. Hey ho!

Then there are the son and father pounding up the hill; at least the son is. The father obviously could not resist starting his sixtieth birthday celebration at the Anchor Inn at Seamouth, and is now paying the penalty; while the son is quietly enjoying his own superior fitness! I find a seat in the shade just before the final gate onto the plateau of the Golden Gap, and choose this to look back towards West Bay and even as far as Sidmouth: I open my sandwiches and munch. A truly fine spectacle of green escarpment

166

running into rugged cliff, tumbling down to a glorious blue sea and sky. A privileged lunch site, and such is the day that most fellow walkers exchange greetings, or, likewise, having struggled with the climb, just pause to admire the view. Of course, more have saved their sandwiches for the top of the plateau where the view stretches in both directions, sweeping on to Torbay, Dartmouth and beyond: the latter reminding me of how far I yet have to go! Having stopped to take in the view again I begin the sweeping descent down well-spaced steps. I pass a man of some years ascending at a deliberate pace that breaks him into perspiring. Some way below I see his wife pausing to regain her breath. When I eventually pass her, as she takes another pause, I stop to applaud her taking the ascent at such a sensible pace that suits her; and confess, when the going is steep, that I count twenty steps, and then have a pause.

'Oh, do you really do that too? It is what I do; I have to!' and her face breaks in to a radiant smile. A problem shared is a problem solved: or at least made more acceptable!

Part of this stretch is National Trust land, with several of the coastal fields running wild. It is astonishing to see an almost carpet of gold with buttercups: but then quite staggering to see that there is a secondary weave of purple, and this is of orchids. Amazing; a benevolence of orchids.

The next dip is St Gabriel's, and well bridged, with a final climb to Cain's Folly. There has been so much slippage along this stretch that there is frequently another secluded world slipped halfway down the high cliff, which gives rise to a totally untouched flora and fauna. I think that I am so engrossed in this that I miss the latest signed diversion inland away from the high cliff. The result is that I descend to Charmouth and find myself confronted by some recent, startling, four foot drops through slippage, with insidious cracks that run into overgrown vegetation. Rather than retracking, I do negotiate these very carefully; and see that there is a new track that is being used along the edge of a grazed field. I am only too pleased to access it safely, then to complete my descent.

I had been in Lyme Regis [and the tourist information office] long enough to know that from Charmouth to Lyme Regis there had been such a considerable fall of the cliff onto the beach that there was no longer a cliff walk and the beach was only negotiable at very low tide. The guides recommend the road diversion. I do this, but catch the 31 bus up to Fern Hill [otherwise it is a not very pleasant walk along the busy road]. However, from just past the hotel at Fernhill, there is a footpath that leads down into Lyme Regis with some fine views of the town and bay. After refreshment I, carrying my backpack of luggage, take the 31 bus going the other way to Dorchester South, a journey worth taking in its own right; admiring the glorious rolling countryside from the top deck. Seemingly there has been a small local retreat at this quiet town; a cluster of young people on the station take fond farewells of each other from what has obviously been an emotionally bonding week.

I catch the train back to Paddington.

17 June 2013: Arriving at Exmouth

Having passed through Exeter a fortnight ago on the way to a holiday in St Ives, [principally to visit the Hepworth Gallery, the Leach Pottery, and Tate St Ives], I finally dismount at Exeter St. Davids from a very full train. The eight coach train is quite unlike any of my previous quiet Monday morning outings, as several of today's carriages are wholly blocked out with reserved tickets, and by the first stop at Reading people are already sitting on the floor at the end of carriages. As there is only one train an hour on this service I cannot but think that there is an obvious solution of more frequent or longer trains [or - re-directing funds from the white elephant HS2 project!].

While it would be easy simply to change platforms and catch an on-going local train to Exmouth, I decide to explore options for returning, as maps tell me that bus and rail stations are juxtaposed in Exmouth, but not in Exeter.

The 'H' bus outside the Exeter rail station is the obvious circular city bus that attracts the heterogeneous population of passengers that you would expect in a large contemporary city; various pensioners out shopping, for whom the bus is duly lowered; the young mothers, inevitably overloaded with buggy and two children; and one extraordinarily large lady who has difficulty squeezing herself over two seats, and then proceeds to delicately unpeel toffee filled chocolates, one after the other! As I am sitting just behind her, I am impressed by my restraint. Me thinks that she has the biggest problem of all the travellers!

A jolly ticket inspector instructs me as to where I should dismount, and there appears an undistinguished bus terminal just across the road, with a double decker 57 that will potter down the estuary of the Exe via Topsham to Exmouth. Here I dismount instinctively at the Esplanade, since it feels like the centre of town, and most people are getting off here [the railway station and the official bus station are visible a roundabout away]. I identify where to catch the 157 bus, which will be my coastal connection to Sidmouth and Budleigh Salterton for the next three days.

Having logged in at the Dolphin Hotel, where I am staying for three nights, I decide to seek out the ferry to Starcross, which I hope to use on my last day – to get me across the river Exe on the way to Teignmouth. In doing so I inevitably discover that the whole of the dock area of Exmouth has been extensively redeveloped into modern apartments and houses, much as the docklands of London have been regenerated, [and east of Eastbourne]. Having found my way through this maze of new developments and waterways, I finally come across what remains of the small old harbour, with the strange mixture of marine management, tourist tatt and enticing fresh fish shops. To the east of this runs the rather splendid sea front of large white-stuccoed hotels and an impressive curve of beach, only terminated by headland cliffs, which will be part of my present walking.

But for the evening I return to eat in the central 'Strand' of Exmouth which looks as if it could have been a rather grand market place, surrounded by buildings now past their prime. Currently it is landscaped to an open space with a central war memorial, presently much decorated with flowers for the horrifically beheaded guardsman [outside his barracks], recently perpetrated by sad, Islamic extremists. But in the relative quiet of the evening the area has become the territory for young skate boarders. I notice a pair where one is showing off, doing all the tricks of flips and turns, on and off the steps and kerbs; while his pal just seems to follow on an even keel. Then I notice that the follower actually has a cam recorder hung low down, and is filming his pal's performance: cool project!

I enjoy muscadet and moules; and feel ready for a little more coastal walking.

18 June 2013: Sidmouth to Budleigh Salterton

Breakfast in the hotel seems to be a haberdashery of visiting workers and tourists: even the couples more often work rather than romance. On my way I purchase my usual paper from a doughty and dumpy lady who is having an on-going conversation with an off stage 'Joe' as to why the white van is parking in the strand again where there are yellow lines; 'E'll cop it alright this time: just you see...', she offers to off stage left. But I don't hang around long enough to find out!

The nine forty version of the 157 certainly brings out the silver brigade, with a pleasant hour's ride to Sidmouth; but also usefully giving me something of a preview of the walk back. In addition I get to view the charm of Otterton and Colaton Raleigh, two inland, chocolate box, villages; along with a glimpse of the driveway of Bicton Gardens and College, [where some colourfully decorated young ladies dismount from the bus]. It seems rather late to be starting a working day: they do look more like design students than catering staff: but of course they could be lecturers these days?

I finally arrive at the gardened triangle in Sidmouth that serves as the main bus station, with memories of the 52B that I never managed to catch, and when the 899 bus saved the day!

The coastal road to Budleigh Salterton, very visibly, rises from the western end of the bay.

The Climb out of Sidmouth.

But since I was last here they have now sculpted a millennium extension to the esplanade, which is a dramatic success, with infills of concrete in the red sandstone, and buttress supports for the overhang; but still bright yellow notices 'beware falling rock'! This exciting stretch ends at a shingle beach, with a zig-zag path leading back up to the road. But another project has converted the meadow at the side of the road into a landscaped walk; the cropped path leading through clusters of large yellow buttercups, mixed with clumps of white clover, while the uncropped grass contrasts the delicate fawn of poa species against the robust heads of the fescues, which are even showing a tinge of purple. This being Sidmouth, some elegant ladies walk here with the most inappropriate, but decorous, footwear, and dogs that fit a similar description. The meadow rises quite steeply, with seats every fifty yards or so, these giving theatrical views over Sidmouth, and of the coastline almost back to Weymouth. But at the end of the meadow the road is rejoined, while the 'old road' can be seen as a fenced off stretch; closed due to subsidence. There is a short stretch on the narrow, hazardous and busy road before a welcome signposted left turn into woods which leads to the cliff edge of Peak Hill with, according to the guide, magnificent views. But such a sea mist suddenly has blown up that not even the sea, never mind Sidmouth, is visible. However there is a pleasant walk through woodland until the path emerges onto the rolling Windgate Common. Foxgloves are unfurling, with their flowers not the spire of pealing bells, but more as the crushed flounces of a flamenco skirt: sea parsley is lime green in its flowering; and the bright blue of speedwell is everywhere.

There are quite a few walkers on this stretch, and the path seems bold enough, but, in following other people I somehow miss a coastal path turning, and at Sea View Farm realize that, picturesque as it is, I do not want to arrive at Otterton, but to head for Budleigh Salterton! Fortunately there is a sufficient network of paths in this area easily to change course towards the coast, thereby arriving at Ladram Bay, which in turn reveals the source of some of the walkers: a large conurbation of holiday homes. In addition to the sand of the bay there are dramatic free standing sandstone pillars, eroded away from the red cliffs, set in swirling seas, their silhouettes disappearing and reappearing in the sea mists.

Once I am past this contrast of the wild cliffs and the domestic holiday homes, it is quiet again. The green corn heads are now emerging; so unbelievable after the poverty of germination earlier in the wet and cold first half of the year. A little later a field, of what must have been winter barley, is well whiskered in its heads of corn, while the light green of the field actually has pale blond streaks; hints of summer's ripening that I can scarcely believe. There soon follows a bold swathe of natural meadowland along this stretch of the path, the pasture dotted with yellow trefoil amongst the grasses, and purple clover, seducing various varieties of bees, with varying assortments of abdominal shapes and striped colouration. Small blue butterflies flutter around, with occasional small fritillaries. Yet most cheering in the clearing mist is the sound of skylarks. I manage only to spot one, but am ministered to by a series, declaring their territory in ascending torrents of song. How fragile their form against the hard silhouettes of the gulls, gliding around to nest on red sandstone shelves in the cliff face.

It is a pleasant and gentle descent to the estuary of the River Otter, meeting a trickle of people who have crossed the river from Budleigh Salterton for a day's picnic. This is no mean undertaking for them, as the marshy estuary of the Otter is a conservation zone, not crossed by a road, or by foot, until a kilometre or so inland. But there is a pleasant walk in the shade of woodland on the eastern side of the river, with a great spread of white ox-eye daisies at the edges of the field, while close to the path the butch, brown heads of plantain are sporting delicate coronas of pale cream anthers. The estuary is obviously a bird migration site with carefully placed, hidden, bird watching huts.

Once the bridge is crossed there is a well prepared path [pedestrians and cyclists!] into Budleigh Salterton with the contrast of a wild, misting, sea marsh on one side and a well mown cricket ground on the other!

A clotted cream ice cream on the quiet comfort of the esplanade of Budleigh Salterton is due reward for the day's walk. Budleigh seems to have a more gently smiling population of pensioners than Sidmouth; which is saying something, for they were genteel enough in Sidmouth!

Just before the post office there are two neighbouring shops: one is called 'the Cosy Teapot', the other, selling ladies attire, is called 'Days of Grace': they somehow sum up this pleasant place?

172

19 June 2013: Budleigh Salterton to Exmouth

Yesterday's mist has transformed into the hottest day of the year, with blue skies to match. No wonder that, having descended from the 157 at Budleigh Salterton, I make the exit hill light of foot. There are various odd little hedged plots to my right, with patches of lawn and superior sheds-come-garden rooms overlooking the bay: perhaps the most superior non-beach, beach huts that I have seen so far.

After some ascent the path narrows and turns a right angle to present an illusion that the walker must go through a magical brown door at the end of the corridor. But on arriving a bold arrow distinctly points to the left, and the narrow path is now hedged by a profusion of yellow and white flowering honeysuckle; its own magic; and intertwines with the 'old man's beard' clematis, save that at this time the old man is but prepubescent tendrils, reaching out to see where it might sport its delicate, small creamy-white flowers. A little further and a small hawthorn supports a pink and white honeysuckle growing three to four metres in height.

For the moment there are few fellow travelers, which is as well since the narrowness of the path makes it virtually one-way traffic. However passing places occur as tidy cuttings with judiciously placed seats, usually dedicated to somebody who has enjoyed retirement here. Whilst the climb out of Budleigh Salterton was steepish, the incline now becomes gentler and more pleasant: but it is somewhat of an anticlimax to emerge onto the West Down Golf Links, with a tractor mowing the greens! So much for the wild beauty of the coast! This is only augmented by the vision of the promontory of Straight Point, housing an all too audible Defence Territory Rifle Range: and out of bounds to the walker. But even this is capped by curving round to Sandy Cove and finding an estate to end all estates of white holiday homes. While the beach below is fairly packed with families, it seems bizarre to have the background rat-a-tat of the rifle range: even the second lieutenant's firing instructions can be heard over a megaphone!

But climbing out of the other side leads into National Trust territory; beautifully preserved coast and natural pasture; with plaques of poetry [!], and informative posters of what went before [dinosaurs, with beetles leading the way from Triassic to Jurassic – as far as I recall]. But the flowers in the meadows are a riot of gold; while the views down to Exmouth Bay and towards Teignmouth and Torbay are quite stunning. Stopping and sitting on an undedicated National Trust seat to assimilate this is a privilege on a day like this.

Thence a gentle descent towards the 'Geostone', a much heralded artifact of Portland stone, dedicated to mark the most western point of this Jurassic Coastal Heritage. [Although from where I am standing there seem to be many more miles of coastal walking on the other side of the River Exe awaiting me!]

Here I meet people coming up from Exmouth, in various shapes and sizes: and it is an easy descent for me, passing the red sandstone of Maer rocks, to the quieter beach and esplanade of east Exmouth: no rifle ranges here.

Old Exmouth, Harbour + beach.

The gardened pub on the Edwardian front is a welcome respite: but, while I am out replenishing my fluid therapy, my fellow imbibers watch s seagull swoop down and take off with the rest of my very welcome cheddar cheese sandwich! Hey – ho. The orcs of Exmouth.

I retire to the comfort of the Dolphin Hotel.

Teignmouth my goal for tomorrow.

20 June 2013: Exmouth to Teignmouth

How fickle the weather! It is back to sea frets and autumn mists today; although it is as near to midsummer as it will be.

This is also the most unpredictable day of the present spate of three days of walking, mainly because I have to cross the River Exe, which at Exmouth is very wide with quite distinct channels. The official walking guide has four alternatives with the

174

ferry to Starcross being the most obvious; but this not running before 10.40. So, making for a relatively late start and a road walk from Starcross to Dawlish Warren, I am at Exmouth pier just after ten, watching other various cruises leave or sail past, including an elderly widower from the hotel who, in yesterday's sunshine, booked for a sail to Torquay and back today; but now faces all the way there and back in shrouded mist!

As I finally see our little ferry arriving, a rather dapper middle aged guy, all in a sailor's dark navy, as if some quayside official, sidles up and says that I look as if I am walking the south coast [the anorak, walking stick, strong shoes, and backpack are a give-away!] and says, sotte voce, that I want 'the river taxi', not the ferry, as the former will take me to Dawlish Warren, so cutting out the Star Cross diversion. This sounds welcome, as it is a road walk from Star Cross to Dawlish Warren; but I wonder about price. He says 'Only a couple of quid'. I wonder whether this is a general or a specific statement. I had noticed another rather lank-haired, bespectacled, individual who is more heavily booted and back packed than I, and so, thinking of splitting costs, ask if he is interested in sharing the water taxi. We proceed, and find that there are three other local people jumping aboard; and it is only two quid each! This little red boat is a real harbor taxi. The day is looking up!

We drop one of the passengers off on his boat which is moored in the estuary, and the boat is then steered into the estuary side of the Dawlish Warren Peninsula, which is one of those strange projections, with similar ones already passed at the entrance to Pagham Harbour, and round the corner at West Wittering. They give rise to particular flora and fauna, and are, quite appropriately, protected sites. We are directed to the front of the boat and, having slung our various baggage onto the sand, have to leap off the bow onto the sand; only some three feet or so; but at my ripe age that suddenly feels quite a leap! Thankfully the wet sand is a soft landing, and I neither disgrace nor injure myself. The little red, flat taxi reverses off the shore, and disappears into the mist with its remaining two passengers.

My companion turns out to be a Mancunian living in London, more than twenty years younger than I, but doing the same coastal walk in greater chunks [although he later admits that his planned, longer walks are further than is enjoyable – simply dominated by trying to complete the coastal walk in the time allocated: so I am quite consoled by my

175

leisurely aims!].

This tip of the Warren is quite 'au naturelle', so we head across a mixture of sand, shells and shingle towards where we can see occasional people walking, rising into sand dunes. There a magnificent run of groynes define the beach on the southern seaward side; without a soul in sight. This was indeed good advice from the dapper guy on the quayside!

But then, as we walk westwards, what do we encounter, but a golf course! Even so it is amongst much wild habitat, with clear paths: we even find some more purple orchids in the mist. Eventually stony or sandy paths formalise into covered surfaces, with various choices of direction. A dog-walking lady kindly directs us to the esplanade of Dawlish Warren, even takes us there; where we negotiate various groups of teenagers, out on this increasingly damp morning, with projects asking people's opinions on the way the peninsula is being preserved. By the third group we declare that we are an unbalanced statistic as we have already been 'done' twice, and given the same answers! Trade is obviously quiet.

However, here we are, heading for Dawlish, much earlier and with more variety than we could have hoped for, already on the esplanade that runs between the sea and the renowned Brunel railway all the way into Dawlish. Moreover the tide is low, even if it is coming in, so there is the prospect that we can make most of this dramatic walk between the sea and the rail all the way to Teignmouth, apart from the jutting red sandstone cliffs, where the train disappears through tunnels and walkers have to go up and over: but these are the far side of Dawlish. So we have a rapid progression towards the shrouded apparition of cream face buildings, making up the frontage of Dawlish. The mist clears sufficiently to see that there might be a very attractive square inland, but with the weather, and Steve having much further to go than I, it is onwards without hesitation.

The Dawlish esplanade ends with a metal bridge crossing over the railway just before the trains disappear into the first tunnel. Having crossed the bridge, the path zig-zags up the cliff to bring you out into parkland close to the A379. This leads along the old road until the houses stop and there is a relatively new well-signposted set of wooden steps that lead down away from the busy road to the cliff edge via meadows and tranquility. How long this part of the cliff will survive I wonder, as part of it is close to

176

the recent subsidence. The narrow, hedged in, path rises quite steeply. We find ourselves virtually in low cloud with a drenching, pervasive, humidity. Steve's glasses become uselessly fogged and, without glasses, he can only see a hand in front. My shirt is suddenly soaked at the front by the penetrating mist. Nevertheless we hear the unmistakable sound of a wren singing and spot a cluster of long tail tits in a hawthorn tree; both of which lift the spirit.

We no sooner rise over the peak than we are reunited with the A379, fortunately with pavement, until we spot the signpost and the rapidly dropping road of Smugglers Lane. A steep incline takes us through a wooded descent, where we see the path going under the coastal rail track, just where the railway dramatically emerges from the second tunnel. Initially the sight of the sea lapping through the bridge makes our heart sink. Surely we will not have to climb back up the hill and walk along the dreaded A379 into Teignmouth?

Under Brunel's Railway.

But no, we are safe from the tide, as the esplanade, and the footpath to it, passing under the bridge, are both set some ten feet above sea level. So, having clambered up the steps, we are all set for another straight set of pounding along the sea and rail scape. Perhaps even more dramatic is the heroic work that is being made against landslip on this stretch. Most of the rail has a ten-foot high wire mesh to catch falling rock. But there is a cavernous area of slippage, the size of a couple of football pitches, where workers are high up in the most precarious positions, cementing and in filling. All this is virtually

177

invisible from the trains whizzing by.

Teignmouth is another tidy, cream fronted esplanade. Here Steve and I part company, an enjoyable partnership, he for Branscombe in the mist, and I for the Kings Arms in Teignmouth, whence refreshment, and a trip back to Paddington; looking out of the window at the sea and the cliffs of that stretch of coast with new eyes! Now I understand exactly where the walker goes under the railway when the footpath seems to end at a cliff face, and what the diversions are in terms of hills, woods, and road traffic when the train heads through a tunnel.

[Storms the following winter caused havoc to this stretch – see below].

15 July 2013: To Teignmouth and onwards…

Suddenly there is a real 'hot spell', and the coast calls again. But the hot spell also means that people in town are packing into Regent's Park, the zoo, the mosque, or Lord's Cricket Ground; all of which pack out the single decker, 274 bus that points me towards Paddington station for my exit. This means that I catch a train an hour later than I hoped, the 11.06; but at least with a French cheese and salami packed croissant to sustain me on the predictably packed, Great Western express. At least I am now sufficiently experienced to know that you rapidly make a dash for coaches E and F if you have not reserved a seat! I even get a window seat and, five minutes later, am joined by a rather nice, plump, shy, widow going to Plymouth, who attempts crosswords while I struggle with sudokus. Somehow we strike up a conversation – prompted by the guy in front of us who occupies a seat with hand luggage when the seating is full; and has the audacity to say that the place 'is taken' when struggling passengers ask if there is 'a spare seat'. But, being british, our indignation goes no further than saying, 'do you think that is a spare seat?' in a quite audible voice! His skin and sensitivities obviously belong to the rhinoceros family.

He maintains his territory until Exeter, where I dismount and transfer to the local rattling, four coach, diesel that shudders, rocks and judders [but it does have windows that actually open to let in the sea air] past the Dawlish Warren of my last outing: but this time the local train draws in to a siding for ten minutes, waiting for the Cornish express to whizz past, heading for Exeter: such is the pressure on this line.

178

The station at Teignmouth is familiar from my last visit and I retrace my footsteps to the esplanade in altogether more cheerful weather. My quest is now to find the Tourist Information Office to try and determine whether, if I cross the river on the Shaldon Ferry and do a stint of the South Coast Path, say to Labrador Bay, I can then find a bus stop for the no 11 bus running on the A379 from Teignmouth to Torquay: Torquay being where I have a hotel reservation for three nights. This hope is in anticipation of shortening tomorrow's walk – so that I do not have to come all the way back across the river to start my walk from Teignmouth to Torquay. But today I am, of course, carrying all my luggage: minimal as it is [one change of clothes [including footwear], waterproofs, maps, a guide, note pad, and a toothbrush!].

Fortunately the tourist information office is empty; and the gentleman on duty recognizes it as a challenge that he has not previously had. But, ringing the bus service, he does open with a distinctly pessimistic intonation of 'let us see if anybody answers'. Out of four different numbers he does get two to answer; but one of those is to give him another number to ring, and the second admits to not knowing the answer!

'But all is not lost: I have another trick or two', the intrepid guide assures me, but more with resignation than expectation, I detect. He accesses an internet map of the A379 which has red dots at certain intervals; but with no code as to what the red dots mean.

'They could be bus stops,' he offers.

'They must be bus stops,' I affirm; 'we must travel in hope', I add, getting somewhat carried away, and aware that now, in the small office, there is a queue of several people behind me.

His response is a hybrid between a smile choked by a frown. The final comment is, 'Sorry I couldn't answer this. Next please.'

Well one must try!

So I head for the Shaldon ferry, asking two charming ladies, who are looking after the Royal Lifeboat counter, where the ferry is, when the signs and the ferry are virtually under my nose. The problem being that I had the image of a substantial ferry, as at Exmouth, when in reality it is a sort of large, motorized, rowing boat, accommodating about 15 people; and gently pottering back and forth when it fills. I scuttle down and am the last passenger aboard the gang plank for this trip. The boat weaves its way through other moorings and the most heterogeneous collection of beach huts, come houses, that I have yet seen, with as many shapes and sizes as variations in colour; with or without variable numbers of small boats; so that the overall effect is near to an anglicised version of a Carribean shanty town: yet not without its own charm.

We simply beach at Shaldon, and the gang plank goes down again to disembark. The walk commences, turning left along the estuary front, a narrow lane running to the comfortable-looking Ness Hotel, where a signpost stops you walking into the hotel's gardens, and an ascent through shaded woodland commences; deliciously cool on this hazy, hot day. The view from the top is of a magnificent sweep, not only of Teignmouth, but back though Dawlish Warren and Exmouth, possibly even as far as a fuzzy Portland Bill: I simply feel encouraged that all that is behind me!

The forward path continues to be shady until, lo and behold, it emerges on to a rather brown looking golf course, splattered with greener patches for putting [I presume!]. Skirting this there is another sequence of shade from which two paths emerge, the coastal path diving down and up again in the distance, and a contour path heading towards the A379. I take the latter, but find that the A379 is a narrow twisting road, which must be hazardous for cyclists and is out of the question for pedestrians: and without any sign of bus stops!

Sticking on my high contour paths [all approved public rights of way!] Labrador Bay is circumnavigated with fine views on such a glorious day. My path passes a field of barley where the stalks and leaves are a distinctly blue –green, but the whiskered seed heads are all a viridian green: a quite electric contrast spread over a field.

Then there is a nearby field with five black grazing cows and one blond beast that are all foraging amongst bracken on the edge of woodland. I cough loudly as I descend from my contour, so that they know that I am approaching. The blond fellow has his head most deeply in the bracken. Two of the dark ladies raise their heads; stare, and return to grazing. I decide that a tuneful whistle is in order. The effect is to alert all the company; and they decide to go off at a canter, with the young blonde monsieur running faster than his dark ladies.

I am pleased that he is but an ingénue, and just there for his good looks [into his other services I will not inquire – but I feel that his pedigree might be quite impressive!].

The next field has a boundary border of great purple thistles, higher than my six feet, mixed in with a mass of bright yellow flowering ragwort that is not much shorter, and both plants meshed in a profusion of bracken. Colourful – but not very productive in agricultural terms. The steep slope is covered in a golden hue of seeding fescue grass, but it would have to be grazed, the gradient being too steep for hay making.

I think that by staying up on the contours I have missed some ups and downs, while sign posts for a 'Maidencombe Circular Walk' remind me that the timetable for the no 11 bus did specify Maidencombe Cross as an official stop. I have travelled rather further than I intended on this 'arrival' day, so I follow this path back towards the A379. Hope above expectation, I trundle along a very short stretch of the A379 actually to find an official bus stop where the road temporarily widens at the top of Gabwell Hill. In the heat of the afternoon a simple bus stop seems almost like a local shrine: and it even has some shade and a sign post to the South Coast Path for me to pick up tomorrow. Moreover, the rather voluptuous, and jolly, lady driver of the number 11 bus does have the more convivial attributes of a Mary Magdelene. 'You alright, mi luv?' she asks with a smile, as my bus pass slides onto the oyster, and I stagger onto the bus. Respite and restoration! Even more so when I finally arrive at the bus terminal outside Debenhams at Torquay, and there is a Wetherspoon's next door with orange and lemonade, plus ice, for rehydration. Two pints disappear in no time.

I think that I walked rather further than I had intended today with all my luggage; more than just crossing the river at Teignmouth: but it is miles covered for tomorrow.

16 July 2013: Gabwell Hill to Torquay

I return to Debenham's next morning, walking through the park of Torre Abbey and along the promenade with the prospect of catching the 9.35, just in time for the grey brigade: and I feel very knowledgeable about directing a 'rambler' spinster who is also catching the bus and supposed to be meeting her group at the Shaldon ferry for Teignmouth. Yesterday's strategy has some pay off!

As there was no bus stop on the opposite side of the road at Gabwell Hill where I finally caught the bus yesterday, nor anywhere for the bus to pull off the narrow road at the top of the hill, I ask the driver if he stops at Gabwell Hill.

'You mean Gabwell', comes back the answer, in a tone that indicates that his breakfast had burnt toast; or none.

As Lower and Higher Gabwell are both villages someway off the A379, I hover a smile; but in view of the queue behind me, move upstairs where I have a good view of where we are on the journey. But not before asking the driver if he will remind me when we get there, and receive,

'I'll probably have forgotten by then', as a gruff answer. Somebody definitely had burnt toast for breakfast.

Fortunately I remember yesterday's bus route and, recognising Maidencombe, descend the stairs to ask, as we are still on the A379 rather than the byroads of Higher Gabwell, …and if the next stop might be Gabwell: most innocently!

'Oh, you want Gabwell do you? Stop after the next one'.

The burnt toast has obviously got through a critical stage of digestion. Surely enough he pulls in at the top of the hill exactly opposite where I caught the bus yesterday, stopping all the traffic behind on the narrow rising hill. I thank him, and stare hard at the sign on the adjoining lane that says in capital letters 'GABWELL HILL'. But I have the feeling that the stare is wasted: and anyway, I am grateful to be back where I left off yesterday!

As I am on a hill, the sea and the coastal path are immediately visible once the busy road has been crossed. But access to the coastal path, although signposted, was not as simple as it might have been; my memory tells me that long legs were useful in circumnavigating the barbed wire that marked off the official coastal path on the edge of a much lower field!

One of the most outstanding features of this stretch of the coastal walk, as I noted yesterday, is that it is heavily wooded; often with the trees going someway down the cliff. This has two consequences, firstly that you are walking in a shady, verdant tunnel much of the time [most welcome on this hot day] and the second is that you do not realize quite how close you are to a fairly precipitous drop on the seaward side. A third result is that you miss the sweeping sea views that I had yesterday from staying up on the higher contours. But the wood is interspersed with stretches along the edges of somewhat brown-looking fields, while there is the distinct up-and-down component for each gully,

182

with clear signposts, at intervals, leading into Maidencombe. The hedges are full of the white trumpets of convolvulus; while its lesser cousin, spreading amongst the grass verges, has a tinge of lilac to its smaller white flowers. Some of the parsley family still have their green panicles; but elsewhere in the sun their older brothers are beginning to burn into brown silhouettes in the sun.

At Maidencombe the guide instructs you to go through the small car park to pick up the next signpost: however the said small car park now has two overspill car parks attached at various corners! One path obviously leads down to the beach; but as I am adopting a policy of staying on high contours where I am given a choice, I decide to follow signs to Watcombe, staying high at all diversions, passing through another delightfully wooded section until emerging onto a green at Petit Tor Point which has a series of theatrically staggered seats to admire the view [very similar to those at the exit of Sidmouth?!]. But here there are firm directions, both in the guide and visibly, to exit the green via the wrought iron gates, to follow the tarmac road to a roundabout, and to turn left into St Mary's Church Road which, after several hundred yards, has a wooden sign post directing you down through woods, and under the steep funicular railway, to Oddicombe bay: with the beach a most pleasant stop for lunch. The rocky coves have water that is translucent in turquoises, greens and blues: and a smattering of people greatly enjoying this secluded cove, with modest but delightful refreshment available. The Cary Arms looks most enticing; but I resist, and settle for a cheese and tomato baguette and a diet coke on the sea front.

It is only looking back from this tranquility that you see how massive the land slip at Petit Tor is. Half of a single house remains precariously perched at the top; the other half gone, and the remainder, with shattered doors and windows, the roof open to the sky. Some tonnage of a slip.

Landfall-Petit Tor Point

The exit from this steep bay is quite a gradient, turning left into high walled passages that give the feel of a very ancient right of way. As this path turns right, through an arch, a broader path leads off to the left through a more open woodland . The latter is the designated route and leads eventually onto a minor road. Further along there is a sign post to go up to Walls Hill; but do pass by any turnings down to the beach here! At the top there is a large open common, with more fine views, and a strange folly with classical pillars and open seats, as if providing protection from the sun and the wind for long skirted picnics of yore. Eventually you come onto a tarmac road, turn left, but still ignore sign posts to the beach and, as the road rises, there is a sign post to woodland on the left where you enter a most unusual 'inland cliff' walk, with the path half way up the face, and, fortunately, with a strongly secured metal hand rail. Downwards the view is into and above the tree tops, while to your right the rock rises vertically. As a solitary walker I almost expect pterodactyls to glide past and to see dinosaurs roaming below; or at least meet a loaded donkey or a mendicant friar coming the other way!

Eventually the cliff levels out while the woods emerge onto a select gathering of houses, generally gated, and I feel the CCTVs are but hidden. Fortunately there is a sign post a path on the road running to Hope's Nose, but it is as well to follow this small road round to Meadowfoot beach, which is a more popular watering place [an ice cream is an indulgence!]. What is needed here is a clear direction to exit via the hill at the west end of the beach. The 'exit' at the extreme west end, past the long row of beach huts, looks tempting, but is a dead end for the walker. However it is a delight for youngsters wishing to dive off high rocks the other side! Not my disposition at this time of the afternoon, or time of life!

The climb out of Meadowfoot is somewhat dispiriting as it rises first into a car park, and then climbs to another green higher up, where families, who have driven there, are playing! So much for leg power! However there are striking coastal views, a coastguard's posting, and a board informing you that this all originally belonged to a wealthy family with a big house and 20 acres of garden. The onward path, close to the coastguard look-out, is meticulously walled and provided with well-maintained stone steps: even the ivy to the seaward side has been clipped! There is definitely an exclusive estate feel. The carefully sculpted path even goes through a look-out tower set in the high stone wall, with stunning views southwards over the whole of Torbay: not difficult to see why the site was chosen as a prestigious, private residence!

All too soon this quiet and secluded walk opens back onto tarmac; admittedly in a decidedly pleasant part of Torquay, and the 'signposts' for the coastal path consist of metal acorns set in the pavement or road: easily missed! But you are not really going to lose your way seriously here anyway.

Finally arriving back at Debenham's and a rehydration appointment, I am very pleased that I had walked as far as Gabwell Hill yesterday. I think the whole walk from Teignmouth on a hot day would have been too far to be pleasantly enjoyed by someone of my vintage.

But tomorrow looks like a flat walk at last! Torbay here I come.

17 July 2013; Torquay to Brixham

Maps and guides decree that this is an easy day of walking; and I do reach Brixham for lunch. But this is because there was no preliminary bus journey at the beginning; and allows me to spend an hour or so in the afternoon walking to and round Berry Point before returning to Brixham for the 12 A bus back to Torquay.

But this is to get ahead of myself. The mediterranean weather continues, with both people, and unwatered grass, looking quite brown.

The first stretch of the walk is on the initially broad esplanade, which is also a combination of the A3022, the A379, and rush hour: but very flat. So until Hollicombe, where there is a diversion in to a large public garden on the site of the old gasworks, the walk is distinctly noisy. However this has the recompense that, away from the traffic in the park, the silence and space hits you. Crossing the railway on a narrow bridge at the corner of the park, the A roads are left behind and the path soon descends to the first of today's sequence of beaches. The first is the tranquility of North Paignton, where the beach is being hoovered with tractors: the beach huts are totalitarian white with a touch of wild indiscretion in that the doors and the eaves can be any colour [even stripes in the odd outlandish case!]. All appears to be quite seemly in North Paignton, with the day's deckchairs and ice creams at an advanced stage of preparation; very few people are around.

A restrained version of a pier seems to separate North Paignton from South Paignton and it may be that the crowds are just beginning to emerge from their variations of 'Full English Breakfasts', but it does seem to be a somewhat more jazzed- up location. A harbour with hotels ends the stretch of beach, while the path goes round Roundham Head, the most gracious feature of which is the grounds of the house of another wealthy, military family, and again with fine views of Torbay, including the next stretch of the seemingly slightly more genteel beach of Goodrington. I pause for refreshment at the southern-most end and enjoy the vista of families celebrating the pleasures of the English seaside in all its glory.

The exit from Goodrington beach almost immediately goes under the delightful, private, steam railway that runs from Paignton to Dartmouth. But then the path, running parallel to it, rapidly rises, with an elderly consortium making their way to one of the hidden holiday home encampments that lies ahead. My metal tipped walking stick taps on the path behind them. One of the elderly ladies emotes;

'Watch out, Doris; there's somebody coming up in the fast lane.'

The two ladies kindly go into single file so that I can pass by. I overtake.

'Did he indicate, Mavis?' is a passing query.

I thank them both and offer the observation that it is an unrestricted zone!

'Careful, Eric; you've got a fast piece coming up behind you,' is the forwarding cry. The three gentlemen ahead, sporting shorts, walking sticks, and various assortments of spindly legs and head gear, are also kind enough to allow me to fast track; without comment.

There are a couple of humps to the west of the railway, with the valley of the last descent leading you under an impressive short viaduct that carries the train over you, on to Churston, while you descend to the even more select and tranquil beaches of Broadsands and Elberry Cove. At each of these beaches I seem to chat to somebody who says how delightfully warm the sea is; and I do begin to wonder if ploughing along the coast on foot is such a sensible occupation on such a glorious day.

The slightly rocky climb out of Elberry Cove leads into the final stretch of cool, deciduous, woodland. But again there is the sudden shock of emerging from this idyll into a densely packed holiday camp of Churston Cove. The road out of this conurbation runs upwards into a shaded area of conifered parkland with fine views over the large marina of Brixham. The narrow road is almost solidly lined with parked cars at this time of the year; but it is a serious number of steps down into the harbour, which in turn, is a hive of activity: a seething mass of lunch-time feeders; and not just the ever-calling gulls. I opt for the nearest 'little shop' and secure the last copy of The Times, a hefty home-made cheese sandwich, and a bottle of Scottish water. The friendly, rather overweight, owner spots the outfit and chats:

'O yes, I've met people coming the other way on the coastal walk; all the way from Minehead, who say that the next stretch was the worst that they had to cope with': he being the sort of person who delivers this sort of verdict with a certain amount of relish; although his outline suggests that he has no direct experience.

I thank him for this piece of information, and decide that it looks too busy in the harbour, so I walk round it and ascend back to the road on the far side, following the coast, and find a quiet seat there, just in the shade, to enjoy my sandwich where I do not have to fight off the predatory seagulls with my walking stick!

I allow the midday sun to pass over before I move up the hill via the pavement, admiring the colourful views over the harbour and estuary. I follow the signs and eventually pass both the Berry House Hotel and another substantial house when you turn up through woods to Berry Head with more fine vistas across the sweep of Torbay. From here there is a fairly open country park walk with both a coastguard station and extensive WWII fortifications; all of which makes something of a tourist attraction, judging by the cars in the car park.

Fortunately a much quieter footpath to the left of the road, after the cattle grid, leads through rough land to the sight of St Mary's Bay from the cliff tops. As this is where I wish to start tomorrow's challenging walk I head inland along a well-trodden bridleway which eventually hits tarmac in the middle of nowhere. But then I happen to meet a helpful and attractive lady jogger, who is kind enough to direct me to Crendy and Rockingham, whose streets to get you back to the centre of Brixham, where a handsome young man points out the obvious bus station, and a number 12 A bus back to Torquay awaits . Apart from the noise of adolescence on the bus [school leaving time!] all is well with the world; and tomorrow another day.

18 July 2013: Brixham to Kingswear

The Brixham newsagent's warnings grow when, at breakfast, the land lady confirms that one of today's climbs - 'just goes on and on; you think that you have got to the top and then there's another big climb', a pause,

'but I'm sure you'll be alright, you're a real walker', and an encouraging smile. I think my returning smile was somewhat fainthearted.

Then there is the objective official guide which classifies it as:
'strenuous, ascent 2887 ft, with two steep gradients'. [I assume this is divided between a series of climbs].

I presume that this also means a descent of 2887 ft, since one generally starts and finishes at sea level; while my perusal of the map suggests that I could go up and down six times in this prospective day – with no contour detours really feasible. Hey–ho! Two up and downs are quite acceptable: but six does seem excessive.

Nevertheless the weather is set for another fine day [with people dying of the heat back in London according to the papers!]. The number 12 bus runs swiftly to Brixham, scarcely stopping at Paignton bus station [which yesterday's returning bus did in the heat] and in the early morning cool I am back up at St Mary's Bay by 10.00 a.m. to resume yesterday's journey. A disparate group [possibly volunteers and a core of professionals?] of ten or so workers are variously busy making improvements to the coast path; which deserves, and receives, commendation. Then I am off along a fairly open path with occasional views down to the early dog-walkers splashing in the sea below, and a good perspective of the next two bays with their interspersed climbs and descents. I am heartened to say that, at this stage, I have seen several more intimidating climbs, with Haute Tous being, as yet, unsurpassed in its scariness. The first peak, rising from the cliff of the bay, is via a good zig-zag path through woods, whence it opens onto the plateau of Sharkham point, thence a good cliff walk to the longish descent into Man Sands, where there are a row of cottages and a wide-ish stretch of beach and shingle. The beck running out of the cove keeps some of the fields of the valley green for cattle, while the sheep are left to graze the rather brown-looking surrounding hills. The beck also gives rise to some marshy areas with a sprinkling of feathery, white, astilbe, and a whisper of magenta willow- herb.

The sheep are on the other side of the valley, where the path is accessed via a gate behind the cottages. The climb out is steep; made more difficult because there are no steps, with no real places to pause and catch a breath. This is when my St Mark's ash walking stick, with its new aluminium ringed tip, is invaluable: it pushes me up very securely! The view from the top is really only to Scabbacombe Head and back to Brixham; the extensive sweep of Torbay, which has been the centre of walking for the last three days, is now behind me, and out of sight. There is now a pleasant cliff walk above Long Sands, and I promise myself a break when I have made the descent to Scabbacombe Sands. The landscape does really roll in sweeping undulations here, some quite precipitous. There is a landrover parked in one of the fields at an angle that would persuade me to leap out of it; certainly not into it!

Studying the map more carefully at my first rest I realize that, although there is no bus access for today's walk, there are two or three car parks at the end of country lanes. These obviously serve to provide access for the more dedicated bathers, and for less dedicated walkers! Scabbacombe Sands seems to be such a one; a smaller bay, and the stream feeding it again supports swathes of astilbe and willow herb, along with the last few flowers of blue irises, most of them already podding into seed heads. With a breeze blowing and a suitable outcrop of stone it is an idyllic pause. The gentle splashings of the few swimmers in the turquoise coloured water do sound very tempting!

Although there is a steepish climb out of Scabbacombe Sands [with some steps],

189

it does only go half way up the hill, after which there is an almost contour walk through bracken and rocks on a narrow-ish footpath amongst a great sweep of a thinly soil-covered, outcrop of rock. Ascending to one of the higher points of this path there is a stile and gate with 'Devon- Gods own country' [I do not remember an apostrophe?] scrawled in green paint on the top bar of the gate. I sit on the other side of the inscribed gate for lunch in the sun and the breeze, looking out to sea, and the odd steamer tripping between Brixham and Dartmouth, the odd white sail, and the enviable seagull just gliding on the thermals and the breeze. The gate scrawl seems most appropriate, with or without an apostrophe.

I begin to meet a few walkers coming the other way after lunch, most looking very prepared for serious walking, but a couple of middle-aged ladies in open sandals, wondering how far they might go: wondering indeed!

The whole of today's walk has been beset by butterflies, a reflection not only on the time of year, but that much of it is National Trust pasture. The small dark Ringlets seem to be the most prevalent, but there are red admirals, peacocks, fritillaries [flying too fast to tell which variety of fritillary!] and one very striking specimen with the fore wings a bright turquoise, while the rear wings are a glinting carmine/orange. While I note this down I cannot subsequently identify it, so wonder if it is something exotic that has blown in on a high wind. It is only a solitary that I see so, unless its mate is quite inconspicuous, I do not see a whole spread of these breeding here.

Meanwhile my walk dips into Ivy Cove, and next into the wooded terrain of Puddcombe Cove, which seems to be attached to a gated hotel, as suddenly there is a stream of people pottering to the edge of the cliff to view the drop down and the angled layers of rock dramatically jutting up where tectonic plates have thrust against each other. But the woodland is welcome shade, even if it is another sequence of down and up!

After another open stretch and Kelly's Cove, with fine views of the Black Rock and the Mew Stone out at sea, along with Froward Point, the path runs into shady woodland, some of it is conifer plantation with a wide bridle path at more or less one level, making for rapid pleasant progress.

My legs are just beginning to feel a little weary at this stage. However there are yet a couple more sets of down and ups in the woodland before the road leading down into Kingswear is reached. It is somewhat dispiriting to find that here there is a final diversion in the outskirts of the conurbation because a landslip has occurred in town! Legs are distinctly weary now. Nevertheless I follow the well-marked diversion for a certain distance, and then espy an elderly couple with a middle-aged daughter ascending some broad steps in a well-used old alleyway. They are pausing [understandably] about halfway up. But I take them to be locals, and shout down to ask if it is possible to descend to the sea front that way. An affirmative has me scooting down, with the elderly lady adding, 'Now you be careful, dear, don't go too quickly: hold the hand rail !'

I thank her and assure her that I will heed her advice. As if I could really rush at this stage of the day! Still, a magnificent walk, with fine views of Dartmouth Harbour as the final corner was rounded. The detour to the WW2 defence points was interesting but, while being a great supporter of Help for Heroes, I could have done with an option not to make that final down and up to see them: and that almost final signpost by the coastguards' cabin was badly placed. This area could be more clearly signposted for the serious coastal walker, as there are several alternatives. But I am of a mind to say, 'All is well that ends well…'

There is a distinct temptation to take the privately-run steam train back to Paignton which, pleasingly, seems to be well supported. But I decide to wait for the 120 bus to Paignton, as it gives me time to restore fluid balance somewhat before I catch it! Then the 12 bus takes me from Paignton to my base at Torquay .

A leisurely trip back to London tomorrow. A return to Dartmouth is another expedition.

Kingswear from Dartmouth Pier

2 September 2013: Arrive Dartmouth and Strete

Technically, I have neither crossed the river Dart by the ferry, nor have I used the private steam railway from Paignton to Dartmouth; both of which I intended to do. But, since this cluster of walks are designed to get me round to Salcombe, I envisaged that a return rail journey to Totnes left me with better bus connections to Dartmouth and to Kingsbury [upstream from Salcombe]. There are also accommodation problems favouring this choice, as Dartmouth is just finishing regatta week, and therefore booked out; while Salcombe seems rather expensive for the lone walker. However Kingsbury is more accommodating. So, with my preference for using a middle base for a few days of walking, I manage to book in to Roxburgh House in the small village of Strete, the B&B being just opposite the King's Arms, which provides food and refreshment.

Of course it now takes me most of Monday simply to get to my walking base. I begin to develop a touch of Frodo [Lord of the Rings?] as the enormity of his task begins to unfold on his journey after the carefree, jolly send off from Hobbit land. I wonder if there is not some pattern of 'journey psychology', with the initial enthusiastic concept/ vision and its associated planning [I think that I either skipped this phase or just slipped into the journey at pending 70] followed by the excitement of finally starting and beginning to realize a dream: then reality, familiarity; and the enormity [everything is relative!] sets in. Step by step; day by day, section by section, the whole thing has a sort modus operandi whereby the 'task' begins to seem larger than the amazement at the beginning?

All in the mind.

It is the glorious month of September; cool misty mornings with dew on the grass: also shorter, so more precious, evenings: the light gentle, clearer; more bestowed than glaring.

The train is fast and full to Exeter, where a half-hour wait for the Plymouth train which has come cross-country form somewhere like Newcastle via Nottingham? It is also curious that while I am awaiting the announcement of the train arrivals and departures from 5 or 6 busy platforms, I am accompanied by loud speaker information as to what buses are departing from the front of the station forecourt. This may well have been due to diversionary services; but I cannot but think how useful this is; particularly as I have worked out that my X81 bus for Dartmouth leaves Totnes station three minutes after the arrival of my train. A tight manoeuvre even if you know where everything is!

The train is not so full, and I have a window seat that allows me a recap of the river Exe and the coast of Dawlish and Teignmouth, hiving inland to Newton Abbot before dismounting at the surprisingly small station of Totnes. Remembering the clear help at Exeter I optimistically ask a young member of the station staff at Totnes in bright fluorescent orange jacket as to where the X81 to Dartmouth might be.

'Mate, I haven't a clue about the buses', is not enlightening: and makes me think that the Exeter broadcast was only for buses replacing trains! Ah well, one must travel in hope!

In fact there is a bus stop immediately outside the station, with timetables, which include the X81. But it does also seem to be the head of a line of taxis waiting for trade; while on the opposite side of the road there is a large sign indicating and saying, 'left to bus stop B, and 'right to bus stop C', without either of the said stops being visible, or any indication as to the destination of the buses at either stop [very Alice in Wonderland! A white rabbit, with a top hat, running between stops, would not have surprised me].

Nevertheless a double-decker X81 does appear, a few minutes late [it is an hourly service] and stops bumper to bumper with the first taxi. Obviously local rituals prevail!

The ride on the upper deck from Totnes to Dartmouth is peerless; the only equivalent being the ride from Wooler to Swanage some time ago. The road, more like a lane, is perilously narrow, but the roll of the countryside, the sweeps of the coast, and the sublime spread of the Mediterranean blue sea are second to none. Of course most of the corn is now gathered, so the patchwork of golden stubble is decorated with stripes of unbaled straw, or dotted with the enormous rolled bales, emphasizing that all is well with this year's harvest.

Dartmouth is as charming as I remember it; a well-boated place on a curving, wooded and castled estuary: still bustling from regatta week. After lunch at one of the many hostelries I return to the buses on the promenade, where the 93 to Plymouth will drop me off at the small village of Strete. The bus seems to be quite full, but does drop about eighty per cent of its cargo at Stoke Fleming which, I later learn, has more copious immobile accommodation sites tucked away. I am welcomed to my B&B with tea and cake in a delightful small garden; a most civilized end to the journey: and end up writing these notes higher up in the far corner of the church graveyard with the sight and smell of new-mown grass mingling with the sea air.

The King's Arms is closed on Mondays; but I came prepared: salmon and cucumber sandwiches from a well-known store in Dartmouth are quite sufficient!

3 September 2013: Dartmouth to Strete

Suitably refreshed, I was early for the 9.38 version of the 93 to Dartmouth. In this I was accompanied by the somewhat gaunt, tweeded, eighty-two year old figure of Brian, with the scuffed shoes of a bachelor, and who, from time to time, withdrew and nibbled a cluster of peas from his left pocket, having clandestinely shelled them in his pocket. Realising I had detected this manoeuvre he furtively smiled and offered 'They keep me going', followed by a pause and a slight shuffle of the scuffed shoes: 'You have to keep planting them every three weeks to keep a good supply', another pause; 'These are a late variety', pause. 'Most people plant them all at once. It's a big mistake'.

The pauses have gone and there is a twinkle in his eye as he decides that I am an acceptable audience: so I am similarly entertained all the way to Dartmouth on the late 9.38.

'Are yer goin upstairs?' he asked as I waited for him to get on. My affirmative was in the expectation that, at his age, he would stay down stairs.

194

'Well will yer carry mi bag up, then I can come up too? I'm 82 yer know' [this being when I discovered his age].

I readily concur, resisting telling him that he is only some seven years older than I am, as I am obviously deemed young enough to carry his bag along with my own walking paraphernalia, to the upper deck. Thereafter I am instructed and enlightened by his local knowledge: that this farm on the right has been in the same family for over two hundred years: that the A road bends sharply here because that apparent cattle trough in the adjacent field is actually on the site of a spring: and that I will come out just here on my walk back, and it is easier to follow the sheep tracks than the steep footpath.

These facts, along with the state of the hay, corn, and silage harvest continuously inform me and the only other passenger on the upper deck until we reach the Dartmouth front again. Having taken leave of Brian [the bus having filled at Stoke Fleming again], I make a quick pilgrimage to the Newcomen [a famous engineer!] Shrine in the Tourist Information Office. An impressive pumping machine is the centre piece, precursor of many, designed to keep the mines dry.

At last I am free to saunter along the quayside, past the Kingswear Ferry, view the fortifications of Bayards Cove and start my ascent via an alleyway of steps to the road leading up to the castle. There are several alternatives here, either staying down to visit the castle and St Petroux church, or a higher course which can cut out the former, and also the up and down to Sugary Cove. The hillside here is well-covered with deciduous woodland so that sea views tend to be glimpses, while the rocky coves and the copious covering of gullies with ivy give a distinct feel of the Victorian Gothic. Escaped blue hydrangeas seem to relish this environment, and seem at their best in September.

A local coming up from Combe Bay kindly stops me from unnecessarily descending to Combe Bay, as the sign posting for the coastal path is not very clear here. So I keep to a good height, viewing a small colony of cormorants out on Meg Rocks, and sweeping views back to Kingswear and Scabbacombe Head, while the long curve of Slapton Sands runs far away to Start Point lighthouse to the west. But that is far ahead – and my present stretch runs into open pasture which is National Trust property, grazed by Corriente cattle, some of which are white with distinctive black ears and muzzle: a sort of bovine-reverse-panda; but quite docile and graceful, with their small, fine bones.

195

I think that this is my favourite type of coastal walking as the broad sweep of the pathway makes for complete foot security, allowing freedom for constant appreciation of the views, enhanced by the lie of the land. True to most NT property there are butterflies a plenty; Large Whites, some Clouded Yellows, with their black edged wings, and the occasional Brown Skipper.

This walk is quite popular as it leads to a car park at Down Farm. Walking south and slightly inland from this the single track road to Stoke Fleming is a pleasant and fairly fast walk; but somewhat hazardous as the sides of the road are often quite high, with nowhere for the pedestrian to go when a vehicle approaches! This quiet road leads directly in to the busy A 379 which you zip across into the Stoke Fleming playing field. There is then a well-signposted diversion through the various lanes and pedestrian walkways of Stoke Fleming, rather than following the main road. But eventually the walker crosses the A 379 again on the far side of the village, sneaking down another narrow lane by the side of the church, passing the wrought iron, stone-pillared, gates of the secluded manor house, and finally running down to open onto the longish stretch of Blackpool Bay: not strictly comparable to its northern namesake as the latter really does have 'golden sands', whereas here it is very fine shingle!

However, as it is still school holidays, this bay is popular – and also has a large car park and accompanying facilities. Thankfully, it is separated from the A379 by sloping woodland, through which the official coastal path wanders, albeit close to both beach and road. Nevertheless it is very clear when it again crosses the A379 by a cluster of thatched cottages [probably all that remains of Old Blackpool?] to run down the side of a field to a small beck with a narrow, original, stone packhorse bridge. I peer over the right side of the bridge, wondering if there might be fish: a boyhood memory of darting shoals. But nothing; it all looks a little too cloudy. However on the left side, downstream, I am rewarded with the sight of a nine-inch, solitary trout, putting in a modest effort to stay stationary in the fast-running current.

I also head upstream, climbing signposted steps to emerge through woodland into open downland, decorated with occasional conifers; one of which has fallen, thus providing a suitable seat for lunch with a sea view!

While sitting here, perusing my map, I am passed by a group of five walkers, each with a seemingly different version of where the path goes in this open downland. I suggest that they continue up the hill to the scarcely visible stile at the top edge of the field. This they variously do; the view dictating that they spread in different direction to take photographs of the bay, the cliffs, and the conifers. By the time that they have reconvened at the top I am replenished and ascend to the stile. After another conference I observe that they have headed off left, still in the field. When I reach the stile I see their dilemma. The signpost, this side of the stile, does indicate that the coastal path is to the left: but the ordnance survey map has the dotted red line running left inside the rather neglected cart track the other side of the stile. I negotiate the stile and wonder who is right as the lane seems very unused and overgrown. However there is a partially hidden sign further on indicating that the 'official coastal path' goes left for a hundred yards down a drive to a private property, then turns right into another open field, whose exit is also somewhat convoluted.

No sign of the other intrepid five walkers anywhere.

I negotiate a short length of woodland, back into a field and then an exit to the busy A379 again; with an immediate crossing into the sheep field that eighty two year old Brian had told me about on my earlier bus trip. At least I now know that I am on the right path! I follow Brian's advice and follow the contour sheep track rather than the precipitous footpath [having observed that the flock is safely tucked in a shady corner of the valley]. Once down the considerable gully, the stream is easily crossed, and I ascend up to the gorse level on the other side, meeting several dog walkers with dogs off leads; contravening clear notices for a field full of sheep!

As I move off into the shade at the top of this stretch I look back and spy the intrepid five walking photographers just emerging to cross the A379: for once I am the hare. I do an obligatory wave of the hand, but do not feel up to seeing how they deal with the next stretch! It seems worse than watching the House of Commons in action. I realize why I choose to walk on my own!

It is then a pasture land walk, populated by larger bovines, seemingly complacent and authoritative in equal measure, to the village of Strete, where more delightful tea and cake await.

4 September 2013: Strete to Torr Cross

Today was really a holiday from walking, partly because I thought that Strete to Salcombe in a day might be more of a penance than a pleasure, and also because I was walking early from the doorstep without the delay of a bus journey. The overall result was that I arrived at Torr Cross in time for coffee and, amidst the short string of cafés that make up most of the sea front, treated myself to a Devonshire cream tea, with clotted cream and jam: which seemed like a wicked variation of having a gin and tonic before 6.00pm. But it was something of a misty morning and almost a day off!

It was also a flat walk to Torr Cross, the most of it being along Slapton Sands. However before the descent to this beach there is virtually a mile of dry-stone-walled A379 to negotiate with some blind corners. The guide book rightly describes this as dangerous. Even periscopes to poke round corners would not solve all the problems as there are some straight stretches which are only one-way in traffic width yet have estate walls that seem to be two storeys high to the pedestrian. The strategy is to look and dart; hovering in between times. I would hate to have to try and navigate a group of walkers through this patch!

But immediately after a wider passing place there is a welcome coastal path sign post for a hedged track leading downwards, away from the road and towards the mile and a half of the Slapton beach. However, just as the track reaches the beach the A379 comes careering in again from the right. Fortunately it is open road here without any enclosing walls and there is even a pedestrian path either side of the road traffic; with each pathway set some yards away from the road. Sporadic vehicles do belt along this open road, but the walker has the freedom to observe midst the sea, sky and sand scape, the rich flora of the tall lavender blue spires of viper buma, its smaller cousin, some second flowering of pink armeria, a scattering of small yellow antirhinums, mixed with the muted mustard of sea parsley.

Across the road lie the inland waters of Slapton Ley, much reeded at their northern end, while the open waters at the Torr Cross end have swans and coots making a living. This is a big contrast to yesterday's cliffs and butterflies: here it is a repeat of Chesil Beach and its inland waters, with appropriate fowl and flora. However I have not come across a stretch of water being called a ley before: perhaps a corruption of lee or lea, and was it a sometime sea marsh meadow..?

The easy walk along the sea side is only interrupted by a cenotaph-like structure, [and attendant car park] that commemorates that this whole bay, along with its neighbouring villages and farms, was totally cleared in WW2 so that the Americans could practice manoeuvres for the D- Day landings. This reminder is augmented by the installation of one of their tanks in the public car park behind the short esplanade at Torr Cross.

WW II tank at Torr Cross

Having savoured my clotted cream scone on the esplanade I view the steps rising at the end of the walkway and I consider heading for Start Point Lighthouse. But I would only have to retrace my steps as it is on one of those isolated corners of the coastline where there is no public transport. Fortunately my landlady at Strete had said that the small village of Slapton was well worth a visit on a return journey; and so it turns out. It involves trekking back along the A379, but this time along the edge of the mere [or ley!] with the track being lower than and further from the road. Then, shortly after the road turns off to Slapton there is a gate leading to a footpath hugging the edge of the ley, through reeds and woodland, with suitably placed seats to quietly contemplate life in all its presentations; sea, sky, ley and inner musings. Today is a holiday!

One reward of this quiet sitting is to see a solitary grebe emerge from the thicket of reeds. I feel sure that a mate and a nest must be hidden somewhere.

The path is quiet, secluded, and a nature reserve; with notices and huts indicating that it is used by local groups: even a college. As the path meanders it eventually passes the first of several substantial houses, rises to a hard-surfaced road and into the village, where a three-isled church dedicated to St James the Great also reveals that the prosperity of the village owes much to De Brien's eminence in the court of Edward III.

Amongst the many attractive houses there are also two attractive inns; one of which provides me with lunch and time to catch up on international news and complete a Sudoku or two.

The road back to the A379 is without event, but the 93 bus, due at 16.30, is a full 30 minutes late; which I discover, along with my two fellow walkers, is due to the fact that school has just started, so the bus is heaving with the local St Trinian's [which, of course, has now gone co-ed]. I dismount thankfully at Strete, and buy the locally made eccles cakes at the local post office to get me round the corner of Start Point lighthouse tomorrow, knowing that the farmhouse that I have booked is too busy with the harvest to be able to provide an evening meal. Tomorrow is a working day of walking! Meanwhile – across the road at Strete to the King's Arms for an excellent crab salad and a glass or two of pinot grigio.

5 September 2013: Torr Cross to Lannacombe Bay

A clear light blue sky, a wisp of high strata clouds, the hint of a breeze: a day made for the work of serious walking. I am well stocked with eccles cakes, sandwiches, and water: also carrying all my luggage. I wave to eighty-two-year-old-Brian as I mount the 9.39 version of the 93 bus [he patiently waiting to make his daily trip into Dartmouth: quietly shelling peas in his pocket as ever] and watch with some trepidation as an elderly lady driver has to reverse in the narrow stretch of the high walled part of the A379 that I negotiated on foot yesterday. Then we zoom along Slapton Sands for me to be dropped off at Torr Cross. No time for coffee this morning. It is straight up the steps, past the old hotel that has been converted into apartments; negotiate the various zig-zags that are fairly well-signposted and described in the guide, to lead on to a comfortable path through headland and woodland. Thereafter there is a vista of the bay of Bee Sands and the prospect of a well-stepped descent.

A young couple are standing at the head of the steps enjoying the view along with a border collie cross that, with pricked ears, is looking down the steps. After exchanging pleasantries the couple instruct the dog, 'Go find mother!', from which I assume 'mother' is ascending someway behind. A further exhortation does not result in the dog moving; so, not standing on niceties, I begin my descent. Surely enough, halfway down, I meet a largeish, white-haired lady, understandably, labouring over the climb. The allusion to the fact that a collie faithfully awaits her at the top also reveals that she is the local rector for all the local churches; this pathway being well endowed with notices advertising Sunday teas at St Andrew's of Bee Sands, 'the Chapel by the Sea', which I am to see, amidst other secular competition, some minutes later. Meanwhile the collie has descended to check out that all is in order, and that 'mother' is not being accosted!

I part with the happy reunion and complete my descent: the beach is virtually deserted at this time of day. The path runs into the shore front street of Bee Sands, with its 'Cricketer's' pub. At the end of the street the coastal path runs up behind the last house to rise over cliffs, giving a good view back to Dartmouth. It soon leads to the bay of Hall Sands. The guide reads as if this is a deserted village. But in fact it is only two or three cottages on the cliff edge that have been abandoned, [waiting to fall into the sea?]. Elsewhere much seems to have been recovered and redeveloped.

Life is beginning to stir here, with a smattering of walkers emerging from cars to tackle this scenic and not-too-taxing stretch of the coastal path. A fairly wide path saunters out of the village towards the Start Point peninsula, attracting a sprinkling of walkers. Here, a younger couple act as hare to my tortoise, as they overtake me, then the young lady stops to take careful photographs of the views. He waits patiently; and I overtake them again; and this is repeated; until it becomes something of a cheery game.

The anticlimax, but perhaps the climax for some, is to reach the peak of the cliff climb before it descends to the lighthouse, only to find that there is a fairly large car park; which siphons off most of the walkers: but probably adds an equal number. From here there is a single track road down to the lighthouse, open for visits today, and run by two tall, impressively competent ladies; one with a very deep voice.

It is an appropriate site to take in the views. Now you can see westwards to Prawle Point as well as back to Dartmouth, and also see the strange wave patterns that the submerged extension of the coast cause, justifying the presence of a warning lighthouse. Sitting watching, I spy a large buzzard out in the bay; an unusual sight out at sea, and one that attracts several pairs of binoculars.

Back-tracking from the lighthouse about a quarter of a mile, the coastal path sign post points to a spiny ridge [it also says 168 miles to Poole and 462 to Minehead; at least I have done the former, and more!]. Crossing over this ridge is something of a shock. Not only is there a very bracing head wind, but the comfort of a tarmac track changes to a very narrow, steep, and irregular path, with it being very apparent that all the contours are quite closely packed, and that the sea, very visibly, is bumping merrily on sharp rocks someway below. Moreover, there is suddenly nobody else in sight. I have a regrouping moment, and am extremely thankful that I have my faithful ash walking stick with me to negotiate the trickier bits of the path, stepping over sharp edged jutting rocks, on a steep bit of downward incline. Thankfully the path widens and levels out by Sleaden rocks where I sit and enjoy my lunch of oranges and the first of the eccles cakes. I am entertained by a cow seal gyrating on one of the rocks just off the coast, while a splendid bull, some nine to ten feet in length, spreads his considerable bulk on a higher rock like a huge, lounging, prop forward. Had I not stopped, and had my binoculars, I might have missed this treat, as the sunbathing motionless bull blended perfectly into his rocky, sea-weeded, background.

While I am enjoying my frugal lunch, a couple pass in the opposite direction, the youngish lady wearing open decorated sandals. I warn of the hazards round the corner; but the rather older partner reassures me that he did it ten years ago with one son on his back, and the other leaping around like a mountain goat. I realise that my stick and I are somewhat geriatric: but am later reassured of my appropriate caution by my good landlady for the night, whose husband farmer also deputises as a coastguard. They had a young man break his leg on this stretch only yesterday. The noble farmer and his son had to climb down and stretcher him to a place where a helicopter could pick him up. Be warned!

Lunch over, two wheatears play their enticing 'follow me – hither and thither' trick of short darting flights, always two rocks ahead. But as they head downwards to the cliff edge I resist their supplications! Mythology is full of such seductions!

It is now a comfortable path again, more or less on a contour, with a couple of beaches down below. The second of these is Lannacombe Bay, and I anticipate there being a path up to Down Farm where I am hoping to stay for the night. Initially I walked past this turning; but it was as well, because on the beach there was a large notice declaring that the coastal path in front of Ivy Cottage was closed due to a recent landslip, with a two-mile diversion initially going up the valley in the direction of Down Farm. I am just so pleased that I had planned not to try and make Salcombe in a day! As it is I am safely ensconced in a pleasant room with a sea view, all in time for a welcome cup of afternoon tea; and, having written these notes, scoffed more sandwiches and eccles cakes, I am early to bed as I knew the farmer's wife was too busy with harvest to offer an evening meal; and there is no local village within walking distance.

6 September 2013: Lannacombe Bay to Salcombe

Early to bed is early to rise: and amidst the quiet of the countryside, there is the sound of men and machines getting ready for harvest, including the arrival of a large, white, twelve-wheeler truck, which, being empty, had considerable difficulty getting a grip to rise up the slight incline on the track. However the noise gets me up early; through a very good breakfast, with delicious local produce, and on my way, with no bus to wait for. Emerging from the farmyard I pass the twelve-wheel truck being heaped full of golden corn. This is modern farming; gone are the reaping and stooking of my youth [thank goodness!]. The harvest is safely in much more quickly; with much expensive machinery replacing the man-power: progress.

Egress from the farm and picking up the diversion take me through some quiet fields, including a steepish climb that brings me splendid views landward across to the moors, with a tinge of purpling heather, and predicated by a patchwork of harvested fields, golden stubble, dotted with the great rolled straw bales from today's machines: the whole landscape a delightful contrast to my diet of sea and cliffs. The hedge of one field also houses a chirping flock of greenfinches; methinks gathering to migrate; this echoed by a group of swallows darting over an isolated farm pond, gathering the last of the summer's insects.

The diversion from the coast is somewhat circuitous, avoiding farmsteads and country retreats; so it is 9.45 before I find myself back on the original path, west of Ivy Cottage. The going is initially good, but then, around Ballsaddle Rocks becomes a jagged, rocky path, much hidden in bracken, which slows me down to bottom gear. It is all about watching where feet are placed: no admiring the view! But fortunately the land soon opens out again and the path borders fields with beef cattle and 'following stock' grazing the 'set aside' borders of harvested corn fields, [set aside= EU regulations?].

Amidst this rugged cliff and agricultural idyll it is something of a surprise to come across the splendor of Maelcombe House, with its paddock sized sweeping lawns and haunches of bunched, blue, hydrangeas; some of them of the lace cap variety. The contrast to this apparent grandeur, in the moderate and modest distance, is to see a camper bathing au naturelle with a bucket of water as a shower: certainly a variation from the seals and buzzard of yesterday!

Today's hare and tortoise game is played with five strapping young ladies, with an obvious team leader, who overtake me in the vicinity of the bather without batting an eyelid. But then two furlongs further on the young ladies have stopped for coffee and the thermos flasks are out: and I pass by. Then as I reach what I think is my half-way of Prawle Point I see that they are back in format and devouring the ground between us. But, lo and behold, on a raised viewing point I see two figures waving to me. As I get nearer and they descend I see that it is the jolly couple of hares from yesterday who kept stopping to take photographs. I do have to blink twice, wondering quite how they can have got so far ahead of me this morning without me seeing them. But all is explained after greetings. They have in fact been camping near to the local village of East Prawle – and had driven back there last night after yesterday's walk. Now they are but indulging in very local scenery before driving back to Bristol. We part with good wishes for our different prospects!

Meanwhile today's five young, female, hares storm past; but it has broken the ice, and at the top of Prawle Point one of the five ladies does volunteer to photograph me with a view of the interesting geology; on my own camera – I hasten to add. I thank her, but say that I am really only interested in the geology – and that there are already rather too many images of self at home! The selfie, with or without scenery, is not my thing! They proceed to hare away, and I subsequently only catch distant visions of their formation marching in the rest of the morning, forever getting more and more distant. It is my day of being the tortoise that does not get there first!

The other good side to all these jollities is that I have arrived at Prawle Point by 11.00 am, when I thought that it might be lunchtime before I arrived. Much of this speed is probably due to the fact that I did not have to spend time waiting for, and journeying on, a bus.

While this good progress gives me an excuse simply to sit and enjoy the view, I am to find that the easy stretch of the walk is behind me. To the west of Prawle Point the coast is dramatically rugged, with the path narrow, up and down, presenting some quite tricky rocky hurdles to clamber over, as yesterday's landlady had warned. I persevere, waiting at passing places for eastern traffic, psychologically feeling that this is not the place to feast on the home-made ham sandwich and apple that the farmer's wife kindly provided for me. I will save them as a prize for traversing this spectacular, if somewhat unnerving section. I negotiate Gammon Head, Ham's Stone, and Pig's Head without reference to the sandwiches, [but somehow am reminded of them!], but under similar geological challenge. This section definitely challenges my sense of vertigo. It is not until I finally descend to the bay below the apartments of the old Gara Rock Hotel that I feel relaxed enough to find a comfortable corner of a stone wall to sit and enjoy the scenery, the golden beach, the bathers in the blue - turquoise sea: and my lunch. I can taste the mustard on home-smoked ham and home-baked bread: delicious.

The upward exit from the bay is broad, and care has to be taken not to get carried up on the well-worn path to the apartments on the cliff top. The coastal path remains somewhat lower and narrower, but does rise to give clearer views of the entrance to Salcombe Harbour. As the river mouth is approached there is a series of options, with one path going up again to Rickham Common. But I take the wooded descent into the bay which circumnavigates a distinctly sandy bay and meanders through expensive looking suburbia to the ferry. Although the river mouth is most attractively wooded and sanded, Salcombe seems more of a monoculture than the buzz of Dartmouth: both are quite trippery after the quiet of coastal walking! I had also found it difficult to find accommodation here – so had booked upstream at Kingsbridge via the 164 bus from Salcombe. I find Kingsbridge to be altogether a place with more variety of character. It is also more suitable for the X81 bus back to Totnes, thence trains to Exeter and London.

I think the season closes here!

2014: MORE OF DEVON

21 April, 2014: a return to Kingsbridge

For some reason it has seemed an enormous break since my last walk. The winter of 2013/4 was the most persistently wet and windy [repeated gales!] for over a century. Because it was Gulf Stream driven it also went with being fairly mild: there was no frost in Primrose Hill, London. But the devastation to the south-west coast from the constant battering was serious [this ignores the flooding of much of the Somerset plain, - but that was not on my coastal walk!]. Brunel's dramatic coastal railway past Dawlish and Teignmouth, that I had passed by last year, succumbed, with stretches of the concrete defences and walkways down, while collapses of part of the rail track severed this important artery of the south west rail network for 6-8 weeks. Even now, although the rail track is repaired and running, there are still extensive repairs needed, [and underway], for the outer fortifications. The impressive walkway between rail and sea that I completed in the mist with Steve last year, will be closed for some time – as I am to learn from other walkers that I meet at Totnes.

All this trauma, the weathermen suggest, might be due to the biennial oscillation in the stratosphere, of forces way above the southern wandering 'jet stream'. The current alignment of these two poorly understood effects [they are but observed rather than explained!] are blamed for the current season of devastation. The whole countryside has been hammered: and the pattering feet of the lone walker are put into due perspective! How powerful the elements are.

However April, so far, has had relatively little rain; and mother earth has rebounded in plentitude. Now the fields are verdant, some pimpled with the yellow flowers of rape seed, which in another week will be brazen in their bright shout. Trees break leaf in delicate pale greens; making exquisite shapes in their tracery.

So I am bound in the Great Western 'Matilda' to Totnes, viewing the still traumatized defences at Dawlish, and arriving and alighting along with a group of four other walkers who are going to Salcombe. We find a taxi driver who delights in telling us that there are no buses on bank holidays! He, fortunately, is joking, albeit a two hour wait; but the group try bartering a reduced taxi fare to Salcombe to no avail. I cross the busy road and spy Castle Road curving up to none other than a castle [!]: whence a short climb through narrow streets and alleyways finds me at a quiet paved courtyard with a large cherry tree in the middle and two benches: moreover the walls shelter from the chilling breeze. A mixture of bluebells, yellow, glistening, celandines, and an odd rhubarb plant add to the charm of the square, as does the view over the town and out to the surrounding hills.

Two hours slip by, a chunk of a Rose Tremain novel and a scan of a score of a Shostakovitch quartet that I have just acquired, more than compensate for the rather persistently noisy kids [including one public nappy change at fairly close quarters!] on the train journey: tranquility restored!

I leave time to wait for the bus, and find out, from the fellow walkers, that the ferry was not available when they had tried the River Avon crossing to Bantham [they are doing the South Coast Walk in the conventional anticlockwise manner]. I hope to get to Bantham on this visit – and make a note to check availability – as the guide recommends; otherwise it is an eight-mile detour on foot up the river Avon, [not to be recommended if you have booked accommodation in advance]!

The X64 to Kingsbridge and Salcombe turns up on time; the freedom pass works its magic, and, even on a single decker bus, the scenery is impressive. I arrive at the Kings Arms, Kingsbridge, while the intrepid four rumble onwards to Salcombe. The hotel has had a change of management since I was last here, and has upgraded. The building has echoes befitting its name. It belongs to that ancient class of hostelry in market towns that were comfortably grand, running through from a bow-windowed formal front on the High Street to a lesser road at the back of the premises for the tradesmen's entrance. Between the two entrances lies a labyrinth of rooms, corridors with inner windows, arches and doors that could have led to kitchens, stables or cellars: yet with a gracefully bannistered staircase rising out of this complexity, as I remember from my last visit when I stayed in a small room on the first floor. But this time I am on the ground floor at the back [en suite stable block?] with a personal [but not private] wooden-decked patio!

22 April 2014: Salcombe to Inner Hope

The place names make it sound more like a spiritual quest than a coastal walk: but it is primarily the latter!

The forecast for the day is 'variable' weather; and so it turns out to be alternating sea mist, sometimes clearing to sun. But the bus station runs smoothly. For today the somewhat infrequent 606 to Salcombe is on time and, having done this trip in reverse at the end of last year, I am reminded of the sequence of narrow junctures at West Alvington, where local traffic is very civilized about giving way; but I do wonder what happens in the tourist season?

As the official guide has prescribed today's walk as 'strenuous', [and my last walk certainly felt that!], I have deliberately programmed a relatively early start, so that by 9.25a.m. I am back at the Salcombe ferry, having confirmed that, although much quieter than my last visit, it is a rather upmarket place with so many shops selling expensive striped nautical attire, or designer dresses. The new houses in the estuary also speak of wealth; although with names such as 'Periwinkle', 'Sunshine Cliff Hotel', 'Fort Charles', one does begin to wonder whether wealth is everything.

While the official guide apologizes for the first part of the walk being on the road, in fact the lane is a quiet, narrow, and relatively verdant, winding route, with attractive views over the estuary; providing that there is no traffic!

The bays of both North and South Sands are tranquil coves, virtually confluent; but with every sign that they are being developed at an equally rapid rate. Nevertheless the National Trust acorn clearly indicates the route to follow, upwards and outwards onto the cliffs. However the instruction to 'keep ahead' at Overbeck car park is somewhat ambiguous, but the acorn sign post is clear, and a younger couple catch me up at that point and confirm that the lower route is the official coastal path, which they had covered yesterday; while today they are taking the high route over the top: a timely meeting for me!

The tarmac rapidly tapers into a rough, narrower path, running into gothic woods where the rich green under foliage of wild garlic is peppered with white flower buds: fortunately too early for perfume!

It is a shame that I hit sea mist here at Sharp Tor, on the very lips of the estuary,

208

as there must be fine views back across to Prawle Point. The ensuing 'Courtney Walk' is a dramatic change, the path and steps being starkly carved out of rocky outcrops, but all safely enclosed either by dry stone walls, or metal hand rails. All very reassuring after the unprotected walk round Gammon Head at the end of last year!

I meet nobody at this stage with the mist and the bleak, craggy rocks a dramatic contrast to the comfortable chic of Salcombe. The stark contours of Bolt Head beg for the relief of some grazing sheep; but the dotted, sporadic grey white shapes all turn out to be rocky outcrops rather than sheep. Nevertheless relief lies round the corner, as it runs into Warren Walk, with my favourite type of open walk through cliff top grassland, where vistas of sea and sky can be constantly appreciated while walking; the most dangerous hazard being the odd cow pat [why, when they have acres of grassland to fertilise, do they choose to deposit their trademark on a well-worn footpath!?]. But this is an enjoyable stretch, covered at a good pace.

It is noticeable that the considerable spread of gorse has been beaten brown by the winter gales. Only on the landside are there shoots of prickly green, bearing a few clusters of their bright yellow flowers. But nature's resilience is not to be underestimated; the pasture is as a starry sky with glistening golden celandines: and the mist has cleared to sunshine: even the sea is now blue green again. I actually spot a small flock of wheatears, popping out of the spread of dead gorse, and dropping variously into the nearby pasture: a real feel that they have just arrived from Spain or North Africa; and are a little wing- weary!

I have a short break [it is too chilly to rest long in the mist, which has reappeared], and observe an outcrop of rock in the sea just past Steeple cove which is home to both breeding gulls and cormorants, the latter in a minority. It is curious to see this sharing; and I would be even more curious to see whether the dynamic is stable, or whether it changes over the years? My intuition is that the gulls are pushing the cormorants out, even as they might take cormorant offspring for breakfast?

There is a steepish descent to Soar Mill Cove, with some slippage of the path inland. The secluded beach has no road access, but there is a Lowry-like splattering of figures, who, I guess, are all from a discreetly hidden hotel, higher up the valley. For the onward walker it is another stint of up and down, with the adjacent, scrubby, hawthorns [hedge size] bravely sporting their small white flowers- April rather than May blossom.

As the sun is trying its best to get back to us, I manage lunch on a welcome seat at Cathole cliff, whence it is a pleasant walk on wards, slightly dipping down and up between West Cliff and Bolberry Down, between which another desirable hotel is located; this also seems to serve as a local car park for walkers doing various circular routes in this area. Heading westward the view suddenly opens onto the headland of Bolt Tail and the vista of Bigbury Bay. The famous Burgh Island, with its dramatic nineteen-thirties' hotel, tidally isolated twice a day, with access only via a very large-wheeled tractor, is visible in the distance, sitting opposite the cluster of houses that make up Bigbury-on-Sea: a future destination.

But I am ahead of myself, for below Bolt Tail lies Hope Cove, host to both Inner and Outer Hope connurbations, and my destination for the day. I have impressed myself that I have completed this walk both enjoyably and in good time: confidence restored. Bolt Tail has the geology of, but only remnants of, an iron-age settlement, bolstered by contemporary stone walling: but even so, looking somewhat scarred by the winter's battering. It is a stroll down through pasture and woodland to Inner Hope, carefully watching a dog-walker emerge from the wood to put his greyhound on a running lease as they emerge into the field full of grazing sheep with new-born lambs. We exchange pleasantries as we cross. A 'rescue dog', he confides, who is very timid. I believe him, but you just never know, and I was glad to see timidity on a lead!

Hope Cove is charming, with Easter holiday families sand-castling and paddling on the beach. It is still too chilly for swimming: and I decide that I deserve refuge at the appropriately named Hope and Anchor Inn until the evening 162 arrives at Inner Hope to take me [as the only passenger] back to Kingsbridge via Galmpton and Marlborough: the bus driver a serious photographer in his spare time!

An evening follows in the King's Arms of guitar, mainly electronic, and folk singing, some American, along with a hearty tapas menu. It is one of those evenings.

23 April 2014: Outer Hope to Bantham: St George's Day

This is really only half a day's walk, but I need to do some reconnoitering for the next stretch, where a ferry crossing to Bigbury is much to be desired in order to avoid an

8 mile detour round the Avon estuary!

I wake to the patter of rain on the window: a tweaked curtain reveals an ominously uniformly grey sky; but the wind is blowing at a fair pace. This is not according to the forecast, and could mean that I am in for a seriously damp day's walking; or that it might clear. Fortunately, by the time that I have caught the 8.50 version of the 162 bus [only three buses a day], and have arrived at Inner Hope, it is the latter; and the sky and sea are as mediterranean magazines portray them: just as I left it yesterday; but doubly appreciated because it could so easily have been otherwise.

I need to pick up this rare species of the 162 bus later in the day at Thurlestone, where it seems to stop at either the church or the school, but not both! So I try to determine from the driver which it might be. He does not quite grasp the focus of my question, but a substantial young fellow, wearing a Warwick University Rugby Club top, googles the timetable on his mobile, nods, and comes up with, 'Oh if you're there, just stick your hand out and they'll stop'. The bus driver concurs: somewhat different from London I think to myself!

Alighting at Inner Hope I re-cover the short path to Outer Hope and veer towards the cliff path out of the village, only to find red striped tape and 'slippage/diversion' notices. The diversion leads up the narrow lane, heading inland, then, just after a right turn to Inner Hope, there is a left hand driveway giving access to houses higher up on the hill. This is the diversion, and runs as a driveway until it peters out into a narrower footpath, which eventually rejoins the original cliff path.

But the pounding winter has really taken its toll here, for, no sooner does the walk open into countryside than there is another diversion – with 'no through way' to Southdown and its beach. Somehow the diversion notice has been moved past the actual new turning. But I meet a couple from the Midlands who have already been warned about this anomaly, and we jointly retrace our steps. The diversion is along a well-rutted cart track [I think they are now definitely the size of tractor tracks!?] that leads on to a minor road with fine views to the coast and across to Thurlestone. So it is fast walking but, with the high hedge banks full of the starry white flowers of goose grass, it leaves you nowhere to go if you meet traffic! The couple from the Midlands zoom like hares into the distance. I am definitely the losing tortoise again.

211

Even after the arrival at Southdown Beach extensive wide diversions are in hand, with access to the beach through the unstable sand dunes being restricted to a single opening. However there is a small café, well behind the dunes, that has survived, where you can restore your confidence with refreshment!

Behind this there is low flat land – which is under conservation as sea marsh; much to be approved! But the downside of this is that, if you walk along the beach to access the cliffs and golf course of Thurlestone, you have to cross the beck that is the outlet for these sea marshes. If the tide is fairly well out [as it was] then it is an interesting judgement of where the lowest spread of the out-going beck water is against the unpredictable in rushes of sea waves; along with how wet you are prepared to have your socks! I observe a younger guy make his mistakes, and I therefore manage rather better. His lady friend remains unconvinced by either of our attempts; so he has the ignominy of having to cross back as well! Travelling solo can have its advantages!

Fortunately the hand-railed steps to exit the beach at the Thurlestone end have survived, although the path across to the edge of the large golf course is also being reconstructed after the winter's damage. The weather now being fine, the golf course is dotted with figures; but it is a fine, and quite popular, walk round the edge of the course; with the occasional buzzard hovering over the cliffs: sea pinks are already in full flower here.

The headland gives fine views across the Avon estuary, to Bigbury, Burgh Island, and coast curving away to the Plymouth Sound.

Burgh Island & Bigbury

Both sides of the Avon mouth seem to be quite popular on this sunny day: walkers of varying ability, various clusters, with and without children, with and without dogs, decorate the hillside and the coast. I descend – feeling something like the man going to St Ives, when, in the relative crowd, I pass the couple from the Midlands coming back up the hill. I think this is the worst case of the 'hare and the tortoise' game to date. It is one thing to be overtaken and eventually catch up: but to meet somebody coming back before you have arrived is the most de trop yet!

Nevertheless I do not let this spoil my enjoyment of the scenery, including the sight of the large-wheeled blue tractor crossings the sands and sea from Burgh Island to Bigbury by the sea. This sand dune entrance to the river is all part of the 'Evans Estate', with frequent notices to remind you of this; and to behave at all times: 'DO NOT' notices all over the place: even warnings about adders!

However, by the land entrance gate to the estate, opposite the ticket sentry hut, there is a small oasis of grass with a couple of seats, one with a gentle view of the river. Here I have my sandwich and water; seeing both small white and orange tip butterflies; while white daisies, yellow celandines, early purple blue ajuga, and escaped pink columbines in the bottom of the hedge, all make me wonder why we strive to make formal gardens.

The village of Bentham is the other side of the gateway; the ticket issuer directs me to the ferry, picturesquely situated down in a bend of the river. Thereafter it is to retire to the very pleasant 'The Sloop' Inn, which appears to do accommodation for walkers as well. Suitably refreshed I climb back over a footpath, starting down the side of the inn and climbs back up the hill to Thurlestone, emerging next to the church and its extensive grounds, which are persistently cascaded by a rookery, based in the winter-scalded firs. This part of old Thurlestone has the sleepy feel of a village; but from afar I could see that there are newer estates attached. Nevertheless I am allowed to muse in this delightful cocoon until the 162 bus does stop at the bus shelter opposite the church; when I put my hand out as instructed!

Thence back to Kingsbridge and the Kings Arms, where this evening is firstly a group of four elegantly attired business ladies of varying ages, then later a larger group of distinctly middle-aged [and more!] men; when suddenly I hear some rather smooth singing serenading the ladies. I look round for a speaker system, only to realize that the male invasion is the local Barber's Shop Singers who have just come in for their evening's fluid refreshment. The ladies are suitably appreciative: and I have a very fine steak and kidney pie from the St George's Day Menu. What more could a chap ask for!

24 April 2014: Prospecting Plymouth

I have completed as much of the coast as I can from a Kingsbridge base and the next section to Plymouth involves crossing three rivers, only two of which have a ferry, while none has a bridge near the coast. As the first two are both relatively remote and not serviced by buses this next outing requires more detailed planning than hitherto. Ferrymen, tides, and forward accommodation all have to be synchronized, as well as working out what to wear to wade across the river Erme, assuming that I hit it at the right time of the tide!

As I have a day in hand I therefore take the hourly 93 bus ride from Kingsbridge to Plymouth to reconnoitre: and a very fine scenic ride it is, with panoramic views across rolling South Hams countryside to the moors beyond: a reassuring and delightful contrast after the coastal walking with its winter scarred cliffs. It is also somewhat easier on the knees and feet; with the bus fairly full of the grey pound – all on freedom passes! It feels like a communal saga outing!

The bus detours and squeezes through several villages en-route, through lanes never meant for a double decker bus; but negotiated well by the intrepid driver.

Finally we are discharged above the Plymouth bus station, whence it is not far to meander coastwards to find the very impressive green open space of the Hoe, which, in addition to impressive statues of Sir Francis Drake and the fallen heroes of the two World Wars, also reveals the beauty of the harbour; no, surely, the beauty of the bay [actually the beauty of the Sound is probably correct]! It is quite magnificent: and therefore quite a trek round monolithic naval fortifications to the entry to the River Plym, where there is a more comprehensible spread of water, redeveloped on the north side to a fairly trendy area, 'the Canary Wharf' of Plymouth, while preserving all the older features. The tourist information, useful for negotiating Plymouth as well as for planning my next trip, is situated at the mouth of the river as part of a museum, and next to the Admiral McBride

214

Inn – where excellent crab sandwiches are to be had; the only company at this hour being three regulars who look as if they have occupied their seats for some years: she sips sherry [sic] with a half-full Tesco bag at her side. She is accompanied by a rather large fellow who looks as if it is not his first pint of bitter, while the third member is as thin as a rake, sips lager, but otherwise, sitting very cross-legged, divides his time between biting his already bitten finger nails and dashing out to smoke a carefully-rolled cigarette, or two. I cannot quite work out whether any of them are married, or which to whom.

Replenished with observation and sustenance, I head back up to the Royal Parade to catch the 1 or 43 bus to the railway station, and thence the train back to Paddington.

2 June 2014: Paddington to Kingsbridge

Marrying life in London, the dates of the suitable low tide for crossing the river Erme, along with forward-booking of limited accommodation options has meant that the lovely walking month of May has escaped me and I am nearly half-way through the year with only a single outing under my feet. But faint heart ne'er won etc.…! So it is the 11.06 from Paddington [the mainly empty 10.06 for some reason has a premium charge – which Mr Grumpy of Sevenoaks, [alias yours indignantly of Tunbridge Wells], finds quite unjustified]. But a seat is found and the three-hour journey begins in relative peace and quiet.

Since there is a gap in the afternoon between arriving at Totnes and catching the X64 bus to Kingsbridge I indulge in refreshment at the Signal Box café which, as the name suggests, is the top floor of the old signal box, now adjacent to a newish footbridge. The café somehow maintains something of a 'Brief Encounter' feel, with its blue-and-white checked oil cloth on the square tables, Windsor wooden chairs, white net pelmets at the windows, photographs of steam engines: and variations of egg, beans chips, and tomatoes compete with fish fingers or sausages: all good café fair.

Refreshed [only by a plain white coffee and an apple and blackberry crumble!] I make my way to the bus stop which is immediately outside the station exit, only to get slightly caught up in a conversation between a rather outgoing, florid, gentleman who has just been to the Hay on Wye book festival [and keen to let us all know] with a late peroxide blonde from Liverpool who ogles said florid gentleman fairly consistently.

215

There is outright support for Niall Ferguson and the UKIP party in no uncertain terms, so that when the bus does arrive I am somewhat relieved to find that I am seated out of conversational range. But it does not stop the other two enlightening most of their neighbours as to their views.

At the next stop a rather smart, bright-looking lady with short cropped grey hair comes to sit near the Liverpool blonde, and they obviously know each other. Introductions follow; but, listening to the conversation, I see the new participant's eyebrows beginning to rise; and after a few 'O really', varied with a few 'How interesting' replies, she falls silent. But the intrepid couple proceed to enlighten us all most of the way to Kingsbridge, where they both alight, having exchanged mobile numbers. There is a collective sigh of relief, and the more elegant lady distinctly reassembles her composure.

I think that the deeply engaged couple were totally oblivious to the extraordinary narrowness of the lane down to Harbeton, a pretty little village, to deliver four children from the Totnes school. The lush vegetation of the hedgerows were so high and close that it was as if the foxglove and the ragged robin were knocking against the windows, while the previous cow parlsey and ferns were now past their best. Quite what happens if something comes the other way I know not.

Otherwise I enjoy what is a pleasantly scenic ride to the now quite familiar Kingsbridge and the Kings Arms. I must say that 'toad in the hole' and a large glass of Shiraz seem a strange combination. But such is the variety of life!

3 June 2014 : the crossing of two rivers: Thurlestone to Battisborough

This is a challenging section inasmuch as buses are scarce and the ferry for the first river has a small boat that only operates between certain hours; the second river is without a ferry or bridge, but can be waded only at low tide: timing is everything.

The 8.50 version of the Kingsbridge 162 bus starts the day's journey, transporting me along with all of four fellow passengers to Thurlestone at the end of the figure of eight, having gone via Marlborough, Galhampton, Inner and Outer Hope, back to Marlborough via South Milton, and thence to Thurlestone, having passed this turning nearly half an hour ago! But this is country life, and I have never had quite such a picturesque bus ride for £1.60. Fortunately on the way we have picked up a few more grey-haired walkers; and two of them, with a Labrador that looks even greyer for its ten years, seem to know the rural way from Thurlestone Church to Bentham - past the church, down the steep slope, pick up the narrow path that comes out at the Sloop Inn, whence left and follow the sign posts to the small boatyard. Here, inquiry eventually unearths the harbour master, who doubles as ferryman, and who promptly disappears to find a boat that might take the four of us across the river. Meanwhile a slim, athletic young fellow appears among the waiting passengers and proceeds, without any inhibition, to strip off in order to wriggle himself into a very fitting wet suit and, having done so, slides into a small white kayak and slithers away as smoothly as a local seal. This pleasurable entertainment detracts us all [perhaps the Labrador was not very interested] but is interrupted by the put - put of our small ferry boat, suggesting that we might imminently be transferred to the opposite bank – which looks to be half a mile away from Bentham. It is already possible to see three or four customers in bright clothing wandering up and down on the far side, there being no obvious pier or jetty there.

Midstream our gallant captain stands up in our small boat to gesture to the waiting passengers that they should move upstream: and then the upright helmsman has suddenly to make a right-angle swerve to avoid a single-man dinghy that is bearing down on us with us on his blind [= port] side. Fortunately we are all safely seated and the captain is nimble; but it crosses my mind that a case could be made for certain vessels to show large 'L' plates when sailing, never mind all this 'port and starboard', and 'motor gives way to sail', malarky!

Having survived this excitement [the novice sailor did shout an apology] we are expertly driven on to the shallows of the sandy beach and discharged, with myself being surprisingly gallant and offering a welcome helping hand to the more elderly of the two ladies; while the second, much younger, lady does but require me to take charge of a disembarking Labrador: said dog immediately taking off at great speed – with me in tow. Just as well that I had settled my fare earlier!

The estuary this side is a maze of paths, and, although I follow an obvious path upwards, I somehow miss a cliff top path. However there is a path through the golf course, with appropriate warnings; but this simply leads out onto a narrow road leading down to Bigbury. It is a busy road too, closely banked; so not fun for walking on traffic wise, even if speedy by foot.

Not suprisingly, there seems to be a sequence of expensive houses going down to Bigbury, with its estuary view over to Burgh Island. The beach seems attractive enough, and well laid out car parks fill the front, whence it is but a short walk round to the Challaborough collection of non-mobile homes, with an equally impressive, and probably more sheltered, beach.

Fortunately it was half term last week, making it almost deserted this week; and so a suitable venue for a coffee break [but no hanging around today with tides dictating!]. The next stretch is to be something of a challenge.

The climb out of Challaborough is via a road that merges into a footpath that has experienced some crumbling, and the ascent to Toby's Point is along the edge of grassland which was radiant with daisies and buttercups, while the wilder parts show a surge of early flowering burdocks, with their candle-like inflorescences flushed with a tinge of pink on green. There are fine views back to the remains of the Iron Age fortress at Bolt Point, and Innner and Outer Hope. But I must press on.

There follows a steep descent to Aymers Cove and the most secluded of all beaches, – since there is no road access. But the contours out of the cove are closely packed; and a stiffish climb out of the valley ensues. An all-too-short walk along the top of the cliff is followed by another, partially-stepped, path down to the deserted Westcombe beach, again with no road access. I begin to find this up and down somewhat hard on the knees. I pause for a while, and view the ascent to Hoist Point. It is as steep as the previous, with a zig-zagging path that seems to go rather close to the edge of the cliff while, set back from the cliff, there is a straight run of boundary fencing up the hill. I choose to take the latter, endeavouring to cover at least four posts at a time [it is very, very steep!] with awkward rests in between, since there is no level ground, with tendons and joints not naturally adapted to pausing on such inclines!

It is with some relief that I reach the top and enjoy a quick, frugal lunch. What a blessing that the weather is fine, scarcely any wind, and the views panoramic and beautiful. If only I could have been hoisted to this point! And, if only I did not have the pressure ahead of a tidal river crossing on foot, I might have enjoyed this stretch more.

But the low tide of the river Erme is ever on my mind. So I say my farewells to the vibrant yellow trefoils, and start a longer, more gradual descent through open pasture where the path initially alternates between wading through waist-high [beware bare arms!] purple flowering nettles, or spiky thistles of the same hue. The open pasture melds into more formal fields, with a large flock of newly shorn Suffolk sheep [with a high percentage of lameness in the flock!] amok in a field of high rye grass: the latter at least polishing my dusty, heavy duty, walking shoes. I have a feeling that all this headland is National Trust property, with tenant farmers?

The estuary of the river Erme is in sight at last! After the two last stiff climbs this downward slope feels something like a cruise. It also reveals a sweeping vista of the sandy estuary of the Erme, with the enclave of Battisborough, my destination for the night, hidden from sight, while the rugged coast runs unhindered and uninhabited, apart from a cluster of buildings at Stoke, towards Wembury Bay on the estuary of the Yealm, and the western most point of the magnificence of the Plymouth Sound. I pause awhile at this truly splendid view.

But this is to see ahead of myself. I have yet to cross the river Erme on foot. By putting pressure on myself I have arrived an hour earlier than low tide. So I am able to enjoy the peace and tranquility of the beach, tempered by the fact that I would like to find the recommended crossing point. A series of Canada geese descend into the estuary while I am sitting. Some go into a synchronized glide as they drop altitude, while others determinedly flap on to a presumed feeding ground further up the river.

219

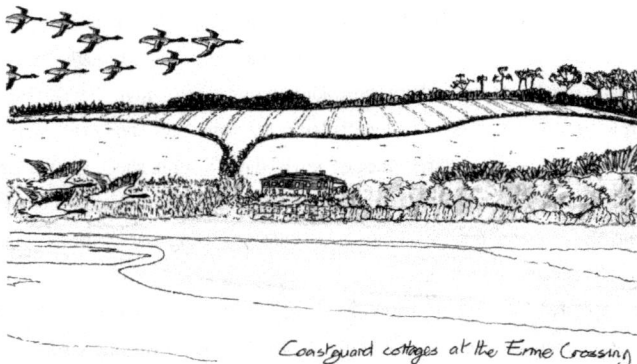

Coastguard cottages at the Erme Crossing

The guide says that there is a blue notice on some rocks, along with a board on the slipway which gives times of crossing where the road comes down to the beach. The latter is obvious enough; but not the sign. [Subsequently I find that it is necessary actually to leave the beach and to start to climb on to the road to find the notice board, framed in blue, which has a clear map of the proposed crossing route]. What is obvious to me on the beach is that there are old ruins either side of the river somewhat further up, which suggest that there might have been a toll bridge at some time. The river is narrower there, some twenty feet or so, even if a little deeper than the flat spread over the sands where the road hits the beach. I opt for the higher crossing as it gives me privacy to change into shorts and canvas shoes. At 4.10 p.m. I wade across this pebbly, stony, but fast flowing, stretch; the water only temporarily higher than my knees. The river current here is quite firm and strong, but the flow is as constant as it is cold, and quite easy to adjust to with the faithful walking stick a very useful prop! I make 'man Friday' footsteps on the other side, and retire to the shrubbery entrance of a private estate to change back into my walking gear.

The day's project of crossing two bridgeless rivers is completed!

It strikes me that since leaving the Challaborough camp I have seen nobody on the walk, and only a few people on the Erme beach, [none of whom knew anything about crossing the river!]. Nor did I see any other person[s] attempting to cross the river!

220

But, as I trek down to the well-fortified row of coastguards' cottages on the western bank [they must have been battered this winter!] to pick up the coastal path again, I meet several groups coming the other way to cross the river. I exchange my experience only to see them all make various versions of wading across the wide sandy stretch, mainly without changing their footwear: although several couples do hover for rather a long time! My guess is that they are all booked in at the comfortable inn in Kingston which is an easily-walkable distance from the estuary beach. It was a strategy [coming the other way!] that I had considered, but the tide times were not helpful. As I ascend further up the path from the estuary I see a similar blue-framed map [the bootprints going in the opposite direction!] clearly indicating the designated route across the flats. Even so I estimate that the water would come over boot level: so it is squelchy feet or barefoot on the pebbles unless you have a spare pair of plimsols!

I watch for a while to see which option the couples take [it is a mixture of both – but none have plimsols!] then I head for the quiet walk through woods, round the low headland, and head for the quiet, sheltered enclave of Battisborough, where the elegantly converted village school, with private access from the coastal path walk, is my destination. It is a secluded, charming spot, set on a slope, so that entering from the higher rear of the house to the living area with its sea views, you go downstairs to the ensuite bedrooms. The only problems are that a single person pays as if they were two [always an irritation if you are a semi-permanent single traveller!] and also that there is nowhere within walking distance to provide supper. But the latter I had anticipated, packing a double load of sandwiches from Kingsbridge: and anticipate an early night to rest a rather tight left knee, and an excellent breakfast in the morning: both of which happen.

4 June 2014: Battisborough to Noss-Mayo

It had rained overnight, freshening the air; and after a delightful breakfast it is a pleasure simply to take the private path across to the coastal path and be on my way so quickly. No bus journey today: the freedom pass lies dormant, but secure, in my pocket.

So I almost immediately go into the climb out of Gulf Cove, with the path edged by tall fescue and rye grasses which, laden with the night's rain, not only obscure the path, but completely soak my trousers below the knee. Not an ideal way to start the day; but the compensations are the clusters of scarlet pimpernels on the way; the supernovae of buttercups and daisies at the top; and, on this stretch of coast, a thorn tree that bears flowers that have both pink and white colouring. I cannot but think that this would be a very marketable addition to any garden! Where they occur in woodland [and they also occur as solitaries on the falling cliffs] the petals fall and lie like confetti from some midsummer wedding that I missed!

The walk is high and rocky, but, thankfully, without the sequence of up and down of yesterday. The Anchorite's Rock is a hefty prominence, back from the path and cliff face, and seems to provide a natural enclosure to the landward side. But a solitary spot: it must be very bleak in winter!

There seem to be hidden coves on this stretch of cliff coast, as I can see the odd small boat and hut down at sea level; but no obvious path down.

Having negotiated the odd electric fence [with no stock in sight?] to mount Beacon Hill, it is not far to the ruin of an archway, which I would have thought might have been a church – since I am still in Anchorite mode. But the succinct guide tells me that this is the remains of a tea room [possibly a Victorian folly?]! I felt the signs and directions for the coastal path route were ambiguous here and, as I was looking for a 'nine mile carriage way walk', I ventured inland a little as I could see the tarmac road with a clear, straight running cart track just below it. Fortunately, as I was going through a gateway, I met a lady exercising a lively [but well behaved] schnauzer. She enlightened me that the path that I am heading for is simply used by the local dairy herd, whereas, for the coastal path, I should have continued past the ruins of the tea room, and swept on towards Stoke Point, staying above the beach and the secluded cluster of non-mobile homes of Stoke Beach. This whole enclave had originally been a summer escape for employees of the 'Cooperative Society' in its hey-day. All this I learn from the erudite lady attached to the schnauzer; and as she has one of the said immobile homes as an escape hole, she is kind enough to both lead me to the top of the cliff and then to set me on my way through the woods running up behind the cliff.

Once the headland is accessed, [local workmen clarify an unsignposted meeting of paths and road!], there follows what is probably the most pleasant and easy section of the nine-mile drive that Lord Revelstoke created for his manse of Membland Hall. He evidently made his fortune building railways in Canada; and subsequently lost it trying to do the same in South America [enough said!]. But, as a singular philanthropist, and at his peak of success, he employed local people to carve out this long scenic stretch running towards Gara point at the mouth of the river Yealm [today I am being less ambitious and staying at Worsell Barton for the night, leaving the crossing of the Yealm until tomorrow]. It is only a shame that the weather is equivocal [meaning showery!] for this stretch of the walk. However, having parted with the schnauzer's owner, I see only a handful of other walkers; but I do see some newly-shorn sheep [– with a much lower prevalence of lameness than yesterday's flock.]: there is the man with the collie shooting round all the rabbit holes: and the two young ladies who, with their camera, flutter like butterflies [rather well-built butterflies!] between the foxgloves; there being an exceptional stretch of 2-300 yards where the slopes and the edge of the cliffs are almost completely covered in the spires of purple foxgloves. It reminds me of a memorable trip to the Kashmir foothills of the Himalayas, where stretches of unspoilt territory were monoclonal cultures of flowering colour, notably aquilegia and primulas.

Then at a curve in the path I meet an American couple trying to decide whether they can go through the 'front garden' of the 'Warren Cottages', rather than the rather narrow and dubious portion of the coastal path which is cliff and seaward of the cottages. The dilemma is solved by two local, venerable, gentlemen, who, approaching from the opposite direction, emerge from the garden while we are holding a conference as to what would be most appropriate. The cottages are obviously holiday lets [or deserted?] with no present occupants. The front patch negotiated I push on, as the weather is distinctly fretting; and the American couple are not moving at 'a suitable pace'! Being civil has its limits!

Gara Point gives a great view of the Plymouth Sound and the estuary of the Yealm, whence it is a delightfully wooded walk to Noss Mayo, where I see the last of the local pink and white thorn and its shedding confetti: is that Titania's veil caught on a thorn, or just an unusual spider's web: surely not the remains of a Tesco plastic bag?

Emerging from the wooded walk each side of the river is lined by old houses, the Swan Inn of Newton Ferrers on one side, and the Ship Inn of Noss Mayo on the other, with the path connecting the two sides actually being accessible at low tide. The other side of this cul-de-sac tributary has its new-builds stacked up above the older quay side buildings. But this part of the estuary is still densely wooded and verdant. There is a touch of the 'Salcombes' about this estuary! It has been found by the silver pound.

Newton Ferrers - low tide

This has been the most civilized of walking days; a great contrast to the demands and disciplines of yesterday: and an equally civilized lunch at the Ship Inn at Noss Mayo is all I have to cope with before gently back tracking and climbing up to the Worsell Barton Farm, which has many charming aspects to recommend it: although there is the 'problem' that I have to walk back to the said 'Ship Inn' for supper, and cope with a fine moonlit walk home by moonlight! Such delightful problems.

5 June 2014: the final day: Noss Mayo to Plymouth Hoe

After such a good yesterday I wake at 6.00 am to a sunny morning, rise to sit in the window seat and drink a coffee while reading some Trollope [Adam Crowe?] with a view across open fields to Wembury Bay.

An excellent home-produce breakfast follows, interrupted by a somewhat ponderous character [charming wife!] who proceeds to pontificate, over porridge [in this weather?!] on the current state of dairy herd products. This man obviously is as important as he knows he is. But our redoubtable landlady more than holds her own; even has a few trump cards inasmuch as she turns out to be organizing the whole of the sheep section for the local agricultural show with over 50 representations. No wonder that I had difficulty identifying the Charollais sheep in the field below my bedroom window [and they were

224

in tip top condtition]. I also learn about a 'rouge' variety that, with their yucky red coloured fleece, constantly look as if they have either been savaged by dogs or escaped from a traffic accident [invent your own story – there were several over breakfast].

I feel that this is all enough information so early in the day, so excuse myself to pack and get on my way. It is an idyllic morning to set off and see the blue sea sitting above the green eared corn: that is until I meet a large tractor, with even wider spraying gear, charging down the narrow, high-hedged, road. I do receive a jolly wave as I manage to clamber like Brer Rabbit amongst the goose grass and faded cow parsley [I surmise that it was the husband of the redoubtable landlady].

As I had passed the signs to the ferry yesterday on my wooded walk to Noss Mayo there is no problem at relocating the narrow slipway down to an outcrop of rock which, with a little concrete, serves as the jetty for several local small boats. More or less at 10.00 o'clock the cheerful ferryman boards myself and two others: they simply wish to go across to Newton Ferrers; where they are replaced by two couples [no prize for working out how many in the boat – but don't forget the ferryman!]. We now all proceed to Warren Point to disembark for the walk to Wembury. They are all on a day return; I to march onwards. My helping hand for the ladies of the outing is even more necessary than on the Bantham ferry, as, in this case, one of the gents is a little fragile too. It makes me feel quite sprightly: but everything is relative!

There are clear signs from the ferry to follow the footpath to Wembury, turning left at the top of the ferry steps, and there are some fine views across the estuary as the path rises quickly to run along the headland of New Barton. This is a fairly popular walk and I seem to meet more people in half an hour than in total for the last two days of walking. There is a distinct element of the dog-walking rush-hour, as first encountered at Broadstairs in Kent, several years ago!

The path soon descends into Wembury via a graveyard, although I think that I missed the signposts here. The beach seems a hive of activity with canoes, surf boards, diving suits, and cafés; but the onward walker has to go inland somewhat to cross the rivulet, partially hidden in beds of reeds. A young man and his lady friend sit at the side of the road in their lycra, he with his knees decidedly gashed.

'Oh, it could have been worse' is his cheerful reply to condolences: and, of

225

course, in this modern age, they have mobiled dad, and are simply waiting to be picked up, with the buckled front wheel of his bike looking fairly unrideable.

Satisfied that they are OK, I move on. The path keeps more or less at river level and proceeds to hug the coast here, but rising slightly to dip into the seclusion of Heybrook, a modern, bland-looking, development from the coastal path: sort of Stepford wives with lace curtains. But the path weaves along until the chalet connurbation of Bovisand, where I judge it expedient to stop at a welcome café for refreshment. It is on this stretch that I have my final hare-and-tortoise experience, as a youngish couple with a lively young collie overtook me somewhere on the walk from Heybrook. They then bumped into two guys coming the other way with two equally lively Jack Russell terriers, where upon there were prolonged exchanges between both dogs and their owners. I silently walked through this committee meeting: not even a greeting. But then, subsequently, the collie couple arrive at the café where I was indulging in a latte and a fine local bakewell tart. The gentleman who previously had overtaken me came up and asked,

'How did you get here? Do you know of a short cut? We overtook you on the way here; but you've arrived before us.'

I deny local knowledge, but choose not to enlighten him that I had walked under his very nose when he was talking about dogs! Power of observation is a curious phenomenon! It reminds me of the psychological test where you are asked to observe how many times a volleyball is moved between players in a short film sequence: meanwhile a man in a gorilla skin walks through the players. Something like sixty percent of observers, while getting close to counting the correct number of passes, fail to notice the man in the gorilla outfit!

The way out of Bovisands is quite tricky to find. Ascending the road and turning left into a car park with a café is easy enough. But then the exit is a narrow alleyway of steps fitted between a block of apartments with 'NO PARKING' blocks outside, and a row of terrace cottages. It all looks rather private – and is easy to miss: but the people at the café are helpful! There is a sign – but it was rather covered with vegetation; while, if missed, the continuation of the road leads to a well gated naval station at Staddon Point.

It is quite a climb of steps out of the alleyway; but I am replenished by the café break. There is a following sequence of a wooden bridge enclosed in a metal cage, running over a gully. This, I imagine, is residue from all this land originally being part of the naval base. At the end of this ex-military zone the narrow path is quite high up on the headland, running very close to the edge. This is not good for vertigo, but does provide quite stunning views of Plymouth Sound, and the beginning of Cornwall.

The high walk runs out onto a hard-surfaced, but wooded, road; and begins to descend. It is in the official directions that there is an eventual walk down through these woods. But I am saved by a bearded man, coming up from working in the woods, who tells me that, lower down in the woods, the path is closed due to subsidence and, had I not met him, I would have had to retrace my steps. Thankfully I carefully stick to the narrow and bendy road, until it opens out onto 'Jenny's Close', a large public green with car park, café, views of the Sound, and acres of open space. So I stride rapidly across the descending slope, passing a large slab of stone, with a National Trust Acorn excavated on it to the size of a wheelie bin! This indicates that you go through a patch of woodland: but then do take care not to follow the main path that swings right as it exits the next viewing green: do keep going down into the lower right hand corner of this second green. Here there is a narrow path that leads into the mixture of suburban housing and industry of Mountbatten Point.

It is possible to walk round either side of the prominent tower [worth climbing for the view and a sheltered garden]. Once round the tower, ignore the rather splendid promenading pier and look for a floating jetty where, amongst all the other large boats, there is a small yellow ferry which will ferry you across to the newly developed ' Canary Wharf' and the Admiral Mc Bride Inn!

Suitably refreshed it is only a stroll round the corner to revisit the magnificent expanse of Plymouth Hoe, shimmering in the sunlight. This seems to be a suitable end to my sojourn; here at Plymouth Hoe, at the feet of the intrepid explorer Sir Francis Drake, [and his notable cousin, Sir Richard Hawkins, true founder of the English Navy!]. I had not quite realized that this was what my pilgrimage was about: for Cornwall, on the far side of the Hoe, is, after all, a different country: even as my left knee also has done all the good and loyal service that a coastal walker needed; but has declared time against steep inclines, down as much as up; and I think I need to pay due heed!

I had raised a glass in the Admiral McBride to all who travel well: what a glorious and varied coast we have, and how I have enjoyed it!

Sir Francis on the Hoe.

END: July 2014.

Additional information.

My diary is no more than it purports to be; written after each day's walk while waiting for, and while digesting dinner! But I recognize that it is something of a hybrid guide book, without in any way intending to be a comprehensive guide, as there are maps and books whose sole purpose is to accomplish that. The most notable of these is written by the South West Coast Path Association, [www.southwestcoastpath.org.uk], and has versions going anticlockwise from Minehead to Poole and clockwise from Poole to Minehead, with the anticlockwise version having the detail of travel facilities and accommodation appropriate for both journeys. It has the advantage that it is regularly updated; which is very necessary with the regular damage suffered by both the wilder regions, and not so remote, areas of the south west coast! It is a very useful guide, but obviously only covers the latter part of my journey.

Otherwise I generally used the 1:50,000 ordinance survey maps, for which I have a considerable affection and collection! However I do realize that both 'google maps', and 'streetmap.com' provide much greater detail, while portable 'sat-navs' on i phones do make the older cartography look a little dated! There is also a very useful A-Z version of the SW Coast, along with the higher resolution ordinance survey maps. Each to their own inclination!

Bus timetables and accommodation can be gleaned from the web, or from local Tourist Information Offices; but the latter can be rather variable; and the former certainly need to be checked for being up to date! There are often seasonal changes to bus timetables. It was most useful to go for county bus service systems in order to see the whole plan of available routes; but this could be frustrating when crossing county boundaries on the coast. So this does need forward planning; a county in advance.?

Times of tides were worked out from either www.tidetimes.co.uk or www.tidetimes.org.uk ; but again, tourist information offices should have details [tide times were only really necessary for the River Erme crossing on foot!].